To Merlin
Whose work has been
helpful to me —
warmly,
Frank 5/87

The Double Strand

The Double Strand

FIVE CONTEMPORARY MEXICAN POETS

Frank Dauster

THE UNIVERSITY PRESS OF KENTUCKY

Scholarly publisher for the Commonwealth,
serving Bellarmine College, Berea College, Centre
College of Kentucky, Eastern Kentucky University,
The Filson Club, Georgetown College, Kentucky
Historical Society, Kentucky State University,
Morehead State University, Murray State University,
Northern Kentucky University, Transylvania University,
University of Kentucky, University of Louisville,
and Western Kentucky University.

Editorial and Sales Offices: Lexington Kentucky 40506-0024

Library of Congress Cataloging-in-Publication Data

Dauster, Frank N.
  The double strand.

  Bibliography: p.
  Includes index.
  1. Mexican poetry—20th century—History and
criticism. I. Title.
PQ7171.D38 1987   861   86-14653
ISBN 0-8131-1618-X

For HELEN, as always

For BOB and NICK, because it
has been such fun all the way

Contents

Preface

This book represents a further step in a longtime fascination with Mexican poetry, a field whose richness and complexity become more intriguing as one comes to realize that it lies within the tradition of Western literature but cannot be wholly contained therein. Mexican poetry—like the land which gives it birth, where at every step one is reminded of the presence of both the Spanish conquerors and the Indian heritage—is made of contrast and conflict. The Conquistadores won the war of conquest, but indigenous traditions are not less powerful or omnipresent for having been defeated, as Carlos Fuentes and Octavio Paz, among others, have said repeatedly. Mexican poetry is rich in subtleties. If Surrealism and other Occidental currents have thrust deep their roots, many Mexican poets, including some who appear to be directly in the European tradition, show unmistakable affiliations in theme and imagery with the pre-Conquest poetry of ritual sacrifice to the gods, who demanded frequent infusions of human blood in order to maintain their efficacy and power.

It is always difficult to deal with problems of literary periodization, and particularly so as we approach more closely our own time. Currents, tendencies, movements are blurred by nearness, and the poets most prized today may be those most ignored tomorrow. A perfect case in point is the Mexican Modernist Amado Nervo, whose international reputation during his life was nothing short of extraordinary, and who is today widely considered to have been, in relative terms, something of a poetic failure. The system implicit in this volume is the generational framework developed by José Juan Arrom in his seminal *Esquema generacional de las letras hispanoamericanas: Ensayo de un método* (2d ed., Bogota: Instituto Caro y Cuervo, 1977). According to this scheme, the writers covered in my introduc-

tory chapter belong to what he refers to as the generations of
1894, 1924, and 1954, after the generalized dates of their early
appearances in print. The first includes those poets born be-
tween 1864 and 1893, and corresponds to the Modernists and
Postmodernists. The Generation of 1924 includes those born
between 1894 and 1923. In Mexico, this translates into the
group known as the Contemporáneos, the Estridentistas, and—
of critical importance in Arrom's development of the theory—
the second half or downslope of the generation, when the gener-
ational characteristics are beginning to be transformed into
something different: the writers centered about the literary
reviews *Taller* and *Tierra Nueva*. Those born between 1924 and
1953 are the Generation of 1954, the postwar writers. Implicit in
this scheme, of course, is a Generation of 1984, including writ-
ers born after 1954; although it lies outside the scope of this
study, such a generation is in fact beginning to be visible in
Mexico.

The writers studied in the five essays here belong to the
generations of 1924 (Huerta, Chumacero) and 1954 (Sabines,
Castellanos, Bonifaz Nuño). Each of the five exemplifies in
some fashion the complexities of Mexican poetry in our cen-
tury. This does not mean that I have attempted to track down
Aztec affiliations, although the archaic metaphorical system
recurs with really astounding frequency. I have sought to get to
the tensions that are the source of their poetry. The poetry of
each displays something quite recognizably Mexican, without
their being in the least regional or picturesque poets. At the
same time, they are all members of the Occidental poetic fam-
ily, the other strand, and it would be impossible to conceive of
them without participation in that family. They have in com-
mon the effort to make poetry out of an inner drive: Chuma-
cero's struggle between the need to communicate love and the
inevitable sterility of the word leading to silence; Sabines's holy
rage that God should permit the outrage of death, and the need
to make peace with this unfeeling divinity; Castellanos's search
to express a woman's anguish in a hostile world without falling
into the excesses of confessional poetry; Huerta's effort to har-
monize the double revolutionary thrust of political and erotic
poetry; Bonifaz Nuño's complex vision of the woman-goddess

in Dantesque and Aztec terms. In a broad sense, they are all poets of love and its ramifications, and in their work they reach out, although in very different ways. They are by no means the only or necessarily the most important poets writing in Mexico in the last forty years, but each of them approaches serious problems of poetic creation and resolves them in an individual, perhaps even unique, fashion.

Whatever may be positive in this book owes a considerable amount to those who have encouraged, taught or simply listened over a good many years. To my teachers, José Vásquez Amaral, who first showed me Mexican poetry, and José Juan Arrom, to whom I owe so much, a special thanks. To María del Carmen Millán and Jesús Arellano, those good friends now gone, and to Porfirio Martínez Peñaloza and the many other Mexican friends who have been so generous; to John Brushwood, Allen Phillips, Merlin Forster, Ed Mullen, Eugene Moretta, and Andrew Debicki, for their comments over the years which have helped focus problems and suggest solutions; to Pedro de Andrea, who has done so much for Mexican culture and for its friends; to Kenneth Brett and John Bennett for kindly having made available to me important materials on Sabines and Bonifaz Nuño, respectively; and to Nick Dauster for his invaluable bibliographical aid and his always perceptive comments, my gratitude. To Rutgers University and its Research Council, my appreciation for the sabbatical leave and the research support that facilitated the preparation and writing. For errors of omission or commission, the responsibility is, of course, mine.

1 The Background: Modern Poetry in Mexico

If the historical study of literature is to be possible, if literature is to be more than an enormous heterogeneous mass of unrelated texts, we must see it as a process whose ramifications extend both forward and backward in time from any given moment or text. In the case of Mexican poetry, we may organize this process around certain key dates. In the majority of cases these reflect the appearance of literary reviews reacting against the prevailing currents and proposing, often rather drastically, a program for the "new" literature. These reviews are so important a fact of Mexican and, in general, of Spanish American literary life that movements are frequently known by the name of their review. These organizational points may have an extra-literary reference as well. Three key dates in modern Mexico are 1910, 1928, and 1968. The first refers to the symbolic publication of a single poem, Enrique González Martínez's "Tuércele el cuello al cisne," which was seen, not entirely with justice, as the end of the formalistic phase of Modernism and the beginning of a great emphasis on the spiritual. The same year also marked the outbreak of the Mexican Revolution, the overwhelming fact of Mexican life, literature, and society. The year 1928 was notable for the publication of the first issue of the review *Contemporáneos*, whose collaborators were to form the single most impressive group of poets in Mexico and perhaps in Spanish America. Not all their contemporaries nor even all later critics and poets express unreserved admiration for them or for their work, but they unquestionably altered the course of Mexican literature, driving it almost in spite of itself into the mainstream of Occidental letters. In 1968 occurred the crushing by government forces of the student movement, an event which has had a critical impact on Mexican society and literature.

MODERNISM AND THE REACTION AGAINST ROMANTICISM

As in all of Spanish America, contemporary literature in Mexico, especially poetry, really begins with the disappearance of an outdated Romanticism about 1910, somewhat after the midpoint of that complex movement known as Modernism. During the 1880s Modernism came as a welcome response to the sterility and routine into which Romanticism had deteriorated. Although the Postmodernists reacted strongly against many aspects of Modernism, and contemporary poetry is remote from the carnival of the senses into which the movement sometimes degenerated, later poets have continued to be fascinated by it, recognizing that, in the Modernists' insistence on the renewal of the poetic idiom and poetic form, Modernism is the source of the modern tradition in Spanish. The Modernists reacted against the stereotyped verbal and emotional formulas and the routine emotional excesses of a Romanticism that had never produced in Mexico poets of the caliber of their European counterparts. They were hardly alone in this; they are, in a broader sense, part of the movement that sprang from such unorthodox European and North American Romantics as Novalis (Friedrich von Hardenberg, 1771–1801), Edgar Allan Poe (1809–1849), and Gérard de Nerval (1808–1855), who were more interested in exploring the obsessive inner world of emotion and feeling than in the rhetorical gesturing typical of so many other Romantic poets. This interest culminated in the poetic explosion in France that produced the ferment of Parnassianism, Symbolism, and the lesser movements that coexisted with them. This is the explosion whose leading figures—Charles Baudelaire (1821–1867), Paul Verlaine (1844–1896), Arthur Rimbaud (1854–1891), Stéphane Mallarmé (1842–1898)—changed fundamentally and forevermore the face of poetry in the Western world.

Romanticism did not simply come to a halt. It still imposed its seal on a good many late nineteenth and even early twentieth century writers, and Romantic tones and attitudes were adapted throughout Modernism. If the Romantic movement itself was at an esthetic dead end, reduced to repeating themes and forms that had been worn out years earlier, the Modernists found also much that was vital in its heritage, as is seen clearly in the first important Modernist literary review in Mexico, the *Revista Azul* (1894–1896). It took its name from *Azul* (1888), the first widely-known volume by the greatest of the Modernists, the Nicaraguan Rubén Darío (1867–1916), and its principle concern was the need for greater formal liberty in poetry. The earliest members of the new movement, which still, after all, had no name and was not always clearly perceived as a movement, took as their spiritual ancestor the Spanish Romantic poet Gustavo Adolfo Bécquer (1836–1870), whose delicate lyrics and short stories in which he explored the tenuous relations between the worlds of dream and reality were much to the taste of the Modernists. In the same fashion they shared the rebelliousness, the doubt, and the exalted individualism that are at the core of Romanticism, and there were foreshadowings of the metric revolution of Modernism in such Romantics as José de Espronceda (1808–1842), although they never approached the extremes of the Modernists.

But if Bécquer was an overwhelming influence on the earliest Modernists, their spiritual colleagues were the French Parnassian poets for whom, unlike the majority of the Mexican Romantics locked into the expression of their individual emotional excess, poetic form was a matter of fundamental importance. The Parnassians attempted to reproduce external reality as objectively as possible, keeping the formal qualities of the poem foremost; this explains the school's close links with painting and the tendency to find subject matter in the works of Watteau or in Japanese screens, among others. Emotion and sentiment were excluded insofar as possible; the poets pursued formal excellence and sculptural serenity. This can all be useful for the perfecting of poetic technique, but in the hands of a less expert practitioner, or of one who takes too literally the prescription to avoid emotion, there is a fearful risk of sterility and preciosity, qualities that are all too visible in much Modernist poetry. At the same time, at its best this kind of technical passion taught an important lesson of verbal flexibility and agility.

Slightly later in arriving in Latin America and far more important was Symbolism, whose principal organ in Mexico, and one of the most important in the Hispanic world, was the *Revista Moderna* (1898–1911), closely associated with the new artistic world of bohemia and so-called Decadentism. The Symbolists preserved the formal excellences of the art-for-art's-sake character of Parnassianism, but they had a far different purpose: the discovery of relationships between the objective, external world and the interior states of the poet. A key word was "correspondences," taken from the title of the poem by Baudelaire: they sought the correspondences between their emotions and the world that surrounded them. Behind this lay the conviction that between the inner and the outer, between the physical world and their psychic universe, there is a relationship capable of being communicated through the evocativeness of poetry. If this bore some resemblance to Catholic doctrines as elaborated by Thomas Aquinas, it was more directly related to the vogue of spiritualism and pseudo-mysticism that swept intellectual circles toward the end of the last century. Where the Parnassians sought poetic freedom, the Symbolists were engaged in a spiritual undertaking that sometimes led them to perilous extremes.

This effort was directly related to one of the most important technical innovations of the Symbolists, synesthesia or the expression of one sense through another. It was perfectly suited for the purpose of attempting to connect dissimilar worlds, as it linked dissimilar senses. Synesthesia was not, however, the only technical innovation; the Modernists were inveterate experimenters, and the reforms of sound, rhythm, and versification carried out by them are fundamental to the process of poetry in Spanish. Following the lead of Darío and the French, especially, the Modernists developed new meters and resuscitated others that had lain forgotten. Some imported such new forms as the Malaysian pantum or the Japanese haiku, or sought a rhythmic renewal through the use of accentual verse or meters based on rhythmic units rather than on fixed numbers of syllables. In their feverish pursuit of novelty in imagery and metaphor, they utilized synesthesia and illogical adjectivization; they rejected the obvious and forthright in favor of the hint, the suggestion; and always the musicality of their verse avoided the Romantic tendency toward declamation and stridency.

There was also a marked social aspect to the development of Modernism. The Romantic heritage of individualism was exacerbated by the growth of industrial society with its emphasis on the practical values useful in the struggle for daily existence. In such a society, there was neither a place for the artist nor interest in his work, so that the Modernists began to develop an art really aimed at other artists. Writers, particularly those who were not financially independent and who were also unable to find the traditional patronage available under older social systems, felt increasingly alienated from such a society. During the early Modernist period this isolation was closely related to the nostalgic emphasis on Parisian bohemia and eighteenth-century French gardens. In Mexico, few of these harassed writers, dependent on bureaucratic or journalistic positions, and even fewer of those economically well-to-do, were in favor of the Revolution and the social tumult it created. Their vision of a world of elegant nobility simply did not harmonize with the irruption of Villa's galloping Northerners or Zapata's Indians fighting for agrarian reform. They were much more comfortable with the apparent relative stability of the Díaz dictatorship, which at least brought prosperity to a portion of the capital, whatever oppression it inflicted on the provinces and the long-suffering rural populace, most of them Indians. In some cases, they even sympathized with or participated in the counter-revolutionary government of the savage usurper General Victoriano Huerta, responsible for the murders of President Madero and Vice-President Pino Suárez. In a very real sense, the Revolution of 1910 did a great deal to bring Mexican Modernism to a rather early end and truncated its more natural development, seen in other nations, toward a poetry more conscious of the American past and present.

If these were the general outlines of the movement, within it there was far more individualism than we might expect. Throughout Spanish America there was a strong tendency toward synthesizing these various threads rather than adhering to one fixed school, so that the leading Modernist poets each developed highly individualized poetic personalities. As José Emilio Pacheco has said, "No hay modernismo sino modernismos: los de cada poeta importante que comienza a escribir en lengua española entre 1880 y 1910. Como los románticos, parnasianos y simbolistas franceses, los poetas modernistas son distintos entre sí y adaptan a su propia circunstancia lecciones aprendidas en otras literaturas."[1] The reader must also recognize that, very broadly speaking, there were two rather distinct periods within the Modernist movement. The first was the more formalist, cosmopolitan, and European-oriented and extended until roughly the turn of the century, although some writers never really abandoned this initial phase. The second was characterized by an increasing awareness of the New World and the development of a continental awareness, although again the extent and nature of this awareness varied greatly from one writer to another, and its development in Mexico was greatly conditioned by the Revolution of 1910.

Among the most important of Mexican Modernists was Manuel Gutiérrez Nájera (1859–1895), remarkable for the elegance and delicacy with which he wrote of the dandyish life he attempted to model after Parisian chic. A man of broad culture, he worked as a professional journalist for most of his life, and his short stories and *crónicas* of the theater and the metropolitan scene developed a new kind of prose of great flexibility and agility. Much of Gutiérrez Nájera's poetry echoes the frivolous gaiety of the world of which he wrote in his prose, but his most lasting work is a subjective and profoundly pessimistic expression of the bitterness of a life that could not be as he wished it. Gutiérrez Nájera sought the delicacy and musicality of a poetry that would express his resigned melancholy; his early death cut short his career before he could really purify his work of the echoes of Paris.

Salvador Díaz Mirón (1853–1928) was at the other pole; where Gutiérrez Nájera lived in and described the gallant world of theater and cabaret, Díaz Mirón was much more emphatic in his work and in his life, which included political exile in New York and Spain, service in the nation's Chamber of Deputies, and several notorious duels, two of which resulted in the death of his opponents and for one of which he served four years in prison. He began in the school of Victor Hugo (1802–1885) and Gáspar Núñez de Arce (1832–1903), of a militant declamatory poetry that saw itself as the herald of social and political redemption. As we might well expect, Díaz Mirón tended toward grandiloquence and hyperbole; yet, in his most thoroughly Modernist period, from about 1892 to 1901, he systematically set about cleansing his verse of this grandiloquence and imposed on himself constantly greater concision. The best poems of this period are nearly impressionistic in their use of detail to suggest description. After 1901 this effort at purification led to an impossible extreme consisting in eliminating all repetition: no adjective could rhyme with another; no rhymes of verb forms with other similar verb forms were permitted; no word, except for particles, could be repeated in the same verse; most difficult of all, perhaps, no vowel could appear twice in a stressed syllable in the same line. The results are often formally remarkable, if somewhat cold and mannered. This passionate rigor is but one of the most striking examples of the Modernist search for purity of poetic form and language, while its relatively late appearance, when other poets had long left such experiments behind, demonstrates the coexistence within Latin America of the Symbolist and Parnassian extremes.

Each of the other leading Mexican Modernists also developed an individual poetic personality. Manuel José Othón (1858–1906) was to some degree a poetic anomaly; the product of a rural conservative traditionalism and of a sterile academic neoclassicism in literature, he condemned the fever for renewal that characterized Modernism as a whole. Yet his best work adopts the Parnassian insistence on formal perfection, and his astonishing "Idilio Salvaje," a sequence of twelve sonnets dealing with an erotic encounter between a traveler and an Indian woman, is overtly Symbolist in its parallel between the physical aridity of the desert surroundings, the spiritual and emotional exhaustion of its protagonist, and the sterility of escape through eroticism. Amado Nervo (1870–1919)—who achieved such international fame as a poet that upon his death in Montevideo his body was transported home in a naval vessel escorted by ships of several other nations—worked extensively as a journalist, lived in the Parisian literary bohemia, and later served in the Mexican diplomatic corps. His poetry is remarkable chiefly for its increasing tone of spirituality. Initially a disciple of Baudelaire, he had been under the influence of the Symbolists and his best poems deal with the struggle between religiosity and the flesh; later, in an odd chronological reversal, he turned toward Parnassian formal perfection. Increasingly, Nervo was preoccupied with spiritualism, with the influences of Oriental doctrines such as reincarnation and the transmigration of souls. The death in 1912 of his beloved Anita, Ana Cecilia Luisa Dailliez, pushed him further toward a poetry of spiritual insistence and renunciation of formal concerns, so that his later volumes are really hardly more than confessional murmurs, and Nervo himself expressed his desire to write a literature "sin literatura." Although it is these latter poems, sentimental and full of commonplaces, that brought him such enormous international popular acclaim, his heritage is much more evident in those earlier poems that expressed his struggle to return to faith, his battle with carnal temptation, and his pantheistic vision of existence.

Enrique González Martínez (1871–1952) is best known for his sonnet "Tuércele el cuello al cisne" (1910), which has been widely interpreted as a denunciation of Modernism and was for a time seen as an attack on Darío, for whom, as for many of the Modernists, the swan symbolized that ethereal beauty they sought. In fact, González Martínez remained a symbolist until very near the end of his life, and his opposition to the swan was rather a rejection of the cult of external beauty, which was in the process of becoming a dead issue by the time the sonnet was written. González Martínez's poetry tends toward austerity, introspection, and an ethical content. Like Nervo, he turned increasingly toward the inner world; unlike Nervo, González Martínez never retreated from formal concerns and in the 1920s experimented with such new currents as antipoetic language and dehumanized imagery. But he never really ceased to be primarily a Symbolist who was tuned to an inner music of metaphysical search for understanding and consolation. This tendency became even more marked in the poems of elegiac simplicity written after the deaths of the poet's wife in 1935 and, four years later, of his son Enrique González Rojo, himself a poet of note.

There were many other Modernist poets, among the most interesting being Francisco González León (1862–1945), Francisco A. de Icaza (1896–1925), Luis G. Urbina (1864–1934), María Enriqueta Camarillo de Pereyra (1872–1968), and Rafael López (1873–1943). A special case, and perhaps not really a Modernist in a narrow sense, was the priest Father Alfredo Placencia (1873–1930), who was unique in his fusion of a personal brand of mysticism with a colloquial manner of addressing a God, with whom he was not always on satisfactory terms. Placencia may well have been a somewhat unorthodox antecedent of such a later poet as Jaime Sabines, whose work consistently reflects religious tensions in a colloquial and often even abusive idiom. Efrén Rebolledo (1877–1929) reflected in his relatively sparse work his interest in Japanese and Scandinavian literature, in Oscar Wilde, and in the Belgian symbolist Maurice Maeterlinck. He was obsessed by a sort of opulent formal perfection. Yet, Rebolledo's best work, *Caro victrix* (1916), is a volume of intense eroticism.

Perhaps this diversity within unity is best reflected in José Juan Tablada (1871–1945), by far the most important of those Modernists who remained devoted primarily to formal questions. Tablada possessed a seemingly inexhaustible capacity for change, for being always at the vanguard of the new movements. He invariably returned from his frequent travels to Japan, Paris, and New York (sometimes on diplomatic service, sometimes in exile for his virulent antirevolutionary writings) full of the news of the latest literary movement. In his early work there are perceptible echoes of various major French symbolists; he also went through a Parnassian period, painting verbal portraits of Oriental screens and landscapes. Self-proclaimed a "decadentista," he wrote "Misa negra" (1898), which scandalized the literary and social establishment. Exiled in New York during a part of the Revolution, he returned to Mexico brimming with the avant garde, typographical experimentation, the haiku. In later volumes he attempted a popularly-oriented nationalistic poetry bordering on local color. An interesting but not a major poet, Tablada was a constant source of information about new currents, in music and painting as well as in poetry. The esthetic and intellectual restlessness that permitted him both to be one of early Modernism's most determinedly decadent poets and also to participate in its death with his introduction of the new currents in 1919 provided an important model for young poets in the years after the Revolution.

Obviously, it is extremely difficult to characterize the Modernists as a whole; there are such significant differences between many of them, such as Othón and Tablada or González Martínez and Gutiérrez Nájera, that they are usually treated as a heterogenous agglomeration of individuals. One recent critic, José Joaquín Blanco, has divided them into four fluid groups: a) Díaz Mirón and the "catastrophe of Romanticism"; b) what he calls "las flores del bien," by which he means the more restrained poetry of those, such as Othón, González Martínez, Urbina, Nervo, and Gutiérrez Nájera, who were comfortable in the world of dictator Díaz; c) Rebolledo and Tablada, with their transplanted decadentism in the French style; and d) González León, Placencia, and Ramón López Velarde, similar because of what he calls their "percepción crítica, cotidiana o irónica."[2] Although this classification offers some useful perceptions, it is also quite problematical, since it lumps a number of otherwise distinct writers because of their willingness to serve in one fashion or another as legitimators of the tyranny, while the other categories are specifically literary. More consistent criteria would alter the pattern drastically. Nor is it at all clear that López Velarde and Placencia really make sense as Modernists. The latter was too isolated and idiosyncratic to really qualify, while López Velarde may have begun in his youth as a Modernist but very early was doing quite different things.

THE REVOLT AGAINST MODERNISM

As I have indicated, 1910 was, for several reasons, a useful date to mark the starting point of modern Mexican literature. It corresponded roughly to the final demise of the outdated Romanticism which, despite the impact of Modernism, had continued to set the dominant tone in Spanish America throughout the nineteenth century, long after its disappearance elsewhere.

The year saw the outbreak of the Revolution, a profound social movement that swept the nation before it and left many institutions changed fundamentally and permanently. The Revolution also produced in literature the subgenre known as the novel of the revolution, with its socially-oriented naturalism that, during the late 1920s, came to be the semi-officially approved literary school. This was also the year of the cultural revolt against the sterility and mediocrity into which the nation's intellectual life had fallen under the corrupt government of the aging dictator Porfirio Díaz. The doctrine of Positivism, which sought to bring the advantages of modern technology to the people of Mexico, had been distorted to enrich a powerful few; its educational variant did away with the "impractical" study of the humanities and the classics without replacing them by a coherent program of technical education. A group of young intellectuals had already set about attempting to reinvigorate this stagnant cultural panorama with the aid of two senior figures of the preceding generation, Urbina and González Martínez. They founded the Popular University and the Ateneo de México, with its organ, the journal *Savia Moderna* (1906), and instituted courses in French and Greek literature and culture. These Ateneístas, as they were known, were not really an important group of poets, despite the presence of figures such as Alfonso Reyes (1889–1959), but they were in many cases the teachers, in the literal classroom sense, of the most important younger writers.

The outstanding poet of this period, Ramón López Velarde (1888–1921), was not really a member of the Ateneo; he was of that group that came to maturity during the later years of Modernism, and his work quite early opened up to new sounds and senses. López Velarde was really an unusual and in some ways an enigmatic poet, both for his work and for the manner in which it has been received. A towering presence in Mexico, although at first for the wrong reasons, he is still almost unknown beyond the national boundaries. He was long considered a poet of nostalgic recollections of childhood in the provinces and of the simple virtues of a way of life that was already rapidly disappearing—a reading one should add, that is difficult to fathom for anyone who has actually read his poetry, yet one that exercised a considerable influence on numbers of other poets who imitated what they mistakenly believed to be his rural themes. When a younger poet, Xavier Villarrutia, published a study of López Velarde, the first serious effort of its kind and still fundamental, the positive overreaction tended to see a sort of Mexican Baudelaire and perceived López Velarde's later poetry as radically distinct from the supposedly simpler techniques of the earlier work. Recent criticism has seen both poetry and poet more completely: the poetry developing logically and quite possibly consciously, and the poet as a profoundly religious man tormented by the passions of the flesh and by the thought of physical death, attracted by the city but deeply rooted in the province of his early life, anguished by an ambiguous relationship with and the early death of a young woman, the "Fuensanta" of his poems.

The dominant structure of López Velarde's poetry is an antithesis that is expressed formally in a series of binary oppositions: religion and the flesh, life and death, love and desire, the province and the city. This tension was also visible in his life; he participated in planning for the forthcoming Revolution but could not bring himself to participate in the movement itself, and the destruction of his beloved provincial cities filled him with despair. His longest work, "La suave patria," which so many readers had seen as a nostalgic recollection of the provinces, is in fact the expression of López Velarde's internal contradictions projected upon his homeland in a poem that is at once an assessment and a highly personal resolution. Love in López Velarde's poems is again a binary ambiguity; the two women are Fuensanta, the immaculate inspiration of his earliest poems, and the tempting sinner typified in one poem by Sara, "blonde Sara, uva en sazón." Occasionally the two aspects are intermingled, but it is much commoner to find them carefully separated, as though the poet were attempting in this fashion to sort out his own inner ambivalences.

One of the most striking technical aspects of his work is the colloquial ironic idiom. If it is not clear to what extent López Velarde was indebted to Baudelaire, it is also unclear whether he was familiar with the poetry of Jules Laforgue (1860–1887), who had such a profound influence on the development of ironic language in modern poetry, particularly through T.S. Eliot (1888–1965) in English and the Argentinian Leopoldo Lugones (1874–1938) in Spanish. The Mexican knew Lugones's work, so it may be that the influence came in that way. This is not a unique problem with López Velarde, whose poetry is so personal and so complex that it is difficult even to guess at some of his sources, even at times some of his meanings. Another key aspect is his extreme use of free association rather than the controlled metaphors linked in series that characterize the majority of earlier poets. The basis of this technique is the unexpected adjective, which López Velarde used in such startling fashion—other poets in Europe were at more or less the same time proclaiming that the adjective was the secret key to poetry. López Velarde was also one of the earliest Mexican poets to use the sense of smell to poetic effect. There is a Modernist echo in his use of rhyme and of Christian liturgical elements as the source for many images; this was a favorite trick of some of the French "poetas malditos," who were so important in the development of Modernism.

But with López Velarde it is never a case of satanism or black masses or the other pseudoreligious flummery that was in vogue earlier. The very ambivalence that tore him between Fuensanta and Sara led him to create images that fuse in startling fashion elements representing the two strands of his life and his poetry. Another characteristic, and one that anticipates a good deal of later poetry, is the highly personal use of allusions and imagery based on immediate experience, so that much of his poetry is all but closed to the reader, who cannot share entirely the poet's intellectual and emotional baggage, the sources of his work. At times these two tendencies combine in poems of strange and even haunting suggestiveness that clearly lead us into a tormented world that frightened the poet, but we are unable to pursue him far enough into the labyrinth of his own immediate poetic reactions to be able to determine more. The extent of López Velarde's influence on later Mexican poets is complicated. On the one hand, his expression is so personal that any direct influence might well have resulted only in imitation. On the other hand, the tortured suggestions of some poems hint at the anguish that would become the dominant theme of

Xavier Villaurrutia, and there are verbal displays that suggest Salvador Novo or Gilberto Owen. In any event, López Velarde served as a constant model of poetic liberty and integrity, in the face of a figure such as Nervo, who carefully excised from his later work any such personalized struggle.

Following the early death of López Velarde, there appeared two groups of younger poets of very different characteristics and interests, the Contemporáneos and the Estridentistas. The latter group formed part of the series (whether we call them Dadaists, Futurists, or whatever) who rejected all existing social and poetic structures in the name of some program. They strove to annul the past and destroy all the idols, although they were often saved from overseriousness by a fey sense of humor; they made considerable use of mechanical imagery inspired by the rapid industrialization and the development of new sources of power and transport. Although the Estridentistas were among the first poets in Mexico to introduce certain technical innovations, they produced little poetry of lasting value; their heritage is rather that of their healthy insolence in the face of all norms and rules.

The Contemporáneos were so known because of the review *Contemporáneos* with which they were associated from 1928 to 1931, although some of them had begun publishing in student reviews as early as 1914, and nearly all of them had been associated with a variety of other journals. They were the total opposite of the Estridentistas, and constitute the most important literary group of the century in Mexico. Like the Modernists, they looked to France, but to the France of the iconoclastic proto-Cubist Guillaume Apollinaire (1880–1918) and the surrealistic fantasies of Jean Cocteau (1889–1963), as well as to Italy and the England of Eliot. The Contemporáneos sought to introduce into Mexico the new literature, music, and painting of the cosmopolitan world. They were, in large measure, self-taught in this undertaking; their logical masters, the Ateneístas, were in many cases abroad, in the diplomatic service, while others were in political exile. Their poetic master should have been González Martínez, as the leading living poet, but his work was so firmly rooted in a Symbolist esthetic that he attracted no real disciples, although the Contemporáneos acknowledged the inspiration of his devotion to his art. The two poets in whom the future Contemporáneos found inspiration were Tablada and López Velarde, the former because he was eternally speaking of the latest books and cultural developments in other nations, the latter because of the inner coherence of a poetry crafted from his own internal tensions. It would be exaggerated but not entirely false to suggest that Tablada was an intellectual model, López Velarde, through his use of irony and sequences of free associations, a poetic one.

Although some, at least, of the Contemporáneos were aggressively intellectual in their pursuit of new ideas in poetry, and the group as a whole was very much avant garde in its general orientation, their spiritual roots, like those of much Occidental twentieth-century poetry, lay in that aspect of Romanticism that struggled with the dilemma of man's inner being and that tended to concentrate on states of dream and madness. If their literary models were Eliot, André Gide (1869–1951), Marcel Proust (1871–1922), or Paul Valéry (1871–1945), they were also influenced by the Surrealists, whose poetry was a direct outgrowth of this branch of Romanticism. When Novo and Villaurrutia began to translate for the theater, they were fascinated by the visions of the subjective nature of external reality of Luigi Pirandello (1867–1936) and by the excursions into a theater of dream and abnormal psychology of Henri-René Lenormand (1882–1951), dramatists closely linked with these new ideas. There has been considerable debate as to whether the Contemporáneos really constituted a litarary generation in the technical sense and, if so, who was their leader/guide and who were the true members, as opposed to hangers-on and friends. A good deal of such debate is really pointless for our purposes. The simple fact is that the group did collaborate on a number of literary reviews over a period of years, reviews that were the focal point for Mexican poetry over several decades, and that simultaneously there were marked differences between the various esthetic practices and theories to which they held. There were also subgroups within what they themselves called "el grupo sin grupo." Carlos Pellicer, José Gorostiza, and Jaime Torres Bodet were just enough older to have been involved with José Vasconcelos in the struggles to broaden the basis of popular education and culture of the very early post-Revolutionary period; it is no accident that two of this group were long-time governmental functionaries, while the third, Pellicer, was perhaps the poet most profoundly conscious of being American in his generation throughout Latin America. The other Contemporáneos were younger, more ironic, more skeptical.[3]

The Contemporáneos have also been criticized by socially-oriented critics, and by others who are not literary critics at all, because of their alleged lack of true national spirit and because of their addiction to French literature. Much of this criticism was not literary in origin; the Contemporáneos were largely urban and middle-class in a Mexico that was increasingly dominated by an establishment provincial or rural in origin, and they were considered too conservative and lacking in revolutionary spirit. In addition, they were youthfully scornful of mediocrity and pretentiousness in literature at a time when the government insisted on a naturalistically-oriented literature of social redemption. What makes all this fairly absurd is the fact that a considerable portion of the material published in *Contemporáneos* related to Mexican literature and art. It was there that Mariano Azuela's *Los de abajo*, the paradigmatic novel of the Revolution, was first widely discussed. Villarrutia was a superb critic of Sor Juana Inés de la Cruz, the seventeenth-century poet, as well as of other Mexican writers; Cuesta wrote penetrating essays on the nature of Mexican poetry, and others of the group experimented with poetry and theater rooted in popular lyric and folktale. Much more important, the Contemporáneos provided a lesson of intellectual and creative rigor that profoundly influenced later Mexican writers, and they were influential in a series of literary reviews, until late in the 1940s, that provided a cultural center about which Mexican letters developed.

Like the Modernists, the Contemporáneos were notable for their diversity within unity. Oldest of the group was Carlos Pellicer (1899–1977). He was the closest to Modernism in his sense of a poetry of visual and plastic beauty, but Pellicer's poetry is extremely sensual, composed of unexpected rhythms and images based on imaginative perceptions of the natural world. He is often considered a poet of great color, but his poetry increasingly represents the tropical state of Tabasco, a land of sea and sky where he was born, and the colors are blue and green. Rather than describe the natural world, Pellicer names it, in a process of magical invocation which recalls the traditional religious role of the bard. At the same time, this process frequently associates the natural world with the human. He made extensive use of pre-Hispanic ritual and myth in his work, and many of the poems relate directly to such myth. Pellicer is also a profoundly Christian poet; his work became increasingly pantheistic and religious, dominated by an almost Franciscan sense of the community of the natural world. This community and the poet's sense of it play an important role in his poetry; among his repeated images are lines such as "Yo que de Tabasco vengo, / con golpes de sangre maya" ("Romance de Tilantongo") and "Agua de Tabasco vengo, / y agua de Tabasco voy" ("Cuatro cantos a mi tierra"), and the poet can call himself "árbol de caoba que camina."

Also from Tabasco was José Gorostiza (1901–1973), who was for many years a governmental functionary, serving as undersecretary and then secretary of foreign relations in the Mexican cabinet. It would be difficult to discover two poets more radically distinct than he and Pellicer. Where Pellicer was prolific, Gorostiza wrote little; where the tone of the former's poetic world was set by the abundant sensual tropics, Gorostiza's poetry is spare. To the sensual immediacy of Pellicer, Gorostiza opposed an intense intellectualism. Gorostiza's first book was *Canciones para cantar en las barcas* (1925); the tendency toward the sparse line is already visible, although there is often a popular tone that recalls some sixteenth-century Spanish lyrics. In 1939 he published the metaphysical *Muerte sin fin*, which uses the image of water and the glass that contains it and gives it form to examine the relationship between form and matter. The shifts between the matter contained and given shape and the form that shapes and contains as they are presented in the poem's multiple levels become also life and death, the poem and the poet, existence and God. Ultimately, existence and water-life-poet-creation are all conceived as matter that is given form by intelligence. But intelligence, form in itself, is not enough; it can imagine itself but it cannot create. In the end, the only

certainty is death, and in the face of this annihilating percep-
tion, the poem opts for a stoically hedonistic attitude. This is, of
course, a simplistic reduction of a poem that functions on
multiple levels simultaneously. In one direction, *Muerte sin fin*
harks back to the Góngora of the *Soledades* and the Sor Juana of
Primero sueño; in another, it is akin to the work of Eliot and
Valéry in its expression of our time's anguished despair of the
intellect. *Muerte sin fin* is a poetic triumph because, despite the
complexity of its metaphysical speculation, this speculation is
carried out poetically, through metaphor and analogy rather
than through logic, so that it always remains a poem and never
becomes a philosophical tract.

Jaime Torres Bodet (1902–1974) was another distinguished
public servant in later life; he served several terms as secretary
of public education, was Mexico's ambassador to France, and
also served as director general of UNESCO. Unlike Gorostiza,
who apparently felt that the demands made on him by public
service were at least a partial cause for his having produced such
a slight quantity of poetry, Torres Bodet published substantially.
Each volume of poetry was a search for expression; each at-
tempted a different style, until with the surrealist period of
Destierro (1930) and the purification of language of *Cripta* (1937),
Torres Bodet began to develop a personal poetic formulation of
the poetry of anguish influenced by Eliot and Laforgue, which
came to dominate his work. Strangely, once he had developed
his own poetic idiom, Torres Bodet's rhythm of publication
slowed markedly, and he did not again publish a book of poetry
until the *Sonetos* of 1949. In *Sonetos* and again in *Frontera* (1954)
the tonic note becomes desolation before the death of those
around us and our own imminent end. The best poems of
Sonetos, such as the sequence "Continuidad," are classical in
their austerity, while in *Frontera* the tone is muted, more minor.
At the same time, there is a sense of resignation alleviated by
the spirit of human solidarity in the face of the misery of
existence.

Within the Contemporáneos there were subgroupings. One
consisted of Salvador Novo (1904–1974) and Xavier Villarrutia
(1903–1950), close friends and collaborators in the literary re-
view *Ulises* (1927–1928) and the important experimental the-

ater groups Teatro Ulises and Teatro Orientación, in which a number of the other Contemporáneos also participated. Novo was polyfacetic and prolific; he published poetry, fiction, plays, travel books, chronicles of past and present Mexico City (he was named its official chronicler), and magazine articles on theater, cooking, and Mexican night life. The majority of his best work was written by the time he was forty; the poetry written between 1934 and 1963, when he again began to write poetry seriously, consists primarily of occasional sonnets. Novo, like several others of the group, was essentially post-Romantic by way of Eliot in his use of irony and colloquial language. His poetry is extremely personal, with an intimate tone that is not entirely hidden by the irony and often the sarcasm that give their characteristic note to his work. These are provoked by the repeated sense of frustration and impotence in the face of a society whose values are increasingly materialistic. At the same time the poet was torn by his own decision to utilize his talents for commercial purposes, a reflection within himself of the same social problem that created the feelings of impotence. In books such as *Nuevo amor*, Novo was able to reconcile these tensions in the figure of the lost love who is simultaneously the ideal betrayed in an uncomprehending world. At his best, Novo is a poet of brilliantly sardonic wit that emphasizes the delicacy and tenderness of his lyric power.

Villaurrutia was in a sense the critical conscience of the group; he was the author of a considerable body of perceptive criticism and of a number of plays. *Reflejos* (1926) consists of impressionistic images of daily life inspired by the paintings of Cezanne and the Japanese haiku, which is rooted in the Zen Buddhist perception of instants of reality. Villaurrutia's mature poetry deals with the history of a death, of the search for a response to the fact of death that would not end in nihilism or madness. He found this response not in the acceptance of death but in its pursuit, as he transformed death into a constant mistress who accompanied him everywhere. In 1946 Villaurrutia published the definitive version of *Nostalgia de la muerte*, an intellectualized world in which mirrors reflect only the poet's same face of always. The volume catches the solipsistic dilemma in which the individual is unable to break through the barriers of the personality to establish contact with any other being. Ultimately, the world of *Nostalgia de la muerte* becomes completely turned back upon itself, for the only contact is with the lady Death whom the poet courts. The intellectual nature of Villaurrutia's poetry and the difficulty of expressing lucidly its theme lend themselves to his extended use of conceptist word-play and antithesis, while the startling metaphors combine to create an unreal atmosphere reminiscent of the work of Villaurrutia's favorite painter, the surrealist Chirico. *Canto a la primavera* (1948) is a major change from this line; although it does not possess the hallucinated unity that marks the previous book, the *Canto* does demonstrate in poems such as "Décimas de nuestro amor" that Villaurrutia could achieve the same concision and brilliance of expression in the new thematics, a fact that might have led to a drastic change in his poetic style had he not died shortly after. In Villaurrutia's work there are echoes of the conquests of Surrealism, particularly in the use of the dream and unconscious states, but his poetic world is one of lucid vigilance in the face of the inability to go beyond the limits of the individual personality.

The Surrealist influence was critical in the development of the poetry of Bernardo Ortiz de Montellano (1899–1949). As the result of his poetic experiments and of the experience of being anesthetized during surgery, the poet came to believe that poetry and dream were analogous and perhaps even related states, alternative means of perceiving one essential reality, and that through them it was even possible to foresee the future. This is, of course, orthodox Surrealist doctrine, within which dream and poetry are regarded as identical, or at most as minimally differentiated states. An essential part of this credo is the acceptance of Freudian psychoanalytic theory and the practice of automatic writing, within which the poet attempted to avoid all conscious control of what he wrote in order that the subconscious might express its truly poetic and prophetic visions. In such an approach there is an obvious danger that overreliance on psychoanalytical concepts may turn the poet and the poem into subjects for Freudian analysis, potential case studies; there is the parallel danger that what is produced in the process of automatic writing may be valued because it is allegedly the

product of the unconscious rather than because it in fact pos-
sesses literary value. Like Villaurrutia and Novo, Ortiz de Mon-
tellano experimented with automatic writing but was aware of
these potential problems and made clear that he was interested
in the arrangement of the images and forms within the dream
and the poem, rather than in any psychoanalytical explication.

Sueños (1933) is an effort to achieve a poetry of dream and
anesthesia, with uneven results. Indeed, there are images of
stunning power and suggestiveness, but a good deal of the book
is close to incomprehensible, even with the aid of the poet's
Diario de mis sueños, a species of commentary. In spite of the
disclaimers to the contrary, he often appears more interested in
the poems' supposed ability to foretell the future than in their
value as poetry. In Muerte de cielo azul (1937), an effort to define
the ephemeral nature of experience and existence, he utilized
the same subject matter and Surrealist focus without radically
altering them but also without permitting himself to be con-
trolled by them. Ultimately, we see him choosing dream as a
necessary antidote to the colorlessness of daily existence. Like
many Surrealists, who considered so-called primitive art to be
closer to the authentic sources of artistic expression because,
like dream, it was not controlled by the logical structures of
Occidental civilization, Ortiz de Montellano was also deeply
interested in the expressive potential of Indian poetry and myth.
In addition to poems using such rhythms, he wrote two one-act
plays that combine avant garde and Surrealist techniques with
indigenous myth.

Gilberto Owen (1904–1952) spent many years outside Mex-
ico in his nation's consular service, and he has never achieved
the full measure of reputation to which his work entitles him.
He was particularly friendly with Villaurrutia. Like him and
Novo, Owen was deeply interested in French and English poetry,
and his sparse work—apparently he destroyed or lost a portion
of it—reflects a taste for Eliot and Mallarmé. Owen's poetry
demonstrates startling images and a considerable reliance on
allusion and wordplay. His most important work by far is Perseo
vencido (1948), a desolate vision of man's role in the cosmos that
sees time as the only permanent force. We are all lost in time and
condemned to perish within it, all metaphysical castaways, as

in the poem "Sindbad el varado." Neither eroticism nor the-
ology offers us a real escape. Where the poetic world of Eliot
ends in a whimper until the poet is able to accept theological
redemption, that of Owen, who was unable to make such an
acceptance, ends with a "Tal vez" that is already an obvious
"nunca." Not entirely a member of the group but united to it by
links of friendship was Elías Nandino (1903), whose work is the
history of a man obsessed by the drive toward religious belief
and the impossibility of finding it. Another facet of his work is
the tortured eroticism which the poet cannot alter but which he
finds morally destructive. Nandino's poetry never exhibits the
degree of control and technical mastery characteristic of the
Contemporáneos, but because he is the only surviving member
of the group, his continued creativity has aroused the long-
delayed interest of the critics. Another tormented personage
was Jorge Cuesta (1903–1942), an obsessively intellectual artist
who sought to create an equally intellectualized poetry that
would effectively suppress the role of the emotions. Although
poems such as "Canto a un dios mineral" are of great expressive
power, the bulk of Cuesta's work is difficult and almost impen-
etrable, and his most appreciated writings are his penetrating
analyses of Mexican poetry and culture.

Perhaps Cuesta's most important contribution to the group,
beyond his role as intellectual goad, was his leading role in the
preparation of their polemical *Antología de la poesía mexicana
moderna* (1928), an effort by a group of very young writers to
deflate some reputations they considered overrated and simul-
taneously to attract attention to their own work. Now, nearly
sixty years later, we see quite clearly that they undoubtedly
were somewhat brusque in their evaluations. At the same time,
the *Antología* pointed out that a good many of the established
giants were in fact considerably less than that, and that there
were younger writers of importance. The Contemporáneos in-
cluded several poets of international stature, and as an active
cooperating group, none has surpassed them in Spanish America
in the twentieth century. In addition to their own creative work,
they established the idea of a literary criticism that brought to
the works studied a broad acquaintance with Occidental liter-
ature and that was applied with rigor. Through their various

journals, poetry, translations, and critical writing, the Contemporáneos introduced the small but growing Mexican literary public to such novelties in music and painting as Satie and Chirico, and to post-Symbolist literature and theater in English, French, and Italian.

TALLER AND THE OTHER SIDE OF THE ROMANTIC HERITAGE

By the mid-1930s there was in Mexico a somewhat younger group of writers, born about 1914, some of whom were frequent contributors to the Contemporáneos' later journals and whose early work in many instances reflects a rather direct influence. They exhibit the same sense of solitude in a hostile or at best indifferent world. The younger writers shared with the Contemporáneos many of their artistic tastes, but they also rejected a good deal of what they perceived as the Contemporáneos' overly intellectualized approach to literature and to life, and by 1936 they were active in their own publications, *Taller poético* (1936–1938) and *Taller* (1938–1941).

The group of Taller came to feel that their elders were too preoccupied with entirely literary matters and with questions of personal style; the new poets sought to make of the poem a vital affirmation rather than a personal document or an exercise in expression. Whether these were really accurate judgments of what the Contemporáneos were about is debatable—after all, at the time *Taller poético* was founded, the oldest of the so-called "older" writers was no more than thirty-seven, the majority were in their early thirties, and Torres Bodet and José Gorostiza had not yet had time to make their significant contributions to public service. But this is, of course, the normal reaction of younger poets against their literary elders, particularly when those elders are themselves still paradoxically engaged in carving out their own creative place. Be that as it may, Taller had two clearly marked directions. First, their poetry was oriented toward society, toward human beings as participants in a social reality. An attempt to change mankind for the better implied a change in society, so that several of the most important members were politically active, although this did not always mean that their poetry was propagandistic. Where the Contemporáneos had experienced the Revolution of 1910 and had responded in literary terms by turning toward a world of creative literature that showed relatively little connection with the turbulent social reality surrounding them, Taller experienced, at a slightly more mature age, the Spanish Civil War and understood that it portended the cataclysm. The result was that they were much more politically committed as a group, and they also were deeply influenced by such writers as the Chilean Pablo Neruda (1904-1973), who had espoused the Marxist and Spanish Loyalist causes.

The other thrust of their work was really a further development of the influences we have already seen at work on several of the Contemporáneos. Where Villaurrutia and others had been deeply influenced by writers such as Novalis and certain aspects of the Surrealists, Taller was fully open to the Surrealists. Neruda and the Spanish poets whom they most admired were all Surrealist-influenced. Another major theme that was to remain visible in their work throughout was the Neoromanticism of D.H. Lawrence (1885–1930), heightened by their passion for the visionary expressionism of William Blake (1757–1827). Love and its complex relationship with eroticism and salvation represented some sort of escape from a world that was rapidly becoming even more intolerable than the most decadent of Modernists could have perceived. The result of all this was that for the members of Taller, love, poetry, and revolution were aspects of the same phenomenon. Like their poetic models, they sought a return to the source and found this source deep in the human psyche; it is no accident that two members of the group, Octavio Paz and Efraín Huerta, are in very different ways the most erotic of Mexico's modern poets.

The most famous member of Taller and of modern Mexican poets is Octavio Paz (1914–), who has achieved a worldwide reputation as a poet and critic. His essays include original and perceptive examinations of the history and personality of the Mexican and of a broad spectrum of modern literature. Paz's earlier poetry is a search for the roots of the Mexican being; at the same time, it establishes the constants that will remain important throughout his work: human solitude, physical love, and the nature of poetic language. Ramón Xirau has suggested that Paz's early poetry is so rich in densely interwoven images that the poems take on an existence of their own, much as though the poetry were a separate reality within which the poet sought escape from the solitude of this world.[4] The work until about 1958 seems to conceive existence in circular or cyclical terms; with *Salamandra* (1962) the emphasis shifts to the simultaneity of human experience, although still rooted in the specifics of Mexican experience. Throughout, Paz is essentially a dialectical poet, attempting to establish relationships between opposed concepts in a fashion that will provide the moment of vision, the escape from solitude and ordinary existence.

From the very beginning of Paz's poetry, love was the only possible solace. His experience as Mexican ambassador to India put him in closer contact with Oriental doctrines that have affected him profoundly, so that his mature poetry is a shifting gallery of approaches to the role of love in a world whose reality is subject to question, as in *Blanco* (1967) or *Ladera este* (1969). The former is a complex poem whose structure recalls that of Mallarmé's *Un coup de dés* in its complicated formal and intellectual structure, which provides for several separate or partial readings as well as a complete or total reading of the entire book. Paz has also experimented with poetry written jointly by several poets in diverse languages and capable of being read in a variety of ways, and with other variations on the poetic word, such as the *Topoemas* (1971), brief binary structures that attempt to capture the dialectical relationships between opposing concepts in a fashion reminiscent of the Oriental ideogram. He is also absorbed by the theoretical question of the nature of poetry and its relationship to the poet; it is hardly surprising that he has been fascinated by the Portuguese poet Fernando Pessoa (1888–1935), who wrote four quite different kinds of poetry under his own name and under the names of three other poets whom he invented. At the same time, in his vision of an antilogical universe within which the visionary image is seen as a means to what limited knowledge we may achieve, Paz has remained faithful to his vision of Surrealism as authentic poetry, although rejecting such tenets as automatic writing. In a sense, Paz is very close to a poetry of mysticism in which the saving element is not grace but love in a very human context.

The other members of Taller were Rafael Solana (1915–), Neftalí Beltrán (1916–), Efraín Huerta (1914–1982) and Alberto Quintero Alvarez (1914–1944). The latter is the most clearly influenced by Surrealism, by the visionary poetry of Rimbaud, and by Neruda. His poetry deals with religious experience, the contact with nature, and anguished love; his early death cut off his development before he achieved a truly individual poetic personality. Solana took other creative roads although his work in poetry, especially in *Los espejos falsarios* (1944) demonstrates considerable technical facility in dealing with standard forms such as the sonnet, which he uses to express the fleeting character of our existence. Beltrán too all but abandoned poetry after a promising book, *Soledad enemiga* (1949); his work is intensely introspective in the face of death and solitude. Huerta continued to be prolific as a poet until his death, and also wrote extensively as a journalist. In his later years his reputation grew rapidly as the critics realized the power of his sardonic verse. Huerta carried the double thrust of the group of Taller to its logical extreme; his unflagging Marxism and eroticism led him to create a poetry that is irascible, colloquial, sarcastic, and sometimes obscene, but that often achieves considerable power in the vein of the great street poets such as François Villon (1431–after 1463).

Only slightly younger than Taller and sharing many of their preoccupations were the poets who initially grouped themselves about the review *Tierra Nueva* (1940–1942): Manuel Calvillo (1918–), Wilberto Cantón (1923–1979), Jorge González Durán (1918–), and Alí Chumacero (1918–). They were far closer to the Contemporáneos' concept of art than to Taller's socially-oriented initial conception, and, like many of the Contemporáneos, their poetic productivity has been small for many years. Cantón soon abandoned poetry for theater, and Calvillo has published little. González Durán, like the members of Taller and so many Mexican poets of the twentieth century, is obsessed with solitude and death, with love as the only escape. Chumacero, who towers over the others, has written almost no new poetry over the last forty years, but the publication of his collected works in 1980 led to a new interest in his work and to the rediscovery that it possesses considerable originality and extraordinary lyrical power, if so dense as to be sometimes almost incomprehensible. Chumacero again is primarily concerned with the solipsistic problem of the impossibility of going beyond the limits of the individual personality; his poetry is haunted by images of sterility and the ultimate failure of any human relationship, of communication, and of the word.

THE WOMEN POETS

Although María Enriqueta had participated in the activities of Modernism, initially few women were active in the literary reviews that were the basis of the succeeding movements until the appearance of the Generation of 1954, when women began to participate fully in the literary activities of the various circles. The result is that during the interval between the end of Modernism and about 1950, women poets in general were either solitary artists or participated tangentially at best in various reviews. Concha Urquiza (1910–1945) held intense religious beliefs that led her to devote herself to religious training and to teaching, and her poetry was nourished in the classics and the Bible. After a youthful rejection of religion and flirtation with Marxism, she entered a convent, but her health failed and she was forced to leave. Urquiza wrote of the search for mystical experience within the confines of the Spanish tradition. Yet hers is a poetry in which the anguish of a fragile sensibility struggles with hope, and the mystical impulse is not always separable from the erotic. Slightly younger than Urquiza were a number of others who were active in *Rueca*, a journal edited by several women writers, whose period of continuous publication extended from 1941 to 1946. Their work is relatively diverse, but most of them share an intense religious search and an active life as teachers and writers.

Emma Godoy (1918–), novelist and teacher, is also a poet of religious inspiration, using an almost colloquial poetic language and an abundant sensual imagery to express the search for God. Guadalupe Amor (1920–), certainly one of Mexico's most productive writers, shares this search for the divine and expresses its conflict with the spiritual sterility of modern life in strict traditional forms such as the sonnet and the decima, dominated by conceptual wordplay. She is perhaps the only one of this group to have been influenced by the Contemporáneos, particularly by the metaphysical anguish of Villaurrutia and Gorostiza. Margarita Michelena (1922–) passed from avant garde abstraction to a delicate lyrical sense, but always her poetry is the expression of a profound solitude that finds only temporary solace in the sense of familiar things remembered. Margarita Paz Paredes (1922–) is considerably different from the others mentioned here; her abundant subjective and highly personal poetry is immediate and approachable, reflecting none of the contemporary innovation and experimentation. She wrote of the oppression and abandonment, both political and cosmic, that she saw about and within her. Her work vacillates between hope for some kind of redemption, a better way, and the sense of despair. None of these writers could be called a feminist in modern terms, and *Rueca* was hardly distinguishable from other journals of the period, except for the number of women authors whom it published and who were active on its staff. At the same time, it was a clear sign that Mexico counted with a number of serious women writers, and it anticipated the burgeoning of women's literature in the 1960s.

THE NEW POETRY: THE GENERATION OF 1954

The true flourishing in Mexico of a new literary generation takes place with the appearance of those poets born in approximately 1925. By the late 1950s they were emerging as a dominant voice, alongside those members of earlier movements who were still active. The Generation of 1954 is a heterogeneous group whose poetry reflects a multiplicity of technical and thematic interests. In very broad terms, it is possible to say that they fall generally into one of two groups: those who, like Paz, see poetry as a form of individual search, frequently with Surrealist and/or metaphysical overtones, and those who, like Huerta, consider it to have a social purpose. It must be remembered that although there were and are subdivisions within the group, generally reflected by those reviews in which they have collaborated, they all know each other and there has been a considerable interaction between them, so that there is a great deal of overlap, and divisions by schools are not really either feasible or enlightening. Rubén Bonifaz Nuño (1923–), for example, is a Latinist by training, which may explain his intense continuing interest in the creation of a poetry of tightly constructed formal unity and thematic coherence and continuity. At the same time, his is a poetry extremely difficult of comprehension, perhaps in part because its creator is accomplished in dealing with the intricate syntactic structure of Latin. To this classical heritage Bonifaz Nuño unites a familiarity with and an awareness of the decisive role in Mexico of the pre-Hispanic inheritance, and his mature poetry is a brilliant effort at a synthesis of the two currents. Jaime García Terrés (1924–) is one of Latin America's most accomplished translators, and his poetry lies in the tradition of the reflective lyric on the transitoriness of life. García Terrés attempts to harmonize the conflicts between opposed concepts that lie at the root of existence. It is an intelligent and measured poetry drawing on the background of European culture, alive with the echoes of the great poets of the world tradition within a general framework of deceptive simplicity.

With Rosario Castellanos (1925–1974) women poets enter fully into the reviews and groupings that are a dominant factor of Mexican literary life. She is best known outside Mexico as a novelist of the predominantly Indian province of Chiapas where she lived until she was sixteen and to which she returned for periods during her adult life. Yet her poetry is quite different; in her search for the meaning of her role as a woman in a male-dominated society and for a poetic persona that would enable her to control her poetic version of this quest, she developed a unique personal idiom that was to undergo a drastic alteration in the years just before her tragic death. Castellanos avoided sentimentalism and prefabricated attitudes, and in her poetry the reader finds the boredom of the domestic world coexisting with and interpenetrating a rich world of cultural and mythological figures. Jaime Sabines (1926–) is a poet of the tradition of Villon or César Vallejo (1892–1938), engaged in a violent battle with a God, whom he insults and implores. He is also desolated by the implacable fact of death, and his finest poetry lies within this double current of enraged defiance and melancholy elegy. Marco Antonio Montes de Oca (1932–) is a poet of astonishing fecundity and richness of invention, whose work is a varied metaphorical kaleidoscope; the cascades of images are for him a means of communication with the mystery of existence and of establishing subjective associations between varying levels of experience. Unlike many of his contemporaries and younger Mexican poets, Montes de Oca writes poetry almost exclusively. He seems to envision his work as a coexisting corpus in constant process of transformation, so that he is constantly revising and correcting his previous work while publishing new poetry at a remarkable rate. Two other poets born in Spain but long associated with Mexico, are Tomás Segovia (1927–) and Manuel Durán (1925–). Durán, active as a teacher in the United States, inherited the Surrealist vision of unreal nightmare, although his poetry is far more purified of nonessentials. Segovia, like many of this generation, is also a talented critic, essayist, and author of fiction; his work is rooted in his own experience of exile, and turns about the twin poles of alienation and perception of the significance of this experience.

The Poetry of Crisis: Tlatelolco, Rock, and After

An extraordinary amount of poetry is being written and published in Mexico today, and a significant portion of it comes from those poets born at roughly the mid-point of their generation. Too young to have experienced the long heritage of social tumult occasioned by the Revolution and the religious civil wars of the late 1920s and the 1930s or to have even vague memories of Mexico's peripheral role in World War II, they are the products of a nation undergoing a dizzying series of transformations. Few of them come from the rural villages, and almost all of them, wherever born, have lived most of their lives in a capital city that threatens to be overcome by its own sheer weight. The center of an enormous governmental bureaucracy as well as the nation's financial and cultural center, Mexico City has gone from a population of some two million in the late

1940s to perhaps nine or ten times that many. It is a city slowly losing the struggle against overcrowding, corruption, air pollution, and inadequate public services. The official revolutionary rhetoric does not hide the fact that governments have become increasingly conservative in the face of spiraling public need. To this picture may be added two further calamities: the terrible earthquake of 1985 desolated even a city accustomed to the occasional tremor, and the falling price of petroleum, upon which recent governments have constructed their plans for economic progress, political stability, and a better standard of living for Mexico, has left the nation with enormous foreign debts it can repay barely if at all. In a nation whose population continues to grow at a disastrous rate and which comments ironically that its most important exports are the Mexicans who, legally or illegally, cross the northern border in search of a better life, these disasters are doubly menacing.

The picture has not always been so threatening. Mexican oil production was envisioned as the foundation of a progressive nation, and Mexico City's rapid growth in the 1960s created a go-go atmosphere which affected many young writers fascinated by youth culture, protest movements, and rock music. But, as the flower-child culture of the United States withered, so Mexican optimism slowly eroded in the face of unmanageable problems. The decisive moment was the terrible Night of Tlatelolco in 1968, when right-wing paramilitary and official forces attacked a demonstration of students. The number of dead has never been clearly established, but it was a night of random violence that was for many Mexicans, especially intellectuals and artists, a sign that the repressive nature of past governments had not really been altered. That this sign was read correctly was borne out by the purging of a leading independent newspaper by pro-government forces. In a city in which artists are often dependent on positions in teaching, journalism, or editorial work, all of which are subject to considerable public and private pressure, the result is an atmosphere of extreme insecurity. The consequence is that Mexican poetry over the last few years, particularly since 1968, has a distinct note of pessimism and of doubt of even the possibility for solutions while at the same time being itself a poetry of great vigor.

Prominent members of this generational mid-point are Isabel Fraire (1934–), Gabriel Zaid (1937–), José Carlos Becerra (1937–1970), Homero Aridjis (1940–), and the Mexican poet of perhaps widest international reputation after Paz, José Emilio Pacheco (1940–). Andrew Debicki has pointed out that there are two major strands to this group's production.[5] The first is intensely subjective, often coupled with metaphysical concerns expressed sometimes through extraordinary metaphorical and visionary richness, sometimes through precise and carefully controlled use of perspective and technique. The other principal vein of this generational grouping is a concern with the relationship of poetry to social problems, spurred particularly by enthusiasm for the Cuban revolution, by opposition to United States intervention in Vietnam and Central America, and by Tlatelolco, which produced a veritable spate of irate poems and which continues to haunt Mexicans as a spectre of what their revolution has become. Although the two tendencies correspond roughly to two different groups of poets, there is also at times considerable overlap.

Pacheco is an important author of fiction, a literary critic, and an anthologist. As a poet, he is prolific and versatile. His work has gone from metaphysical formalism to a more colloquial idiom and he has experimented widely with montages and personal versions of other poets from the world tradition. A constant theme in Pacheco is the uncertainty and impermanence of a decaying world. Although he searches for a balance between permanence and flux, Pacheco's poetry seems drawn to the vision of time as constant change within which we are trapped without anchor. Aridjis, like Pacheco, has published extensively in prose fiction and in poetry; like many of these younger figures, he resists classification because his poetry seems to embrace all life and existence. Underlying it is the theme of love alternately satisfied and wanting. His favorite forms range from short and apparently simple strophes to long rhythmic lines nearly indistinguishable from prose poems. Fraire's thoughtful and rigorous work is in the metaphysical tradition of Villaurrutia and Gorostiza, although she has been deeply influenced by North American poets such as Eliot, E.E. Cummings (1894–1962), and William Carlos Williams (1883–

1963). She creates images that relate on another level to inner states such as love or the creative process. Zaid, who has also written widely on literature, politics, and economics, is a poet who seeks to express the exact nature of the contradictory world about him. His poetry is carefully structured, with an almost mathematical sense of order and a biting ironic humor. Becerra's poetry is populated by darkness, empty rooms, the memories of the dead, and a terrible sense of loss, in a kind of purified Postromanticism, without falling into the clichés of such poetry.

For the poets who view poetry as a means to social action, Efraín Huerta has served as a model. Best known of these are the five poets known collectively as *La espiga amotinada* after the title of their first joint volume (1960): Juan Bañuelos (1932–), Eraclio Zepeda (1937–), Oscar Oliva (1937–), Jaime Augusto Shelley (1937–), and Jaime Labastida (1939–). Although they have a common approach to poetry and life, they have not written collective poetry. *La espiga,* written while several members of the group were living in the remote conservative state of Chiapas, where they had gone in a rejection of modern society, includes a collection of poems by each. In 1965 the group published a second volume, *Ocupación de la palabra,* following the lines of their earlier publication. They reject the notion of poetry for poetry's sake and take the position that art has a social function and must be dealt with in group fashion, a position they maintained in their second volume but later largely abandoned. Although they are all committed to the idea of poetry as protest, there are substantial differences between them, both formally and in terms of the attitudes inherent in their work; none of them writes poetry reduced to propaganda.

If Aridjis, Pacheco, Montes de Oca, and the others are now the established figures of Mexican poetry, there are other younger poets who also have much to offer and who are pursuing widely varying paths. It would be impossible to treat them adequately here. One example is Elsa Cross (1946–), for whom memories, such as those of the Provençal or early Italian poets and of their spiritual brethren the Cathars, combine with the echo of poetry in English to create hard-edged poetic visions that reflect a more modern anguish as well. Another is David

Huerta (1949–), son of Efraín Huerta, who creates a poetry far more disciplined and traditionally literary than that of his father. They are only two of the many younger poets whose plaquettes and books are widely available and whose poems fill the literary reviews which, after a lapse of a few years, once again thrive despite disaster and economic hardship. Gabriel Zaid, in his incisive and amusing introduction to the anthology *Asamblea de poetas jóvenes de México* (1980), refers to his bemused stupefaction when his cherished belief that in any given decade there can be only ten or a dozen poets of some importance came face to face with the fact that in 1979 knowledgeable people in Mexico identified a total of 549 born in the 1950s and 1960s. Worse still, he found it impossible to reduce the massive list to less than a hundred who were more or less visibly superior to the rest. He also found a total of 213 literary reviews, newspapers, and other periodicals that have published the work of poets born after 1950. Sandro Cohen, himself a younger poet of note, published in 1981 a somewhat more restrained selection of the work of poets born after 1940; he includes 54. It seems clear that, in spite of earthquake and crisis, Mexican poetry continues to flourish.

2 ALÍ CHUMACERO
The Inner Landscape

Although anthologies and histories of literature invariably refer to him as one of the leading figures of this century, Alí Chumacero could be called the invisible man of modern Mexican poetry. His production is extremely sparse: three slim volumes and a handful of other poems published in journals and collected in the *Poesía Completa* in 1980.[1] Critical studies of his work are far from abundant: a few articles and reviews, some of considerable value, but in total very little. Even the publication of the collected poems and the subsequent receipt of the 1980 Villaurrutia Prize for Poetry, the most important of its kind in Mexico, produced little critical response aside from newspaper reports. This virtual oblivion is almost certainly due to two factors: the undeniable difficulty of the work and the fact that Chumacero has long since abandoned poetry and makes almost no public appearances in the literary world. The *Poesía Completa* adds only a few very early poems; Chumacero has apparently written nothing in over thirty years. And yet the reader who turns to this almost forgotten work finds in it a complexity and density of expression seldom equalled.

The difficulty of the two earliest books, *Páramo de sueños* (1944) and *Imágenes desterradas* (1948) is due in great measure to the nearly total lack of anything that might be called anecdote or external reference. This is a poetry so stubbornly turned inward, toward the writer's inner personal world, that frequently there is no anchor for the reader; the principal character is always the poet himself. As Andrés Henestrosa has said, "Alí Chumacero es una dramática dualidad, un adolorido conflicto entre el corazón y la inteligencia."[2] In some of the poems we can see only the general outline of the movement of the creative mind. Years later, the author was to say, "A veces caigo en el error de manejar elementos demasiado personales que le dan a mi poesía cierto esoterismo . . . Justamente ahora, por la aparición de *Poesía completa*, acabo de leer toda mi obra y la encuentro muy poco comunicativa y un tanto hermética."[3]

This inward view is rooted in Chumacero's frequently stated belief that all poetry represents the psychic state of its creator. In a review of the poetry of Antonio Machado, which serves as a point of departure for the closest Chumacero has come to a statement of a personal poetics, he speaks at length of this concept: "Toda poesía pone a prueba nuestra sensibilidad, haciendo que nos encontremos o nos neguemos en ella que al fin es un espejo, certero o no, donde la imagen reflejada asegurará la presencia nuestra dentro, en el azogue más íntimo del cristal."[4] The vocabulary here will be familiar to the reader of Chumacero's poetry: mirrors, images, glass, words that speak of surfaces resistant to penetration but at the same time related to seeing, to the search for autovision, for recognition, for self within the work. In his critical writings Chumacero was obviously cognizant of the inner tension of his creative work, in which this search forever struggles against the almost insurmountable barriers of the effort to communicate. The seeker here is the poet, but the reader too will recognize himself. The poet alludes to this when he speaks of "la calidad poética, el valor universal, el que debe entrañar toda poesía, la comunicación más vasta, profunda y humana donde se afirma la legitimidad, la validez y el vuelo de ella,"[5] dimensions pointed out as well by Alfredo Roggiano.[6] But this suprapersonal extension does not prevent Chumacero's poetry from being essentially an inner drama, even in the last volume, which is much more outwardly directed. It is exactly in this internalization that we find the communicative dimension, in the effort to coalesce in words the poet's psychic movement. Chumacero understands this, as we see when he refers to poetry as a sort of portrait of our deepest inner being:

La poesía es eso más que nada: imagen de algo; y ese algo somos nosotros con nuestro paisaje interior y la naturaleza circundante que al fin y al cabo se convierte en interior también, más o menos asimilada,

más o menos incorporada a nuestra personalidad, a la manera de man-
ifestarnos. En este sentido cada poeta, por más exteriorizado que sea,
posee "su" paisaje propio, inconfundiblemente matizado de par-
ticulares sensaciones, poblado de originales colores y sonidos. Cada
sensibilidad recoge como le es dado entender, las fuerzas que integran el
paisaje y los recuerdos de estas fuerzas que a su vez se integran a los
recuerdos de las ciudades, de los campos, de las selvas, de los mares y los
sujeta a una especie de decantación, a un proceso de especiales com-
binaciones conceptuales que den al fin con el sello de la personalidad
del poeta, con el timbre intransferible que hace a las cosas ser nuestras.[7]

This conception of poetry as the expression of the poet's
individual interior landscape becomes almost obsessive;
Chumacero turns to it repeatedly in other critical essays. In
another review, he comments that "No hay más estricta biog-
rafía de un poeta lírico que la lectura cronológica de sus poesías
completas. Porque él maneja en su verso lo más arcano de su
experiencia vital, su existencia misma. La condición única de su
poesía radica en su vida, y no difiere de sus actos privados sino
en la limpieza de la expresión, en la forma de trasvasar al mundo
eso que, contra su voluntad, requiere en especial una diferente y
radical manera de manifestarse."[8]

It is worth emphasizing that for Chumacero this process is
contrary to his will. The poet *must* express this inner drama,
whether he wish or no; over this aspect of his work he exercises
no control. This is really the great paradox of every poet's work;
he must, by the very nature of poetry, write out of his own inner
struggle. Yet, at the same time, he is trapped between the effort
to communicate and the difficulty of doing so through symbols
and images that are comprehensible to the reader, if at all, only
in terms of this individual inner world, what we might call a
total psychic configuration.

El poeta es un hombre que elude en buena parte todos los problemas de
la sociedad, es alguien que se refleja a sí mismo al escribir; general-
mente escribe sobre la mínima importancia que tiene esta sociedad; la
poesía lo dignifica, lo salva de esa miseria en que vive; el poeta es
tímido, es cruel a veces, es resentido; ante la sociedad tiene una posi-
ción muy adolescente. La poesía lo salva, lo descarga de sus culpas, es
como la confesión para el cristiano. El poeta se encierra, transforma

todo aquel mundo confuso y lo hace palabras escritas y vuelve a ser un hombre en paz consigo mismo y con los demás.[9]

Chumacero carefully avoids confessional sentimentalism, the great danger of such inward-directed poetry. On the contrary, his work is almost totally lacking in personal notes or autobiography in its various superficial dimensions. Through an effort of conscious control he succeeds in eliminating anecdotal references and transforms his poetry into a testimony of inner movement. In one of his most important critical essays, he develops his notion of these relations between form and content, that is, between poetry and life:

Si establecemos diferencias entre lo que es *un hombre* que vive y lo que internamente constituye la *imagen de un poeta*, el hombre viene a ser el contenido que el poeta utiliza para tomar existencia: víctima y victimario que conviven en una constante lucha, en un acalorado diálogo cuyo triunfo pertenece a quien tiene la palabra. Y la palabra es la principal y única arma del poeta. El hombre resulta vencido y, por paradoja, más pleno de existencia bajo el triunfo del poeta. Uno y otro, a fin de cuentas, se realizan totalmente y se confunden en la poesía escrita. Forma y contenido se erigen en una común verdad que los sintetiza.[10]

This then is Chumacero's poetry: a constant struggle with the word to force it to take on form and give us a faithful image of inner being in movement. It is an austere and concentrated poetry, the portrait of an entirely subjectivized inner landscape.[11] What I attempt here is an examination of this landscape in a search for the roots, that "untransferable tone" which distinguishes every authentic poet.

Páramo de sueños received the Rueca Prize for 1944, to a unanimous critical reaction that it reflected a devastating sentiment of solitude. José Emilio Pacheco, one of Mexico's finest poets and critics, commented that "La desolación, el sueño, la nostalgia confieren al desplomado peso de los años un prestigio de ruina al que el poeta enfrenta sus palabras."[12] The book was written under the double shadow of death and anguish, Chumacero's dominant thematics. "Sus temas principales ya quedan claros en *Páramo de sueños* y en *Imágenes desterradas*:

son la angustia engendrada por el tiempo y la muerte, la desola-
ción producida por nuestro mundo enigmático, y la búsqueda de
significados en una realidad llena de momentos pasajeros y de
recuerdos perecederos."[13]

The poet recognizes this trajectory; even more, he sees it as
the only one possible, when he asks, "¿qué otra cosa nos puede
entregar un viaje hacia nuestra intimidad, si no desolación y
tristeza?"[14] Critics have repeatedly pointed out the resem-
blance of this desolate credo to much of the poetry of Xavier
Villaurrutia, who created a nightmare vision of a solitude so
extreme that it threatens to fall into radical solipsism, and of a
personal and inviting death ever present. Aside from thematic
similarities between Chumacero and Villaurrutia, there are fre-
quent direct echoes, as in "Vencidos," in the lines "Porque nada
delata que existamos / en esta soledad del pensamiento" or in
"Espejo de zozobra," with its vision of the solitary being con-
templating itself in the "espejo de sueños," to find itself face to
face with the death it bears in its blood. This poem is a special
case, since in addition to echoes of Villaurrutia's anguish, there
is a conscious allusion to José Gorostiza's masterful meditation
on death and existence, *Muerte sin fin*. The lines "Estoy junto a
la sombra que proyecta mi sombra, / dentro de mí, sitiado . . .,"
echoing the key image of Gorostiza's poem, show how clearly
Chumacero understood the poetic tradition within which he
wrote, with its radical sense of individual solitude and its roots
in the Aztec poetry of death that celebrated the ritual sacrifice
to the ever-demanding gods. There is also at times a family
resemblance to two other young poets of his own generation,
Octavio Paz and Efraín Huerta, in the passion of solitude and the
effort to escape the quicksand of solipsism through the immedi-
ate human contact of love and the flesh.

The theme that dominates the book, and one that is wide-
spread in modern Mexican literature, is this presence of death,
its fatal necessity. The poems offer an abundance of terms such
as *herido, mortuorio, miedo, sombrío, amargo, doliente, tumba,
silencio, cadáver, duelo, letal, naufragio, insepulto, ataúd,
olvido*—a whole spectrum of images related to absence and
death. The poems tend strongly to present these images in an
almost abstract fashion rather than to situate them within the

experiential context of a presumed implicit speaker. In this respect Chumacero differs widely from Villaurrutia, whose poems, in general, offer a specific context. Presiding over this gallery of solitude is the figure of the beloved. It is she who gives the few instants of relief, in a poem like "Poema de amorosa raíz," of a more traditional form and idiom, perhaps because it is quite early; Chumacero calls it his first poem and dates it in 1938.[15] It is quite precocious, since we can still respond to the gentle elegiac beauty of the final lines.

> Cuando aún no había flores en las sendas
> porque las sendas no eran ni las flores estaban;
> cuando azul no era el cielo ni rojas las hormigas,
> ya éramos tú y yo.[16]

This sense of fulfillment is almost unique in Chumacero's work. Another rare example of amorous happiness is "Amor es mar," where "Llegas, amor, cuando la vida ya nada me ofrecía / sino un duro sabor de lenta consunción / y un saberse dolor desamparado, / casi ceniza de tinieblas; / llega tu voz a destrozar la noche." The poem is really rather traditional in its use of love as the response to despair, and it is also one of Chumacero's most accessible. This is an example of the very few cases in all Chumacero's poetry of solitude transcended, and it establishes a basic imagery of *olas/playa* representing the two lovers which becomes increasingly important and which also takes on more complex significance in other poems. It is also nearly the only use of sound to characterize the beloved: "Olas de luz tu voz, tu aliento y tu mirada / en la dolida playa de mi cuerpo," a technique which later evolves into its own antithesis.

On the basis of a few poems of this general sort it has become customary to say, as does Ramón Xirau, for example,[17] that Chumacero finds escape from his solitude through love, although Debicki is more exact when he says, "El amor se presenta como un modo, no siempre logrado, de encontrar significados."[18] The fact is that poems like those mentioned are notably rare in *Páramo de sueños*. There are a number with an amorous or erotic content, but none of them express in this same way the simple truth of the overflowing life of the lovers. The most frequent tendency, on the contrary, is toward showing the uselessness of love, its inevitable failure in the face of the threat of death. A metaphor basic to the entire book appears in "Ola," where the wave approaches the beach as a human approaches a lover. The erotic nature of the image is obvious, and it was a cliché of the films of the 1930s and 1940s that were unable to be as sexually explicit as today's films, due to the drastic censorship to which they were subject. But even this erotic contact is resolved into the inevitable solitude:

> y sabe cómo al fin la arena es tumba,
> frontera temblorosa donde se abren
> las flores fugitivas de la espuma,
> resueltas ya en silencio y lentitud.[19]

After the act, all that remains is the same silence. Water is a traditional symbol for salvation in Occidental literature, ranging from the salvation of the spirit through redemption or grace, to the life-giving force of love. Chumacero uses this traditional figure, but he characteristically reverses its meaning. In "Mujer en la playa," written in 1938 but not published until forty years later,[20] he was already using the equation of wave/beach/love, but in *Páramo de sueños* he almost always adds the missing term: death. It is not coincidental that Chumacero's early work makes such extensive use of marine imagery; the silence, the distortion of natural perceptions, and the seeming inability to burst into freedom of movement almost give the feeling of an underwater world. "Ola" is resolved in a key image which helps clarify the underlying significance of the repeated figure of the water as lover and of the sand as beloved. At the instant of sexual contact, the instant when the wave breaks upon the shore, each learns "como al fin la arena es tumba, / frontera temblorosa donde se abren / las flores fugitivas de la espuma, / resueltas ya en silencio y lentitud." The wave is shattered into "the fugitive flowers of froth" which are scattered on the silent sand, as the man becomes lost and scattered in the silent and unresponding woman. The frustration and eventual destruction of the erotic impulse develop in many poems into a fear of love/creation, since they by definition produce only further frustration and even death, so that symbols traditionally associated with love and creativity are given here a reverse meaning. Thus, beach and sea come to signify eroticism, but a sterile eroticism that leads only to solitude and, finally, to death. Humankind desperately pursues this contact because the alternative is the ever-present mirror where "hallamos dentro sombras silenciosas / o una paloma destrozada" ("Vencidos"). But this is a double bind without a possible satisfactory resolution, since the search undertaken to escape solitude leads only to the exasperation of despair.

> . . . es la lentitud
> y el sentirse arrojados sobre el lecho,
> como el cesar y el impedir,
> lo que alimenta nuestro amor
> y el incansable continuar entre los hombres,
> del dolor de la carne enamorados.
> Igual que rosa o roca:
> crueles cadáveres sin agonía.
>
> ["Vencidos"]

In this sterile desire repeatedly associated with death, at times the beloved herself seems dead. In "Diálogo con un retrato," which calls to mind Sor Juana Inés de la Cruz's stunning sonnet "A su retrato," the beloved fades away, leaving the lover in a universe without support or center. Perhaps because she is dead, perhaps because this is the necessary fate of any human relationship, she has become her own portrait, pure impenetrable surface; she is absent. In this absence, the poet sees that which haunts him, the fear that her fate is the same; in her image he finds only "la imagen / de todo lo que nutre mi silencio, / y mi temor de ser sólo una imagen." Even when she is present, they are merely bodies that have become enemies; the amorous connection is, in the best of cases, double-edged. The relationship fails in the face of what the poet calls "mi funesta amante" and "esta soledad de tu desnudo" ("Mi amante"). Beloved, but also enemy, and always in the process of escaping, when she is not already absent.

The most frequent of the physical senses in *Páramo de sueños* is touch, but there is another and more important sense because of its nearly complete absence: sound. Chumacero's work is a poetry of silences, and behind them, of absence. Actions are soundless; the rose that falls "deja una huella: pie que no se posa / y yeso que se apaga en el silencio" ("A una flor inmersa"). Even physical contact seems insulated in this strange world; a kiss is "como profundo aroma silencioso" ("Ola"). This lack of sound is related to the repeated images of glass and mirrors; just as these reflect the one who looks into them, the absence of sound reinforces the absence of communication. There is an almost complete lack of external action in *Páramo de sueños*; the individual poems capture a series of interrelated frozen emotional states through the repetition of images of silence, sterility, lack of communication, and death. In "Vencidos" human beings are "mudos cadáveres precipitados / a una impasible tempestad." Even the vision of self is vain: "al mirar un espejo / hallamos dentro sombras silenciosas." In "Anunciación" sleep comes as an anticipation of death, "Inserto en soledad / de palabra vertida / que apenas hiriera el silencio." It then arrives "sobre el lecho, silencioso, / negando su sonido." The relationship between sleep/silence/death is clear in poems such as "Anestesia final," when the poet describes himself navigating "la boca atropellada de silencios, / como si labios húmedos / cayeran en mi huella / deletreando ausencia entre las manos." The only sound is barely perceptible: "El sonido, ah cómo sabe a río, / urdido como estrellas apenas presentidas, / resbala por la piel de mis espaldas." And the same poem ends with this clear statement: "Así me voy perdiendo cercado en mis contornos, / cercano a mi silencio / cuando navego en aguas de la muerte." This silence weighs on the entire book. In "En la orilla del silencio" we are at the moment of facing imminent death, at the final mystery "donde la voz no alcanza a pronunciar / el nombre del misterio. // Ahora que a mis dedos se adhiere temblorosa / la flor más pura del silencio, / inquebrantable muerte ya iniciada." In the same poem, "un solo y único sollozo / germina lentamente, apagado, / con un silencio de cadáver insepulto."

The standard response to this lethal solitude to which we are condemned by our destiny as human beings is love, or at least

the variant of an erotic relationship, which gives us the passing
consolation of a few instants of intense human nearness. This is
the response of the majority of Chumacero's contemporaries in
Mexico, and in the cases of Huerta and Paz it continues to
characterize their poetry throughout. But in *Páramo de sueños*
this relationship takes on unexpected dimensions. The woman
is a body which "sobre el lecho se nos vuelve / cadáver multi-
lado en el recuerdo, / como mentira íntima / o rosa desde siglos
viviendo en el silencio" ("Jardín de ceniza"). The desperate
surrender to her leads nowhere; "su placer nos sostiene sobre un
mentido mundo," but uselessly. Any rescue is only temporary;
woman, after all, is "flor ahogada," also a victim of the water
which is for Chumacero a representation of our total mortality.

> y mi aliento en tu savia navegaba,
> y tu voz en mi pulso se moría
> como sombra de ave agonizante,
> transformando mi cuerpo en sueño tuyo,
> en vivo espejo abandonado
> o silencio que cruza los espacios.
> ["De tiempo a espacio"]

In "Desvelado amor" Chumacero created an extremely slippery
poem in which there are various expressive codes. The subject
appears to be as much despairing love recalling an apparently
dead beloved as an examination of the useless silence of any
attempt at expression. The two experiences are equivalent and
equally fruitless efforts at breaking out of the silent well in
which the speaker dwells. Neither speech nor human contact,
neither poetry nor love, the two supreme efforts at creativity, is
of avail. The voice, the word, communication through language,
are useless to him. In the same way, love is hopeless; literally or
metaphorically, she is dead. Facing love, as facing language, the
poet is sunk in total sterility. There are several unexpected bits
of wordplay, again reminiscent of Villaurrutia; the parallelism of
the first two lines and the phonetic identity between their
initial words (*cayó-calló*), techniques which the older poet used
to express opposite or contrastive meanings, here stress the
final similarity between the two experiences: the word fell
virgin, nude, i.e., unused; for language this is absolute sterility,

death, just as the "virgen desnudada" fell (and fell silent) be-
neath the body of the speaker.

Perhaps the most finished version of this vision of woman is
"A tu voz"—exceptionally, for Chumacero, who prefers longer
poems in freer metric combinations, a sonnet—which contrasts
clearly with such earlier poems as "Amor es mar."

> Erígese tu voz en mis sentidos
> tornándose en mi cuerpo sueño helado,
> y me miro entre espejos congelado,
> y mis labios en sombra doloridos.
>
> Cuando hablo, mi dolor a ti se vierte,
> cálida flor de ceniciento aroma,
> y tu voz a mis labios ya no asoma
> sino en duro temor de viva muerte.
>
> Porque tu sueño en mí su voz levanta,
> y enemigo de luz y de sonido
> destroza la palabra en mi garganta;
>
> así al fin en tinieblas alojado,
> ciego de ti, tal un árbol vencido
> flota mi cuerpo entre tu voz ahogado.

Now a direct relationship is established between the poet's
solitude and the woman's voice. Instead of provoking in the
speaker the joy of "Amor es mar," it produces a frozen sleep,
slowly taking complete control and robbing him of all possibil-
ity of communication. He sees himself frozen among mirrors,
his lips—source of communication—pain him. In the last verse
his drowned body floats on her voice. In this game of mirrors
which is Chumacero's poetry, this lethal voice may be equally
that of death or of increasing poetic sterility or of the woman
who in turn may represent death and whose anticipated contact
becomes fatal. In any event, it is all much the same; all three are
one, because they are three distinct visions of the same underly-
ing problem, the impossibility of breaking through the solip-
sistic barrier, of breaking free from the restrictions of the in-
dividual personality. Again, there is really no anecdote or action
which takes place; the poem objectifies an emotional process,
even a fixed state.

Perhaps the most complete version of this impossibility is "Diálogo con un retrato," pointless before it is undertaken, since the other party to the dialogue, by definition, is lacking voice or communicative abilities. When we look into the mirror in our fruitless attempt at self-knowledge, we perceive only a two-dimensional surface without depth. In the same way, others also lack depth beneath their surface, at least in our efforts to communicate with them. In both cases, the object we contemplate simply sends back our own image—pictorially in the case of the mirror, verbally in speech. All dialogue is this, a monologue without hope of expression or comprehension, an intimate reflection of the speaker. "Porque ¿quién eres tú sino la imagen / de todo lo que nutre mi silencio, / y mi temor de ser sólo una imagen?" *Páramo de sueños* is a volume filled with anguish, ruled by the spectre of a love which is useless and finally dead, by a beloved and an idiom dead and drowned. Behind them, always, like the mirror that returns the same vision of one's self, the silent statue, the still and finally alien woman.

Published in 1948, four years after the appearance of *Páramo de sueños, Imagenes Desterradas* employs the same themes and, up to a point, the same techniques. As Raúl Leiva has shown, "En todo el libro se escucha el paso del tiempo, su latir sosegado hacia la muerte. Pero es un tiempo en permamente disolución, en combustión interna, que se desgaja contra los acantilados del olvido."[21] The two sections into which it is divided are "Tiempo desolado," of six poems, and "Tiempo perdido," of fifteen, among them one of Chumacero's longest and most important, "Amor entre ruinas." "Tiempo desolado" continues the anguish and solitude of the first book, but with a change of emphasis. Now the threatening shadow of time appears ever more menacingly until it becomes dominant, especially in the four poems "El nombre del tiempo," "Pureza en el tiempo," "Viaje en el tiempo," and "Recuerda . . ." The anguish is less absorbing, less violent, although no less desolate. The same vocabulary appears, although not so obsessively, in lines like "los besos fúnebres de la amante lejana" ("Viaje en el tiempo") or the ocean as symbol of that which ends ("El nombre del tiempo"). Again we see the frozen water and the deformed voice of memory ("Recuerda . . ."). Nevertheless, the tone is more reflective, and in the two poems "Narciso herido" and "El nombre del tiempo" there appears for the first time the questioning of God.

In "Narciso herido" the speaker is once more before the mirror which gives back the same eternal image, his own. The poem is extremely obscure, and directed to a *tú* who is not really identifiable to the reader; it seems to be a god who is as inept as the poet in attempting to remedy solitude: "en mí te niegas tú, pues yo no existo." In "El nombre del tiempo," the *Tú*, now capitalized, has obvious superhuman dimensions, since "Solo Tú sabes de las olas de los aires de la nada; / si el viento ha de caer eternamente / convertido en esquirlas y áridos sudores." But at heart nothing has changed, since this omniscient *Tú* is but "purulento resplandor."

The section "Tiempo perdido" is one of Chumacero's most desolate creations. It opens with one of his most impressive poems, "Amor entre ruinas," a hymn to the impossibility of love's aiding us to survive the shipwreck. Silence is insistently opposed to the intensity of physical love: "nuestros desnudos abren el cauce del deseo / desbordándose en alas y gemidos de silenciosa aroma." After love, "la violencia es sólo yeso destrozado / en la inmovilidad yacente del silencio." Certainly the figure of the silent mistress and the idea of the sterility of love when confronted with a desolate world are hardly new, although Chumacero's polarization adds a new element. What is most surprising is the conjunction of the mistress with death, which we saw in *Páramo de sueños* and which is repeated here. There is a constant question in dealing with Chumacero's work. First, why is this beloved always related to death? Second, why is there such an extraordinary and almost literally fatal attraction? Inevitably, she recalls La Belle Dame Sans Merci, the fatal beauty so beloved of Romantic poetry, although not all may recognize in her the outlines of another, much more archaic and more disturbing beauty, Robert Graves's White Goddess. What is the meaning of this attraction? And above all, since the poet knows her fatal force, "y no miro a tus ojos / por temor de encontrarme asesinado."

We are familiar with the Baroque usage in which words such

as "death" were used as synonyms for the sexual climax. In Villaurrutia's poetry the dialectic of love-death and the person-ification of death as the beloved depend heavily on such word-play, and in Chumacero it is possible to find an echo, perhaps a deliberate use, of this technique. What is most important is that, deliberate or not, the love/death relationship becomes the fundamental resource of this poetry, the basic binomial of its poetic structure. In "Amor entre ruinas" we see the failure of the flesh; after love, there is only the return to solitude: "soy un balbuceo, / un aroma caído entre tus piernas rocas: / soy un eco." But behind this, there is something worse: she *is* death, the enemy. Not only is there no salvation in her, she herself bears us toward death, because she is of flesh and contaminates us.

There is a clue in "Elegía del marino," a remarkably roman-tic poem of lost love which lives among memories. But again, this is a love lost because of death.

> Un aire triste arrastra las imágenes
> que de tu cuerpo surgen
> como hálito de una sepultura:
> mármol y resplandor casi desiertos,
> olvidada su danza entre la noche.
> Mas el tiempo disipa nuestras sombras,
> y habré de ser el hombre sin retorno,
> amante de un cadáver en la memoria vivo.
> Entonces te hallaré de nuevo en otros cuerpos.

The poet is obsessed with the corruptibility of the flesh, with our ancient destiny of also becoming carrion, and this despair contaminates everything he touches. But it is not his destiny that murders her, but the other way round; when she is there, it is in her absence from death, and repeatedly it is suggested that she is the enemy: "oye cómo por tu piel florece / ya madura la sombra de la muerte" ("Poema donde amor dice").

"Inolvidable" is another key poem; it deals in a traditional form with love disappeared but remembered.

> Decir amor es recordar tu nombre,
> el ruiseñor que habita tu mirada,

> ir hacia ti a través de lo que fuiste
> y cruzar el espacio suavemente
> buscándote cristal, desnuda forma
> caída del recuerdo, o solo nube.

But how are we to reconcile these elegiac lines, lovely as they are, with the last five of the poem?

> En vano lejanías, o la muerte
> del tiempo entre tu cuerpo agonizando,
> porque en música pura estoy rendido
> cuando al sentir conmigo tu tristeza
> sobre mis labios mueres, amor mío.

There is an obvious allusion to Villaurrutia, and particularly to those poems in which Villaurrutia speaks to death in amorous and even erotic terms. Of course, the two final lines can be interpreted once again as conventional erotic vocabulary, but this does not explain the entire poem. On the contrary, what we have here is this conventional idiom directed to a memory, to an absence, eroticism elevated to a fact in itself since the other party is missing. Perhaps the only reference to her voice in positive terms in the entire book occurs in "Palabras que nacen del vacío," when the poet speaks of

> . . . aquel tumulto que su palabra era,
> bajo mi lengua detenido eternamente, pálido
> invasor de los símbolos, música ardida
> que equilibra la flor del pensamiento,
> en ráfagas de sombra hoy viven,
> en muda calma claman su soledad vencida,
> sobre el misterio de la tierra, abandonándose
> al recuerdo anegado con su ausencia.

And this voice is in the past tense, lost in absence.

Between the two earlier books and *Palabras en reposo*, published in definitive version in 1965, there are substantial differences. First, the latter is a much less personal book; where the other two deal almost exclusively with the inner states of the poet—or of his persona—and there is almost no connection with the external world, there is now often an objectively identifiable situation. Where the earlier work imprisoned emotional states in images of solitude and silence, the reader is now drawn into the game of identifying the specific situation of the concrete world in which the action of the poem takes place. Chumacero has even spoken of an "objectivization" of the poem[22] and we begin to come across characters who seem clearly other than the poet-persona. Identified in various titles are *el peregrino, el amante, el solitario, el viudo, la viuda, el hijo natural, la virgen, la mujer, el suicida, el poeta, el proscrito, el perezoso, el soltero,* and *el desconocido.* This appears to be a substantially different poetic world, but this change is deceptive if we anticipate a greater accessibility of communication, since there is also a further syntactic concentration, an even greater pruning of excess elements. In addition, this is a less static book than the others. Far from being anchored in one individual given situation, it gives an impression of movement toward a deeper poetic comprehension of the totality of human experience. The result of all this is that *Palabras en reposo* is, in many poems at least, considerably more complex. Where the earlier works require a concentrated reading because of the difficulty of giving them a more or less specific semantic value, the later volume requires even more because it is such a concentrated vision, purified of the lingering remnants of Neoromantic rhetoric.

Several critics have pointed out another change, the increasing intellectualism, which is really another face of what I have suggested. For Leiva, "El poeta realiza ahora una poesía de ideas más que de emociones."[23] Jesús Arellano was much blunter: "Que Alí Chumacero sea poeta ni siquiera lo discutimos; pero el caso desespera en la mayor parte de este libro, pues hay que desentrañarlo pacientemente para poder sentirlo un poco; si no es que luego resulta opaco, monótono a veces, otras con vaguedades y pocas accesible. Al fin, muy al fin, gusta por su arquitectura, por su dominio y precisión; no como poesía sino como habilidad mental, y ésta es necesaria mientras no obstruya la sabia libertad de aquélla."[24] What disconcerted these and other critics is what Debicki singled out as in a certain sense a progress: "a menudo una imagen lleva a una idea, y de lo sensorial se pasa rápidamente a un tema universal."[25] It seems clear that there has been a change of poetic orientation. Where the poet earlier expressed the anguish of the amorous situation in the face of the impossibility that love lead to anything vital and lasting, he now examines his theme in less personal, even more abstract terms, in order to relate it to a deeper human dimension, that is, with the human race in all its anguished solitude before the implacability of death.

Palabras en reposo also consists of two parts, "Búsqueda precaria" and "Destierro apacible." It is tempting to suspect some atypical authorial laughter, since the words are absolutely not at rest and there is nothing peaceable about the exile. Among the most important poems of the first section we find "Responso del peregrino," the first of a group of six which all bear titles relating to the sound of the voice: "Imagen de una voz," "Palabras del amante," "Prosa del solitario," "Monólogo del viudo," and "Paráfrasis de la viuda." There are also two others with related titles, "Epitafio a una virgen" and "Alabanza secreta." "Responso del peregrino" develops something new, the religious element. From the first line we find a tone reminiscent of the Song of Solomon: "Yo, pecador, a orillas de tus ojos / miro nacer la tempestad." All this first section is an exaltation of woman—"María te designo . . ."—and more than anything else recalls the stylized figures of the Virgin in a child's catechism; it is a sort of transfer into verbal terms of a visual image. She is a "manantial de gracia" and "Elegida entre todas las mujeres," "pastora de esplendores" and "cítara del alma." And the speaker asks forgiveness of this virgin, while she is "erigiendo en olas / el muro de mi salvación." We almost suspect, in this echo of so many lines from the earlier work in a poem which has an obvious religious context, that the poet has drastically altered his characteristic theme and that he is using the same techniques and images to construct an antithetical result. But the metaphorical system of the poem collapses in an ironic crash. In addition to the initial irony of finding this sort of language in a notoriously sensual poet, the discovery that this symbol of purity and salvation is creating from waves the wall of his salvation leads us to the exact opposite of what we have momentarily expected. As we have seen, in Chumacero's work waves and sea represent the unresolvable tension between erotic impulse and implacable death. When we find these lines

imbedded in others of a totally traditional religious type, we
suddenly perceive that behind the first response there is an-
other. In fact the whole system of religious references contra-
dicts itself; while he paints her as the purity which can confer
salvation upon him, he sings to her in these words.

> María te designo, paloma que insinúa
> páramos amorosos y esperanzas,
> reina de erguidas arpas y de soberbios nardos;
> te miro y el silencio atónito presiente
> pudor y languidez, la corona de mirto
> llevada a la ribera donde mis pies reposan,
> donde te nombro y en la voz flameas
> como viento imprevisto que incendiara
> la melodia de tu nombre . . .

There is little of the prayer about all this, and a good deal that
recalls once more the eroticism of the Song of Solomon.

In the second section of "Responso del peregrino" the poet
offers a vision of his own death. It begins with some truly
apocalyptic lines, asking to share life with her in spite of the
negative vision of what may come to pass. And one day his death
will take place. It must be emphasized that a 180 degree turn has
taken place, since the earlier books dealt primarily with *her*
death and only secondarily with *his*; now he realizes that his
turn will come, with "el turbio fragor / de las beatas, como
acordes: / 'Ruega por él, ruega por él.' " In the final section, he
pleads that she pray for him at the final judgment, "a la hora
solemne de la hora / el día del estupor en Josafat." And once
more there is a crushing reversal; everything leads us to believe
that he expects they will be reunited at that time beyond time,
but it will not be so.

> Sola, comprenderás mi fe desvanecida,
> el pavor de mirar siempre el vacío
> y gemirás amarga cuando sientas que eres
> cristiana sepultura de mi desolación.
>
> Fiesta de Pascua, en el desierto inmenso
> adorarás la tempestad.

So unbelieving is he that the contemplation of Paradise is forbidden to him. But *she* has been somehow altered, and now she will, paradoxically after the suffering, long for the tempest of the flesh.

"Imagen de una voz" follows the themes of the other books; it appears to be the memory of the voice of a woman disappeared, or perhaps dead. But there is a difference; where previously she was a silent body, she has now disappeared entirely, leaving only the memory of her voice. "Palabras del amante" is much the same; he recalls only her words. There is a new and surprising vocabulary: the memory of "hoteles vacíos de sucios corredores" gives a tone of moral despair which echoes Eliot and presages the bitter world of "La noche del suicida." "Prosa del solitario" presents another novelty: it is one of the few poems of Chumacero with a perfectly visible anecdotic line, and it includes a woman of flesh and blood who empties her coffee cup and undertakes "su cotidiano ir hacia la calle." She even speaks, to ask him to wish her luck. But once again there is the ironic twist, since it is through her voice that the failure is communicated: "El oído sabía el germen de su luto / al presentir las frases masculinas, / murallas de fulgor y cementerio."

"Paráfrasis de la viuda" seems to be one of the last of the book's poems to have been written and employs a vocabulary more reminiscent of St. John Perse than of the more Mexican influences visible in the earlier poems. It does not appear in the first edition, and its publication in 1980 on the page facing the "Monólogo del viudo" suggests a relationship between the two poems. They do in fact represent the familiar sense of loss, but the situation is more specifically identified with the death of an individual. The "Monólogo" treats the return to an empty home, the difficulty of dealing with the daily objects left behind by the departed one, in symbols of religious overtones, culminating in the procession of "túnicas tornadas en emblemas" which mark his forehead with ashes, a familiar Christian symbol of loss and mourning. The "Paráfrasis" is more obscure, and appears to recreate the ambivalent emotions of the widow, ranging from loss to hatred because she has been abandoned. Nevertheless, it culminates in lines which strongly recall familiar attitudes.

Porque conoce ahora, al respirar
el perezoso ruido del desastre
ardiendo sin arder su cabellera,
cómo sobre el recinto funeral
de la almohada túrbase el silencio.

We have here the reverse of what we have seen so many times: the woman sunken in silence, not because of her death but because of his. The initial line alludes to his virile voice, so that the last verse is made up of contrasts; the reader, as in so much of Chumacero's later poetry, anticipates one conclusion and is offered another. But one element continues true: voice here is life, and its absence is death.

The last of these poems dedicated to the word, "Alabanza secreta," also does not appear in the 1956 edition. It traces a radical alteration of focus: the woman presented here is no moribund silent figure but a complete woman, proud in love and in her independence as a free being. With reason is she named Debora, for a great patriot and the only woman judge of Israel. Old now, she lives still in her memory.

Perdida entre la gente, derrotado
color en la penumbra, suelta el esquife hacia la nada,
mas su imagen un cántico profiere, brisa o trueno
pretérito sonando en el solar airado del cautivo.

This section ends with two more poems not included in the first edition, which also have in common the fact that they are visions of woman, albeit drastically different one from the other. "Mujer ante el espejo" again recalls Sor Juana in its vision of a woman in whom "alternan castidades segadas / y el perenne danzar de Salome" and for whom time begins its task of undermining the flesh: "cierra los párpados y deja al tiempo agonizar / porque la estatua al fin presiente su derrumbe." "La imprevista" is thoroughly different, a love poem of a traditional type in spite of displaying Chumacero's typical vocabulary and techniques. The speaker tells lost love to return, since—and here again the ironic twist we have learned to expect—"sobre el vacío caen las palabras." After all, the word is sterile and nothing can save us from solitude.

The section "Destierro apacible" begins with "La noche del suicida," another of the author's few longer poems. Like all those of some length, it consists of three parts. The first presents the fact of the suicide and the horror before the act, which is again referred back to the supposed author ("el fúnebre espacio que me espera"). In vain he speaks of

> el milagro
> de un cuerpo que incendiaba la penumbra,
> la furia de los dientes, a cierta hora hermosos,
> los cabellos perdidos, el sudor.
>
> Todo en silencio a la quietud navega.

The second section gives us the pitiless vision of a world which impels toward self-destruction. All this portion of the poem presents the inferno of the "nauseabundo olor de ardientes madrugadas," with "inánimes mujeres / que pudren la palabra amor en las habitaciones." It is the terror of a death in life which cannot be less horrifying than real death. In the final section, Chumacero creates a world in which there is only "la desierta jornada, escalera sin fin / que no conduce, inmóvil en la orilla / de un tiempo desolado." Sight focuses on someone who does not exist, "alguien que abandona la ciudad / rumbo al río del nunca más volver." In the last lines, the poet confers a greater dimension to this horrendous vision when he expands this "someone" to "us."

> Leve humedad será nuestra elegía
> y ejércitos de sombra sitiarán para siempre
> el nombre que llevamos.
> Porque solo un imperio, el del olvido,
> esplende su olear como la fiel paloma
> sobre el agua tranquila de la noche.

An intolerable act is referred back first to the speaker, then to another, and finally to all of us, because we are all lost in this ruinous truth.

This cosmic despair has completely replaced the desperate love of the first two volumes, and the biblical tone serves only to reinforce the gloom of this wasteland of the spirit. In "Mar a la

vista" the vision of horror is repeated, and the resuscitation of
Lazarus is transformed into empty vanity. By means of a skillful
verbal shift, the speaker is identified with Lazarus, but a Lazarus
who has small reason to give thanks to anyone. In lines that are
among the most startling he has written, Chumacero leads us to
the perception toward which he has been moving since the
beginning, that we are all Lazarus, without hope of any re-
deemer.

> En medio de la arena, frente a un mundo
> sin más consolación ni movedizos
> resplandores, mi mano determina
> la invariabilidad, el ir llorando
> sobre un cadáver condenado a muerte.

This is the naked terror which we see in the greater part of these
poems of the second part of *Palabras en reposo*. The struggle
against death continues, but the focus has shifted; she, the
silent woman, has disappeared, and the speaker is entirely
alone, except for "la huella sudorosa del alquilado amor"
("Vacaciones del soltero"). The title of "Salón de baile" recalls
some key verses of Salvador Novo's "Diluvio." Although there
are profound differences between the two poems, they share a
basic metaphor of the world as a dance hall. But where in Novo
the tone is of ironic nostalgia for a hall closed forever, Chu-
macero repeats the topic of the tavern, the brothel, and alcohol
as the only conceivable responses to an intolerable dance of
death. Perhaps the most striking example of this despair is "De
cuerpo presente," whose title uses the Spanish phrase for the
vigil before the dead to suggest that even before death there is
really little difference between the two states.

> Yo no estaré presente. La ilusoria
> marea irrumpirá, letal y fría,
> en olas conmovidas todavía,
> a anegar de ceniza la memoria.
>
> Fuego abatido, cólera desierta,
> la urna en sábanas al fin vencida
> olvidará su resplandor: la vida
> ayer a su cuidado amante muerta.

Indiferente imagen, su apariencia
no será abismo sino roca o viento
de soledad, sosiego y permanencia;

cuerpo no más, vacío de pecado,
inmutable al pavor del pensamiento:
solo estará, en sí mismo acostumbrado.

The poem consists in a series of images of the body: *fuego abatido, cólera desierta, / la urna en sábanas al fin vencida; indiferente imagen; cuerpo no más, vacío de pecado.* Perhaps the critical lines are 7 and 8: "la vida / ayer a su cuidado amante muerta," with its possible variant functions of *amante*, either "cuidado amante" or "amante muerta" or both simultaneously. These lines sum up much of Chumacero's poetic theme: the mortality of the body, which is at best a simulacrum of the inner being, which in turn is destined for death, the uselessness of love. The entire poem is a chain of images which constitute an objectified reflection of the poet's emotional state.

There is no doubt that Alí Chumacero's poetry is extremely difficult, and that between his first two books and the last this difficulty increases markedly. But it is not a matter of capricious obscurantism. The material with which the poet struggles is the movement of the mind, of consciousness, a voyage of cognition toward an ever more crushing perception of the desperate situation which we must live—and die. What we see, from the two early books rooted in eroticism as a frustrated means for achieving some meaning to existence, to the final examination of this frustration as a symbol of the absolute cosmic abandonment of mankind, is the slow despairing process. Within this despair, and giving it form, we find the three poles of contrastive tensions: 1) the theoretical position of poetry as communication, to which Chumacero adheres, versus the increasing obscurity of his own work; 2) the perspective of this world as a spiritual desert, from which one may only escape through salvation by woman, and the impossibility of any such salvation because of the absence of any relationship lasting more than an instant;

and 3) the spur of the flesh in the face of the recognition that the flesh too is a mirror of death and leads us to it. These are the tensions we see reproduced in Chumacero's poetry, the vision of a mind on a slow journey toward the oblivion which is inevitably ours as well.

3 EFRAÍN HUERTA
The Sword of Eros

Efraín Huerta was born in Silao, in the state of Guanajuato, in 1914 and died in 1982. A member of the literary group centered around the journal *Taller* in the late 1930s, to the end of his life he remained faithful to this initial orientation, seeking always a poetic expression fusing eroticism with political rebellion. During a career that culminated in the receipt of the Villaurrutia Poetry Prize in 1975, the National Literature Prize in 1976, and the National Journalism Prize in 1978, Huerta was, without doubt, the front-rank Mexican poet most openly committed to a far-reaching sociopolitical change. He repeatedly avowed his faith in Marxism, and this faith produced a substantial body of social poetry. He saw poetry as an extension of life, and demanded for it the same absolute liberty that he demanded in politics. The result was a poetry of testimony, and at the same time of sometimes ferocious eroticism. Perhaps more than any other contemporary Mexican poet, his life as a writer is marked by this effort to express political commitment without falling into the rhetorical bombast that characterizes so much committed poetry. Huerta struggled to harmonize these apparently conflicting ideas of poetry which led him to a radical rejection of traditional notions of the sanctity of poetry and poetic language. This commitment continued undaunted by the swiftly changing complexities of the modern world, and is a marked theme of his poetry, at least from *Poemas de guerra y esperanza* (1943). In light of the later official Soviet rejection of Stalinism and its excesses, Huerta would probably have preferred to be able to ignore some of this work because of its unabashed adulation of Stalin. On the other hand, Huerta was sufficiently strong-willed, or perhaps still unrepentantly devoted, to include in

Poemas prohibidos y de amor, at least as late as the third edition
of 1978, such poems as "Descubrimiento de Moscú," from *Los
poemas de viaje* (1956). It includes the following rhythmically
atrocious lines.

> Allí vive, allí piensa, allí es más joven y más digno,
> allí es el único hombre del mundo que sabe lo que piensa,
> y a quien los pueblos de la URSS
> llaman el padre de todos los pueblos de la URSS.
>
> Se llama José Stalin y es un hombre mayor de 70 años.
> Pero vale por siglos.

Odd language indeed for 1978. Mauricio de la Selva has objected
to this poem, saying that "lo objetable no es, precisamente, el
tema ni las afirmaciones sobre Stalin sino la construcción dis-
cursiva, ajena a lo que podría denominarse oratoria de la poét-
ica."[1] This fudges the objection on two grounds: de la Selva does
not object "precisamente" to the remarks on Stalin, but this
leads us to suspect that he has some reservations there without
really expressing them. More important, he seems to miss the
point of what Huerta has done. Totally aside from our evalua-
tion of the poem or our agreement or disagreement with its
political content, and whether or not the evaluation is based on
that content, Huerta has consciously attempted to *avoid* any-
thing that might be called "oratoria de la poética." Most critics
would agree that the poem is a failed effort to do something
original, but it hardly seems appropriate to criticize Huerta for
having made the effort.

    This problem of shifting political winds is a difficult one for
the politically committed poet, who is no safer from them and
from the uncertainties of tomorrow than is the political com-
mentator. Along with the potential embarrassment of the de-
ification and subsequent desacralization of Stalin, there is the
irony of reading today such phrases as "Varsovia socializada,
hecha cristal por los campeones del trabajo" ("Palomas sobre
Varsovia, II"). The Solidarity movement has given the line a
meaning Huerta could not have suspected when he wrote it. In
any event, much of Huerta's overtly political poetry suffers
from a considerable degree of awkwardness; some of it reads like

quotations from official handouts or press releases. One may be appalled by the slaughter of helpless people and still see little poetic merit in the habit of ending a poem with a slogan such as "¡Lídice victoriosa!" ("Elegia de Lídice") or "¡Magnífica Varsovia, / sereno momumento a la paz, / insignia de victoria!" ("Palomas sobre Varsovia, III"). Even if we recall that the poems were written as much as fifty years ago, it is wryly amusing to read the diatribes against "esos bárbaros de cerebro de piedra / maniobras de víboras cristianas; / contra esos que provocan a la URSS" ("Presencia de Federico García Lorca, 3") or the canonization of Alvaro Obregón:

> Nuestra guerra civil es pavorosa,
> es dura y es amarga, mas tu huella
> será en definitiva el buen camino.
> . . . .
> Tu experiencia de símbolo está en pie: los tambores
> del indio yaqui grave y sudoroso
> atruenan la república, y hay en tus ojos grises
> serenidad de líder amoroso.
> . . . .
> tu natural virtud, aquella planta
> de noble origen rancheril y obrero.
>
> ["Canto a Obregón"]

Naomi Lindstrom has pointed out the dangers inherent in this brand of social poetry when she reminds us that it is so anchored in the objetive world outside, so tied to an external social referent, that the poems tend to lose their autonomy as poems.[2] There is also the further danger, she adds, that the reader, without a fairly thorough knowledge of the specific circumstances, may, for all practical purposes, be excluded from the poem.

In the evolution from the traditional lyric themes of love and solitude which are prevalent in his earlier poems, Huerta developed a style that is often colloquial, frequently jarringly aggressive, sometimes (particularly in the later work) overtly obscene or pornographic. This is certainly a deliberate choice, as well as a possible function of the poet's personality. Given Huerta's commitment to social change, he was determined to use his poetry to shock, to challenge, to threaten, on both the

political and the poetic levels. Julio Ortega characterizes it as
"un entendimiento radical de la poesía, ya anunciado por Oc-
tavio Paz para su generación: la poesía como aventura de realiza-
ción trascendente. Para Efraín Huerta, esta aventura opera desde
una actitud testimonial, confesional, y por eso el lenguaje será
para él una materia que deberá corporizar, dar forma y violencia,
a una vida también asumida radicalmente, en sus tensiones y
urgencias."[3] Lindstrom has commented on the liberating effect
of such language: "These poems are pro-liberation in wide-
ranging and sometimes diffuse ways. The freeing of language
from prudery and fossilization is often in the foreground."[4] She
goes on to draw some interesting parallels: "The insistence on a
cultural liberation involving the creative and the erotic imag-
ination suggests a parallelism with Herbert Marcuse. And, in-
deed, it would seem to agree with Marcuse's assertion that even
a Playboy-style eroticism can be a liberating force in society. A
rather locker-room spirit pervades some poems."

These qualities inevitably provoke reactions by critics and
fellow poets. Rafael Solana points out the use of the adjective,
not for adornment but to jar the reader, as well as the unusual
vocabulary and the insistence on using poetry for its semantic
values rather than being concerned with rhythmic or other
formal properties; he remarks that the two principal aspects of
the poems are "la desagradabilidad y la preclara excelencia
poética."[5] Curiously, Solana also says that Huerta "carece por
completo del sentido del humor,"[6] a startling indication of the
change in Huerta's later work, much of which depends heavily
on raucous laughter. José Emilio Pacheco has called his tone "en
vez de musiquita y de teatrito, sequedad, aridez, acidez. . . .
Poesía absoluta, radicalmente impura. Quiere abarcarlo todo, y
todas las cosas entran y salen sin pedir permiso."[7] Perhaps the
best and most concise summing-up of this aspect of Huerta's
work within his total production is given by Octavio Paz:

Muy joven aún publicó una serie de poemas en los que, cegados por la
literatura, sus amigos no vimos sino unas imágenes sorprendentes
mezcladas a otras que prolongaban el surrealismo hispanoamericano y
español. Ciegos y también sordos, pues no oímos la voz que hablaba por
boca de Huerta—la otra voz, blasfema, anónima, la voz maravillosa de
la transeunte desconocida, la voz de la calle. Despúes Huerta escribió

desafortunados poemas políticos. Ahora, en una milagrosa vuelta a su
juventud, ha publicado varios poemas que continúan, ahondan y en-
sanchan sus primeros poemas.[8]

In the over twenty years since Paz wrote these words, they have
proven even more apt; after the publication of *Poesía* in 1968
Huerta enjoyed a rebirth of creativity and public and critical
favor, and in the last works, especially *Transa poética*, Huerta's
idiosyncratic version of social poetry achieved a high, if some-
times startling, level.

It is somewhat inexact to speak of Huerta's political poetry as
if it were distinct from his other work, since it is characterized
by the same constellation of interests. Huerta himself does not
seem to have had any clear sense—nor should he have needed
one—that there were different things happening in different
works. Although the "brief explanation" he included in *Poesía,
1935-1968* clearly states that he omitted from the volume "de
manera voluntaria los poemas 'políticos' (¡"Mi país, oh mi
país"!, "Elegía de la policía montada," "Barbas para desatar la
lujuria," etc.), que espero juntar en un libro que se titularía *Los
poemas prohibidos,*"[9] the fact is that *Poesía* includes a number of
poems which might well be considered political, especially
those from *Poemas de guerra y de esperanza* and *Los poemas de
viaje.* There is also a section of apparently new poems called
"Responsos," which includes several dealing with Che
Guevara. Huerta did in fact publish *Poemas prohibidos y de amor*
in 1973, and it includes the poems he cites above except for
"Barbas para desatar la lujuria," which was republished in *Los
eróticos* the following year. The 1973 volume also includes a
number of poems that are hardly political in any sense. Al-
though it is tempting to suspect that Huerta was perhaps trying
to establish subcategories of poems that are overtly propagan-
distic and those that express a more personal emotional com-
plex, the system breaks down in the face of the mixture of both
kinds of poem in the same volume. Given Huerta's apparently
haphazard system of organizing his works, and his seeming lack
of concern about publication—see for example the case of "Río
San Lorenzo," which was probably written in 1953 and first
published in the *Anuario de la poesía mexicana, 1954*[10] but

which puts in its first appearance in one of Huerta's books in
Transa poética in 1980—the division may simply have been the
product of whim, or of a typical Huerta disregard for anything
smacking of the literary.

There is another and extremely important arrow to Huerta's
bow, one that fewer critics have really studied to any extent: his
love or erotic poetry. Jesús Arellano underlines this double
trajectory: "Dos características directrizan su obra: el amor y la
rebeldía contra las injusticias. Su primera etapa, apoyada en *Los
hombres del alba*, es amorosa y ya se dejan ver sus instintos de
protesta; su segunda, sellada con los más recientes poemas, es
rebelde, y no olvida que el amor es una necesidad en el
hombre."[11] The terminology here is difficult, for the version of
love we find in Huerta is anything but the idyllic vision the
words usually connote. As Andrés González Pagés pointed out
of Huerta's first book, *Absoluto amor* (1935), "No se halla en ese
libro, como hubiera podido esperarse de un joven de vcintiún
años de los años treinta, una poesía romántica, idealista, propia
del adolescente que está 'enamorado del amor', sino una poesía
que consigna la entrega a mujeres reales."[12] Huerta's antece-
dents are not in the Renaissance Garcilasos, with their crys-
talline streams and lovely gardens inhabited by gentle damsels,
but in the great outspoken erotic poets: Villon, Neruda,
Baudelaire, Rimbaud.

There are, nevertheless, occasional love poems of a tradi-
tional type; we even find some reminiscences of the medieval
alba with its strong erotic flavor, such as the lovely "Alba desde
una estrella" from *Estrella en alto*. "Alba" has the flavor we
would expect—"en el alba las rodillas desesperadas de una vir-
gen"—but soon the dawn takes on another dimension, one that
again relates the love poetry to the social poetry, what José
Emilio Pacheco has called a "creencia a toda prueba en el nuevo
día."[13] Without entirely ceasing to be the traditional moment of
lovers, the dawn becomes a vision of a better world. The change
is clearly visible in the two books that use the word *alba* in their
titles. *Línea del alba* (1936) is a subjective work dealing with the
typically early Huerta themes of love and solitude; in *Los
hombres del alba* (1944), without abandoning entirely the earlier
themes, there is a clear shift toward a wider focus with greater

emphasis on broader human themes. Dawn is now a time of future hope for Huerta's beloved city: "para amarte mañana cuando el alba sea alba / y no chorro de insultos, y no río de fatigas, / y no una puerta falsa para huir de rodillas" ("Declaración de odio"). In "Buenos días a Diana Cazadora," one of the poet's most impassioned songs to his city, dawn is a frozen moment from which to contemplate the new day symbolized by the famous statue of Diana. But the dawn is also the highly ambiguous moment of "Los hombres del alba," neither day nor night, a moment when the world is trapped somewhere between good and evil. Dawn may be the moment of hope, but it can also be the moment of despair, in an ambivalence typical of Huerta.

> Que el alba, que el alba siempre:
> río de hormigas verde
> y mentiras
> y saliva
> y odio.
>
> ["Mensaje"]

The symbolic meaning of dawn for Huerta is visible in his comments on his poem "Los perros del alba," also called "Poema para un ballet." The author's belief in the continuing validity of the comments is visible in the fact that the poem was written in 1948 and originally published in the journal *Prometeus* in 1949, and twenty-four years later included in *Poemas prohibidos y de amor*. The author's remarks include the following: "De la ingrata quietud nocturna, se pasa al desorden, al caos de la luz que es el alba, llegándose por fin a la armonía y disciplina de la mañana."[14] This is Huerta's vision of the future, a vision anchored in his double erotic and social commitment, and the dawn has an obvious revolutionary aspect. It also seems to reflect his concept of poetry, since it is analogous to the shift from traditional romantic, night-oriented poetry in his earliest work, to the vigorous, often violent, imagery of the mature work. It is fruitless, but intriguing, to speculate whether Huerta's poetry, had he lived to see the new political dawn he so ardently desired, would really have come to reflect this "harmony and discipline."

One of the most important and lasting manifestations of love in this poetry is as absence. Repeatedly, the poems present an absent lover, and often these are among Huerta's most unabashedly erotic creations.

> Labios como el sabor del viento en el invierno,
> dientes jóvenes de luna consentida en la llama del abrazo.
> Se endurecía la noche en tu garganta.
> Espacio duro de tus senos. Amarilla y quemada,
> la inesperada sombra de tus piernas en las alas de los
>   pájaros . . .
>
> ["La estrella"]

The dominant note is of amorous nostalgia, often giving a coloration of despair to the poet's attitude.

> Entre lirios azules y aristas de recuerdos
> envueltos en pañuelo de seda,
> todo lo que es mi vida. Deshecha
> en una raya de la noche,
> en ese vidrio que sangra en la ventana,
> sobre tus hombros.
> Entre la luz y el cadáver de una hora,
> mi vida. Sin cantos, sin esquinas.
>
> ["Pausa"]

At times this longing is so acute that it produces a brilliant image: "Es una herida de alfiler sobre los labios tu recuerdo" ("Los ruidos del alba"), "amor en ruinas, muros / de vegetal ausencia" ("La lección más amplia").

> ¡Oh geografía del ansia, geografía de tu cuerpo!
> Voy a llorar las lágrimas más amargas del mundo.
> Voy a besar tu sombra y a vivir tu recuerdo.
> Voy a vivir muriendo. Soy el que nunca estuvo.
>
> ["La paloma y el sueño"]

Perhaps more frequent is the creation of virtual meditations on absence, often addressed directly to the absent lover, as in the *cantos de abandono*. It is important to note the essential continuity of Huerta's poetry; in "Protesta y rendimientos," written in 1970 and published in *Los eróticos y otros poemas* in 1974,

the poet takes this same matter, turns it upside down—he is
now the absent one—and uses it to express something resem-
bling a tragic insight, a perception of his own self and soul.

Cuando, Teresa a solas, te abandoné en aquella humedad,
y yo empecé los viajes súbitamente inventados,
pensé que no debí amar tanto y tan mal;
vamos, que mejor hubiera sido querernos de una manera
     exquisitamente estúpida,
porque la Estupidez (del árbol pasmado todos hacen leña)
es la madre de los desmadres—y someterse después de la protesta
es tanto como alcanzar corriendo con la lengua de fuera
la abominable paz del rendimiento.
                              ["Protesta y rendimientos"]

An essentially romantic poet, Huerta was equally capable of
writing poems of love triumphant, such as the lovely definition
of "La poesía enemiga" or even the nearly unique "Este es un
amor," but this verbal and emotional delicacy was not to en-
dure. The love relationship is presented in increasingly erotic
terms, whether it be the humorous vision of the impact on his
senses of a young woman ("Sandra sólo habla en líneas gener-
ales") or the overtly physical focus of "Apólogo y meridiano del
amante." These varied aspects of love appear throughout Huer-
ta's work, but in the later creations there is a pronounced shift
toward the erotic and away from the nostalgic. A typical earlier
poem would be "Vals del clavel," with its "clavel de cobre del
deseo":

Bajo el signo del vals y el olor del clavel
estoy viviendo. Queden, allá en penumbras,
los dorados mensajes y las estatuas vírgenes.
Estoy en mi elemento, y mi elemento es
la madurez del alma y el deseo cuesta arriba.

In the later work the irony is more piercing, the details more
physiological. After the traditional love songs of an earlier mo-
ment—"Y tú me das la dicha / y tú me das el pan" ("Ordenes de
amor")—there is now a new bluntness. By the time of publica-
tion of *Los eróticos* the dominant tone has become sarcastic, as

in the encounter with a fellow bus passenger whose corporeal
presence and daring physical contact are as devastating—or
perhaps even more so—as the assaults perpetrated by thieves
and muggers.

> La del piernón bruto me rebasó por la derecha:
> rozóme las regiones sagradas, me vio de arriba abajo
> y se detuvo en el aire viciado: cielo sucio
> de la Ruta 85, donde los ladrones
> me conocen porque me roban, me pisotean
> y me humillan: seguramente saben
> que escribo versos: ¿Pero ella? ¿Por qué
> me rebasa en esa forma tan desleal? ¿Por qué
> me faulea, madruga, tumba, habita, bebe?
>   ["Juárez-Loreto"]

This is a poem that subverts the entire tradition of amorous
poetry; the object of desire is equated with the muggers because
of the flagrant physical contact and its effect on him. Indeed, she
is even worse then they; she assults him in the most arrogant
fashion. The vocabulary reinforces the poem's conceptual
framework; we are simply not accustomed to thinking of the
subject of an amorous or even an erotic poem as "la del piernón
bruto," and the last line casts her in the same light as an overly
aggressive athlete before making clear the sexual context. Or
there is the remarkable "Afrodita Morris," with the punning
allusion to Neruda in the "dulce miniatura de tus machu-
pechos" and a musculature that sows pandemonium.

> Cuando un fregabundal de albañiles te miran
> Y los andamios son ya castillos en ruinas
> Los pasajeros de autobuses fallecen de escalofrío
> Y los decesos (desexos) se suceden como un tropel de
>   alfajores
> Imposible sería, erectamente hablando,
> Decir tu nombre porque nadie lo sabe y
> Porque pocos conocen tu eminencia hipotenar
> El aductor medio el definitivo sartorio
> Los nombrados internos y externos
> El crucial peroneo lateral largo
> Y los delicados crural anterior, ah, y el sóleo.
>   ["Afrodita Morris"]

This must certainly be one of the few poems extant in which a poet has contrived to express the overwhelming sensuality of his subject while simultaneously parodying the fundamental silliness of the whole business through a listing of medical terminology, interspersed with a sigh truly worthy of Romeo. The seeds of this poetry lie in the earlier work, as Octavio Paz points out. "Hay que hacer notar que la actual poesía de Huerta sigue por las huellas de algunos de sus mejores poemas anteriores: el aspecto coloquial, lo anecdótico, el erotismo, la cotidianidad, la violencia y, en raras pero deslumbrantes ocasiones, la piedad. Tal vez lo más característico de esta nueva poesía sea su rasgo de *antisolemnidad*, que faltaba frecuentemente en sus poemas anteriores."[15] In fact, this "antisolemnity" gives a humorous tone that does not always hide an aggressiveness that sometimes becomes hostility. The blatant eroticism of poems like "Dolora de la perseguida hasta donde por fin" or "Milonga libre en gris menor" involves attitudes of hostility and even, at times, of physical violence that weaken any notion of an attachment beyond immediate physical gratification. This aggressivity is not new; in 1955 Rafael del Río had commented on Huerta's "furia más belicosa y más sollozante."[16]

Although these attitudes develop over a number of works, they are concentrated to a singular degree in *Transa poética* (1980). "Siempre mía" seems a poem of fevered eroticism until we recognize in the key imagery the pre-Hispanic ritual in which the victim's chest was opened with the obsidian knife and the heart extracted as a sacrifice to the gods who needed the blood for sustenance. The Aztecs called the wars of conquest aimed at capturing victims for this rite the flowering war because the heart was systematically represented as a flower. In Huerta's poem the erotic experience is incarnated in the characteristic metaphors of this rite of violent adoration.

> Criatura hecha de besos, criatura siempre mía:
> una orquídea en tu cuerpo me llama desde siempre,
> y yo la bebo entera con mis labios-cuchillos
> y me muero de fiebre sobre tu pecho abierto.

Less obvious, perhaps, is the frenzy of Huerta's most overtly erotic work, the "Manifiesto nalgaísta", an extraordinary

melange of eroticism, phallic imagery, free-wheeling savage
irony, and what looks very much like poetic free association,
almost a sort of latter-day Dadaist or Surrealist manifesto. Here
too there is barely concealed violence. This aggressive in-
sistence is really only an intensification of something visible in
the early poems. For example, in "Los ruidos del alba," from *Los
hombres del alba* (1944), we find the partner described as "la gran
llama de oro de tus diecinueve años." But this passionate image
is extended to the "madera blanca incendiada" of her body and
her "nombre mordido, / carbonizado." This violence is visible
in the poetry almost from the beginning as a love-hate relation-
ship between the lovers. In "Poema del desprecio," from *Los
hombres del alba*, we find the following statement of profound
despair:

> Laten palomas grises en la orilla
> de todo amor, y al aire que nos nutre
> vuele la gris pasión, vuele el silencio
> roto en rudas astillas musicales.
>
> (Ruina y melancolía, sudor de fiebre,
> amargura de abismo: eso es amor.)
>
> Del gesto de aquel hombre que solloza
> brota una espiga sorda, desnutrida,
> una doliente espiga, frágil, suave,
> una verdad perfecta: es el Desprecio.

And again:

> Junto a la flor del odio y el amor,
> la tierna flor del ansia y el Desprecio.

These may all well be the predictable results of youthful despair,
but that does not alter the fact that love and hatred are here
inextricably mixed in another of the ambivalent pairings that
underlie all Huerta's poetry. In the 1956 edition of *Estrella en
alto*, an uneven volume that includes some of Huerta's best
work, there appears a sonnet, "La voz," that is not in *Poesía* and
of which the poet said in the introduction to the latter volume,
"Se suprime un soneto hecho por encargo" (p. 7). Be that as it

may, "La voz" is a traditional and unoriginal lyric based on the Romantic confusion/identification between love and death.

> Que no me mates tú, que no me enferme
> tu lejana quietud de mediodía;
> que mi voz halle sitio en tu armonía
> para borrar el ansia de perderme.
> Dame la vida, en fin, dame tu muerte.

It is intriguing to wonder what "encargo" might have produced such a thoroughly unlikely poem, but no matter how different it may seem from the rest of Huerta's production, we see again a bit of the ambivalence toward the love object that becomes so characteristic. The continuity of this ambivalence is visible in "Para gozar tu paz," a new poem incorporated into the *Poemas prohibidos*.

> Sólo cuando el pecado es la guirnalda
> y la atadura, la cadena infinita
> y el profundo latido; sólo cuando
> la hora ha llegado, y tú,
> joven de rosas y jazmines,
> miras al horizonte del deseo
> y dejas que el tesoro de seda y maravilla
> sea la noche en mis manos,
> sólo entonces, dorada,
> todo me pertenece;
> las hierbas agitadas y el viento
> corriendo como el agua entre mis dedos:
> aqua de mi delirio, eterna fiebre,
> espejismo y violencia, dura espina,
> pedernal de la muerte, lento mármol,
> millón de espigas negras.

Again, the flowers and the flint hint at the Aztec ritual. Huerta uses the combination of a traditional Occidental vocabulary associated with the love object and archaic Aztec imagery to express once again this uncertainty in the face of the experience of love, or at least of the erotic experience. The moment of culmination is slowly transformed into a vision of violence and suffering. The image does not last, the tone reverts, but underlying the poem is always the echo, the trace of this uncertainty, this absence.

Aggressivity of this kind characterizes Huerta's humorous poetry, which becomes a much more important part of his production in later years. We have already seen the sarcastic humor of "Juárez-Loreto" and "Afrodita Morris"; the "Poemínimos" of *Los eróticos* and *Circuito interior* rely primarily on abrasive shock for their epigrammatic effect:

> Los lunes, miércoles y viernes
> Soy un indigente sexual;
> Lo mismo que los martes,
> Los jueves y los sábados.
>
> Los domingos descanso.
> ["Mansa hipérbole"]

Ricardo Aguilar remarks that "La actitud del poeta se torna hacia el sarcasmo, el albur, el retruécano y el chiste franco."[17] I am more inclined to see the roots of this in Huerta's earlier poetry than is Aguilar, who asserts that there is no humor before the "Poemínimos," but in any case his remarks can certainly be extended to more than these brief epigrams of which he speaks. Indeed, his comments on the techniques of the *poemínimos* read almost like a description of the new poems included in *Transa poética*, which includes no *poemínimos* at all: "Se vale de nuevas técnicas: de la lengua callejera, llena del pueblo, del neologismo, y así sus alusiones humorísticas toman el camino del humor negro y de la abierta descripción sexual. // Se ríe de lo grandioso tanto como de lo insignificante indistintamente."[18] As we have seen, this is really Huerta's fundamental technique, but the *poemínimos* carry this tendency to a savage, if grandly funny, logical consequence: "Lo escrito / Escrito / Está / Y al que / No le gustare / Que por un tubo / Se regrese / *A la fuente / De gracia / De donde procedía*" ("Bon voyage"). The humor is even more marked when we realize that he has used the future subjunctive, normally relegated to legal documents and official pronouncements. Nor does the poet spare himself, as we see in this ironic comment, which depends on the reader's knowledge that Huerta customarily used the crocodile as his humorous persona: "Siempre / Amé / Con la / Furia / Silenciosa / De un / Cocodrilo / Aletargado" ("Tótem").

Not all the "Poemínimos" are so sarcastic; occasionally there is a flash of the true wit that is sister to compassion and reveals understanding, as in the echo of Neruda's "Walking around" in "Tláloc": "Sucede / Que me canso / De ser dios / Sucede / Que me canso / De llover / Sobre mojado // Sucede / Que aquí / Nada sucede / sino la lluvia / lluvia / lluvia / lluvia." Or these: "Como / Dijo / Don Wolfgango: / Tengo / Dolor / De muelas / En / El / Corazón" ("Weimar"). Such punning allusions to other poets are numerous, as in "Benaventina": "Por / Soñarla / Quien / La sueña / La llaman / La / Biensoñada" or "Manriqueana": "Nuestras / Vidas / Son los / Ríos / Que van / A dar / Al / Amar / Que es / El vivir." And occasionally there is a glimpse of the man behind the savage mask, as in the revealingly rueful "Viudo infinito."

> De la melancolía
> De Sophia y de Brigitte
> De Jacqueline y Soraya
> De Marie Laforet
> De Ira de Fürstenberg
> De mi acelerada mujer
>
> Viudo del alba
> De la también
> Infinita miseria
> De ti
> De ustedes
> De mí mismo
>> Y de la Poesía
>> Claro está

Or the equally rueful punning salute to Neruda, one of Huerta's most admired models, in the last line of "Variaciones sobre una misma Telma," which is also the simultaneous recognition of the erotic source of their common inspiration.

> Yo soy un amoroso lastimado
> y sólo me consuela el proyecto
> de escribir en mis últimas horas—pero ya!

> un libro de también malos versos
> autobiográficos que se llamaría,
> ah caray,
> *Grupusculario.*

Víctor M. Navarro, in a lucid review of *Textos profanos*, a collection of Huerta's essays originally published in magazines and newspapers between 1966 and 1975, remarks that there are in Huerta's work "cinco elementos centrales: la ciudad, la mujer, la eterna contradicción: amor-odio, paraíso-infierno, la caracterización poética del habla cotidiana, y el desenfado por hacer la 'gran literatura.' "[19] It would be artificial to take this as a list of disparate themes; Huerta's poetry tends to slide back and forth, using the various polarities as though they were, in their different areas, equivalent: the ambivalent attitudes toward the city and woman, toward love and the physical relationship, the creation of the opposition of literature and ordinary speech. Navarro also comments acutely on "una poesía que recupera el habla cotidiana (de la calle) y que hace de la mujer amada-desamada centro fundamental del ejercicio de creación." This love/hate ambivalence is not restricted to the poet's attitude toward women; one of the most frequent and lasting themes of Huerta's poetry is his double feeling toward the sprawling megalopolis of Mexico City, as Raúl Leiva has noted. "Mas en esa lucha que el poeta mantiene en esta tenaz búsqueda de la poesía, no es sólo el amor quien le mueve al canto: también el odio, el desprecio y otras formas de pasión excesiva. A la ciudad de México, donde el poeta agoniza y sueña, le dedica cantos de odio y de amor."[20] In "Declaración de odio," published in *Los hombres del alba* (1944), there is a bitter vision of his tarnished city, "ciudad de ceniza y tezontle cada día menos puro." The poem is a virtual catalogue of the urban abuses, the moral and social ills of a city out of control. But underlying this violent rejection runs a thread of love for the city which cannot be hidden, and which is oddly linked to a nebulous concept of "lo nuestro." The poem ends in a denunciation of those who are not devoted to this vague "lo nuestro" and a song of hope for a better city.

Pero no es todo, ciudad de lenta vida.
Hay por ahí escondidos, asustados, acaso masturbándose,
varias docenas de cobardes, niños de la teoría,
de la envidia y el caos, jóvenes del 'sentido práctico de la vida,'
ruines abandonados a sus propios orgasmos,
viles niños sin forma mascullando su tedio,
especulando en libros ajenos a lo nuestro.
¡A lo nuestro, ciudad!, lo que nos pertenece,
lo que vierte alegría y hace florecer júbilos,
risas, risas de gozo de unas bocas hambrientas,
hambrientas de trabajo,
de trabajo y orgullo de ser al fin varones
en un mundo distinto.

Así hemos visto limpias decisiones que saltan
paralizando el ruido mediocre de las calles,
puliendo caracteres, dando voces de alerta,
de esperanza y progreso.
Son rosas o geranios, claveles o palomas,
saludos de victoria y puños retadores.
Son las voces, los brazos y los pies decisivos,
y los rostros perfectos, y los ojos de fuego,
y la táctica en vilo de quienes hoy te odian
para amarte mañana cuando el alba sea alba
y no chorro de insultos, y no río de fatigas,
y no una puerta falsa para huir de rodillas.

This fragment, like the entire poem, contains a considerable amount of the political rhetoric typical of much of Huerta's production during the 1940s and 1950s, but, strangely, there is no real identification of the evil "viles niños." One presumes that they are future businessmen, probably, given Huerta's general attitudes, in the employ of American corporations; they might also be those poets, less devoted to revolution than he, whom he so detested. The interesting aspect of the poem is its use of derogatory sexual imagery to characterize these enemies of "lo nuestro," a characteristic usage that breaks with all traditional notions of the "poetic." If love and an even violent sexual relationship with a woman were somehow for Huerta equated with political freedom, it was only to be expected that he would characterize those associated with the establish-

ment—literary, political, or economic—in terms of their spine-
less autoeroticism. In the same way, political attitudes are
categorized in terms of love and hate, another clear example of
Huerta's essentially emotional and nonintellectual poetic at-
titudes.

A poem from the same volume is "Declaración de amor," in
which Huerta makes clear his hatred for those who have turned
the city from its people, that is, those who use its economic
resources for their own benefit rather than for the good of all.
Put in these terms, the theme promises little, but nevertheless
it is one of Huerta's most successful poems in its loving evoca-
tion of a city and a land. And always, the ambivalence.

> Cuando llegas, rezumando delicia,
> calles recién lavadas
> y edificios-cristales,
> pensamos en la recia tristeza del subsuelo,
> en lo que tienen de agonía los lagos
> y los ríos,
> en los campos enfermos de amapolas,
> en las montañas erizadas de espinas,
> en esas playas largas
> donde apenas la espuma
> es un pobre animal inofensivo,
> o en las costas de piedra
> tan cínicas y bravas como leones . . .

Just as love becomes aggression, here Huerta's beloved city,
presented as though it were a woman, becomes the object of
both love and hate, and always missed, "la antigua, / la agotada
raíz de la ciudad" ("Esta región de ruina").

In "Avenida Juárez" there is a clearer symbiosis than usual of
the twin themes of the city and politics, especially Huerta's
anti-Americanism. The principal tourist avenue of Mexico City
is inundated by an endless torrent of uncomprehending and
presumptuous foreigners. The poet walks the city

> perseguido por las tibias azaleas de Alabama,
> las calientes magnolias de Mississippi,
> las rosas salvajes de las praderas

> y los políticos pelícanos de Louisiana,
> las castas violetas de Illinois,
> las *bluebonnets* de Texas . . .

Given what we have seen of the obsessive nature of Huerta's poetry, it is hardly coincidental that he chose so many feminine words, especially flowers, to name the hated tourist phenomenon; once again rejection walks arm in arm with attraction. The poem rises to an angry crescendo of hatred, to end in the poet's despair as he finds himself "tirado a media calle / con los ojos despedazados / y una arrugada postal de Chapultepec / entre los dedos." There is much truth here—the tourist abroad can be a fearful thing to behold—but the poem is hardly a balanced or fair portrait of either American tourists or American culture. Huerta is not interested in balance or fairness; this is the same kind of instinctive violent reaction that we have seen in the love poems. For Huerta, they are all much of a kind, as he recognizes in the poem "Circuito interior," which is dedicated to "Nuestra Señora del Metro."

> Porque estar enamorado, enamorarse siempre
> de una vaga ciudad, es andar como en blanco;
> conjugar y padecer un verbo helado;
> caminar la luz, pisarla, rehacerla
> y dar vueltas y vueltas y volver a empezar

The poem presents the geography of the city as a sort of horizontal metaphor for the city's existence, so that expressing one's love for the city takes the form of a pilgrimage through its streets or, in this case, its Metro stations.

The whole conception here is very much as though the city were a woman. This is hardly surprising, since one of Huerta's most frequent techniques is the use of feminine imagery. For example, he objectivizes in this way such phenomena as restlessness: "Por la noche se precipita la inquietud en mis brazos" ("Andrea y el tiempo"); clouds and morning: "los senos oscuros de las nubes, la mañana se recoge la falda" ("La invitada"); dawn; "la grupa tierna y suntuosa de la madrugada" ("La poesía enemiga"); night: "sus pechos de innumerable belleza" ("La arboleda"). This is so firmly rooted in Huerta's creative process that in shorter poems it is often difficult to tell whether he is presenting a woman in images drawn from the material world or humanizing nature and the surrounding world in feminine imagery. This is not simply a process of personification; there is at times a real dialectic between woman and the external world, whether it be the natural world or the artificial world of human beings. This symbiosis dominates the early book *Línea del alba* (1936), but it is still the basis of such important later poems as "Estuario," written in 1963, the lengthy "Apólogo y meridiano del amante" of *Los eróticos* and the long meditation on the meaning of Mexican history, "Amor, Patria mía," of *Transa poética.*

The extent of this intermingling of the erotic with what we might call the civic aspect of Huerta's work is perhaps best seen in one of his most aggressively outspoken creations and one which verges on pornography, "Barbas para desatar la lujuria," a poem that also displays a characteristic ambivalence between the sexual and the violent. First published as a plaquette in 1965, it was, curiously, not included in either *Poesía* or *Poemas Prohibidos.* Its point of departure is some allegedly pornographic photographs of a Mexican actress, but it also uses as a structural reference the initial section of Joyce's *Ulysses,* of Buck Mulligan's shaving. The poem is a heterogeneous mixture of sexual references, comments on the photographs, inside jokes alluding to Huerta's poet friends (and others not so friendly), a heavy dose of antiamerican politics, and sarcastic references to numerous Mexican institutions. A supreme example of satire directed at very nearly everything and everyone, it is questionable whether in a few years, when the topical allusions are no longer so readily identifiable, the poem will be even legible, much less of any real poetic validity. But more than anything else, "Barbas para desatar la lujuria" shows clearly how the political and the erotic are two sides of the same coin and how, underlying this double-sided theme, lies the aggressive violence toward the external world which is at the heart of so much of Huerta's work.

Beneath the sarcasm, the occasional grossness, and the deliberate effort to shock the bourgeoisie—it is surprising in how many ways Huerta combines Romantic attitudes with some of the doctrines of the Modernists—we see a man who is suffering for his land and his people. He is perhaps at his best when he abandons the mocking mask and reverts to the familiar imagery of the Flowering War and the Aztec pantheon, as in "Elegía de noviembre"[21] or these stunning lines from *Línea del alba:*

> Cuajada de cadáveres de lunas,
> soberbia parturienta de plata.
> fruta todavía niña:
> cuelgan de tu cintura los insomnios,
> los gritos de las vírgenes te ciñen.
> ["Cuajada de cadáveres de lunes"]

She too is woman, but not flesh and blood. This is Coatlicue, goddess of fertility and of human sacrifice, and her identifying skirt of human skulls. Perhaps we may find here the secret of Efraín Huerta's radical ambivalence; perhaps here too still beats the Indian heritage in all its complexity. Certainly, over the years, in his idiosyncratic fashion, Huerta returned insistently to the old themes and even the old images.

> Agua dulce, agua amarga,
> agua de soledad, agua de nada,
> agua quebrada para el verde amor
> y la amarilla piedad:
> agua sin sombra para el aire
> de esta región llamada
> la más transparente de la sangre.
> ["Agua de Dios, I"]

The complexity of Huerta's expression of his feeling for his land is visible in his last line, an allusion to Alfonso Reyes's famous description of the Valley of Mexico, "la región más transparente del aire." For the reader familiar with Mexican literature—and reality—, the line awakens memories of Reyes's words and the nostalgia felt by those who have seen Mexico's hideously polluted contemporary reality in which the sky is barely visible. But the allusion is also to Carlos Fuentes's famous novel *La región más transparente,* which also took its title from Reyes, and which, like Huerta's poem, refers to the political and social contamination that has taken place since the 1930s. Later in the same poem, the lines "la patria es / impecable como un asesinato al pie de las ruinas" allude both to Ramón López Velarde's magnificent *Suave patria*, as they parody the earlier poet's vision of a province still pure in its heritage of tradition, and to the dark Aztec ritual of sacrifice atop the pyramids. Perhaps here more than anywhere we see the fusion of Huerta's eroticism with the ancient rite: "Acércate, abre las piernas del viento / y húndele tu puñal de purísima obsidiana." And the poet, trapped in a world of tourists, asks bitterly, using once again images from the ancient lost culture, "¿Entonces soy el perro poeta de rodillas / o el jaguar vencido, hincada la man-díbula en la tierra que nada engendra?"

It is this clear vision of two radically different worlds jux-taposed that is so impressive in "El Tajín," first published as a plaquette in 1963 and included in both anthological volumes, *Poesía* and *Transa poética*. The poem consists of three brief sections; they establish the mood and atmosphere of the deso-late, ruined temple-pyramid, where all is dead, so much so that even the three visitors (the poet, his son and his friend) fall under the spell: "Muertos estamos, muertos / en el instante, en la hora canicular / cuando el ave es vencida / y una dulce ser-piente se desploma." The images are all of silence, of blindness, of solitude and disaster; the concrete objects are all symbolic of the destroyed Indian heritage: skulls, daggers, the serpents and birds that are so inextricably fused in pre-Hispanic myth. In this ruin of what the ancestors had created is the seed of our future ruin; as they disappeared, leaving only traces, so we shall disap-pear, leaving only traces. But within this vision of the inevitable mortality of every being and every civilization, there is a para-doxical tranquillity, as though saying that the final rest may not be totally catastrophic. The recognition and acceptance of this vision of an ancient world now dead—and even so perhaps more permanent than anything that surrounds us now—may explain the violent ambivalence of Huerta's poetic attitudes. Only in rare moments is it given to humankind to perceive and accept such a vision.

As we have seen, for Huerta poetry is, among other things, a means for expressing his rejection of everything he sees as corrupt or inauthentic. His scorn is not reserved for those he considers lackeys of capitalism; his contempt for some poets is as constant a theme as is his admiration for certain others. The most frequent charge is that they are unrepentant bourgeois.

> . . . tus poetas publicistas,
> ¡por tus poetas, grandísima ciudad!, por ellos y su enfadosa categoría de
>   descastados,
> por sus flojas virtudes de ocho sonetos diarios,
> por sus lamentos al crepúsculo y a la soledad interminable,
> por sus retorcimientos histéricos de prometeos sin sexo
> o estatuas del sollozo, por su ritmo de asnos en busca de una flauta.
>
> ["Declaración de odio"]

Aside from several obvious allusions to older poets less committed to insurrectionary poetics and politics than Huerta, this is a blanket condemnation. If we were to exile every poet who had written the kind of personal poetry damned thus, it is doubtful that anyone at all would be exempt, certainly not Huerta himself, as can be seen in poems like "La rosa primitiva." But Huerta was unconcerned with matters such as consistency; within the parameters generated by his political and social commitment, his is a poetry of emotional attitudes and reactions, of the feelings of the moment. Poets who did not share his beliefs were a convenient vehicle for objectifying his hatred of and distrust for the foreign capitalist system that he saw taking over and destroying his city. This attack on poets appears again in a curious poem entitled "Un hombre solitario," devoted to the anonymous man who left flowers at Stalin's tomb on the anniversary of the discredited dictator's death. The episode passed unnoticed—or suppressed—and Huerta laments that "nadie sabrá nada sobre él, entre millones de sombras silenciosas y chillidos de poetas egocentristas." Jaime Labastida has suggested that the anonymous figure was Huerta himself, showing the continuity of his political convictions.[22] One might add that this probably apocryphal attribution would demonstrate the singularity and the paradoxical internal coherence of Huerta's poetic vision.

A few writers escape this reiterated attack: Whitman, García Lorca, Virginia Woolf, Alberti, Neruda, Hemingway, Kafka,

Darío, Roque Dalton, and the Mexicans Margarita Paz Paredes, Jaime Sabines, and those writers, born about ten years later than Huerta, led by Jesús Arellano and gathered about the review *Metáfora:* altogether a heterogeneous assortment. Poetry for Huerta is Father Hidalgo's proclamation of Mexican independence ("Amor, patria mía"); it is "palabra Poesía, / que es una torre de funcional erección, / y ay de quien lo ponga en duda" ("De los desnudos será"); an open metaphoric recognition of the intimate relationship between these two aspects of his own subjective drives. Those who disagree "tienen el seco olor de las estatuas" ("Avenida Juárez") they are "el poeta callado en su muro de adobe, / mientras la dulce patria temblorosa / cae vencida en la calle y en la fábrica" ("¡Mi país, oh mi país!"). Huerta puns abundantly on the names of T.S. Eliot, whose political beliefs were diametrically opposed to those of Huerta, and the conservative opposition political party PAN (Partido de Acción Nacional) when he speaks of the "poetas elotes tiernos calaveritas apaleadas / poetas immensos reyes del eliotazgo / baratarios y pancistas / grandísimos quijotes de su tiznadísima chingamusa" ("Manifiesto nalgaísta aleluya cocodrilos sexuales aleluya"), or "alguna poetisa peruana o mexicana en su salsa" ("Para que aprenda [Hildebrando Pérez] a tomar un caballito de tequila"). And yet, so often behind this violent front there appears a flash of rueful despair that would arouse an echo in any Romantic: "el rojizo hastío del poema / siempre tan mal pensado y peor escrito" ("La gran trampa"). This is the same poet who repeatedly condemns this sort of emotion, and who wrote "La oración por Tania," where the rage at the murder of a young girl by the Nazis produced this outburst:

> ¡Odio, odio fiel!
> ¡Odio perfecto! Respiración, sacudimiento.
> Odio a la terrible mentira y al saqueo,
> odio al devastador y al incendiario,
> odio petrificado, odio purificado,
> odio por centenares de razones y sangre.

Throughout this rapid overview of Huerta's poetry, it has become obvious that at any given point in his career, and regardless of any immediate subject matter, there is at work an

operative principle of contradiction, of internal tension, what
Ricardo Aguilar called the fundamental duality of life and
death.[23] Although concentrating on the *poemínimos*, Aguilar
perceives this duality throughout and extends it to include the
love/hate dualism as a manifestation of the basic pattern. By
now, however, it is clear that this duality, if it can truly be called
that, is a basic principle embracing the entire vital system of
Huerta's poetry on every level. It is not only the mocking para-
dox, although such paradox is frequent enough, but the funda-
mental ambivalent character of so much of Huerta's imagery.

> Pero el amor es lento, pero el amor es muerte
> resignada y sombría: el amor es misterio,
> es una luna parda, larga noche sin crímenes,
> río de suicidas fríos y pensativos, fea
> y perfecta maldad hija de una Poesía
> que todavía rezuma lágrimas y bostezos,
> oraciones y agua, bendiciones y penas.
>   ["El amor"]

Only a poet for whom the contradictory nature of all human
existence was clearly visible could write such lines. It is this
that permits Huerta to see both sides of the hated/loved city.

> Amplia y dolorosa ciudad donde caben los perros,
> la miseria y los homosexuales,
> las prostitutas y la famosa melancolía de los poetas,
> los rezos y las oraciones de los cristianos
>   ["Declaración de odio"]

Such lines are no accident, any more than the lyrical catalogue
of contradicatory aspects of "Destino de la tarde" or the ironic
message that "Alguna vez los hombres del subsuelo / dirán que
la melancolía / es una gran bandera libertaria" ("Acerca de la
melancolía"), or the sardonically sad vision of Mexican politics
in "Puebla endemoniada":

> Pero por esta patria, oh Puebla,
> que es a pesar de todo nuestra patria,
> te envío
>   un poco de mi amarga alegría.

It is this sense of contradiction that lies behind the agonized irony of the "Dolorido canto a la iglesia católica y a quienes en ella suelen confiar" or the negative litany of the ferocious "Elegía de la policía montada," both from *Poemas prohibidos y de amor*, arrows aimed at elements that Huerta considered arms of repression, but using phraseology and terminology characteristic of the church. It is this same sense that has, paradoxically, made Huerta's poetic process one of fusion in which opposites become identified, so that what he says and the manner in which he says it become very nearly the same thing. It is, in sum, this sense of contradiction that has made Efraín Huerta one of Spanish America's most intensely committed social poets and at the same time a lyric poet of sometimes overwhelming intensity, a man who sings both lyrically and savagely, a man who has seen the double face of love.

4 JAIME SABINES
The Quarrel with God

Jaime Sabines is something of an anomaly in modern Mexican poetry. He has succeeded in earning a living from activities outside literature and has remained economically independent of the literary establishment, which tends to rely on professorships, fellowships, editorships, and a whole battery of similar economic support systems. A good part of Sabines's adult creative life has been spent in the state of Chiapas where he was born in 1925, remote from the intense and sometimes superheated literary relationships that characterize life in the capital. All this probably explains why so many critics saw in his earlier work a poet of the provinces, a spiritual heir of Ramón López Velarde, who was really something quite different and, in many ways, remote from Sabines. Sabines seems much more an heir of Baudelaire in his agonized portrayal of modern alienation. As Ammen Alwar has said, "Sabines is essentially an urban poet whose work is suffused with a harsh or dark way of looking at things, a sense of alienation, pain. When a lyricism comes into his work, it enters against that background of pain, so it seems well-earned."[1]

There seems to be no real change or development in Sabines's writing; a few slight modifications or shifts of emphasis have not substantially altered his apparent disinterest in any formal aspect of poetry or his stress on death and the bitter, corrosive nature of life trapped within the borders of time. This may possibly explain the almost total absence of any published work since *Nuevo recuento de poemas* (1977).[2] Or, as is suggested by the reading of *Nuevo recuento de poemas*, Sabines may have undergone a crisis of disillusionment with poetry, even a poetry as fiery and combative as his own. In any case, some of the most impressive of Sabines's work is among the earliest, and it is really quite disconcerting to read a study of the earlier books, such as Armando Armengol's "La iniciación poética de Jaime Sabines,"[3] and to recognize that the critic's comments are valid for even the *Nuevo recuento.*

Sabines's work tends to startle the reader accustomed to the verbal elaboration or the dance of images of much modern Mexican poetry. The poet to whom he is closest is probably Efraín Huerta, in his conception of an oral poetry, his rejection of technical virtuosity, and his tone of anger at injustice of various sorts. This apparent relative simplicity has led many to regard Sabines as some sort of poetic primitive, with the result that they ignore his complicated and sophisticated use of irony and contrast: "En efecto, en esta obra increíblemente clara y directa, todo está a la vista, todo en un solo plano aparente. La principal característica de esta poesía es su inmediatez, su absoluta carencia de toda ocultación, su ser-para-nosotros."[4] This seems a considerable overstatement; if there is a good deal of truth, there is also a quantity of exaggeration. Sabines is certainly not a "difficult" poet in the sense that his meaning is cloaked in obscurity; he is remote from the tradition of hermetic poetry. At the same time, he is a far more sophisticated and complicated artist than one would perceive from the remarks quoted above. Andrew Debicki, for example, has pointed out the complexities of Sabines's use of irony and point of view.[5]

This attitude toward Sabines's work has been fostered in large measure by his use of daily terminology, by his stubborn avoidance of anything that seems even remotely "literary," and by his unabashed willingness to use street language to achieve his desired effect. This latter is what Alí Chumacero has called "Esa afán de nombrar la vida diaria"[6] and José Emilio Pacheco spoke of as "una voz natural que celebra lo diario con las palabras diarias."[7] The result is a powerful but tender, sometimes explosive, poetry that varies notoriously in quality and tends to discomfit the critics. He is sometimes seen as a social poet, which seems a graphically incorrect reading, and is often compared to César Vallejo, with much more reason. Mauricio de la Selva has spoken of the "diluido tono vallejiano de Sabines: lo referente a los muertos, huesos, lluvias, domingos, lunas, ara-

ñas, cadáveres, angustias sin salida."[8] A few further charac-
teristics must be added: the towering rage against an unjust
universe and an unfair divinity that impregnates nearly all
Sabines's poetry, and the duality of flesh and death that does
recall López Velarde, and through him, the spiritual ancestor of
both, Charles Baudelaire.

Many of these contradictory and at times even confused
readings of Sabines's work may stem from his own comments
about his poetry. In an essay entitled "Sobre la poesía" he gives
us the following view of poetry, or at least his own: "Todos los
poemas de un poeta no son más que fragmentos de una carta
siempre inconclusa, escrita a un amigo desconocido. El poema
es así, el testimonio de las horas del hombre sobre la tierra.
Canto o lamento, queja o protesta, grito o balbuceo, el poema
debe de ir siempre oscuro de hombre."[9] In the same essay he
shows clearly his affiliation with Neoromanticism when he
says, in words visibly learned in antecedents as remote as Jules
Laforgue, that "El poeta es el payaso sufriente." And, he adds,
"Pero no hay que tomar muy en serio a la poesía. La poesía
ocurre de todos modos como un accidente, un atropello, un
enamoramiento, un crimen: ocurre diariamente, a solas, en la
soledad purísima, cuando el corazón del hombre se pone a
pensar en la vida."[10]

One of the few truly negative appreciations of Sabines's
poetry is the introduction "Algunas palabras" which appears in
the brief anthology of his work prepared by Sabines himself,
Poesía de la sinceridad.[11] Signed by José Casahonda Castillo, it
apparently was really writen by Sabines. Either it is an out-
rageous spoof, perfectly in character for a poet so little con-
cerned with the formalities of literature and the literary world
and so much a spiritual heir of the great poetic rebels, or it is the
expression of Sabines's profound doubts about poetry and his
own creativity. The burden of the remarks is that Sabines has
relied almost exclusively on sincerity as an esthetic standard in
his effort to "construir esa poesía cuya condición principal ha de
ser no parecer poesía."[12] In this attempt, the author asks," ¿se
ha preguntado Sabines a dónde lo conducirá esta insistencia de
de-formar la construcción poética? ¿No está corriendo el peor de
los riesgos: el de conseguir, después de todo, no hacer poesía?"[13]

To judge from these comments, whatever his intent, Sabines was fully conscious of the dangers of the artistic road he had chosen to follow. In his summing up, Sabines—if indeed he was the author—seems to predict a negative future for his own work. "El afán de sincer idad, de decir la verdad escuetamente y sin rodeos, es un afán honesto, pero no necesariamente un ejercicio poético. La poesía es la verdad con emoción, y la emoción sólo se contagia con artificio. Si le quitamos al arte el artificio, ¿qué queda? Queda solamente la invalidez del hombre."[14]

Such paradoxical comments provoke a series of questions that cannot be treated here, the most important among them being the nature and extent of this (according to Sabines), supremely important sincerity. If in fact he was speaking honestly in such negative and contradictory remarks, it is clear that he suffered from profound doubts about the nature of his poetic undertaking. If the paradoxical nature of the comments indicates an extension of the self-mocking persona common to much Romantic poetry and never totally absent from Sabines's work, we would then face the serious question of the extent to which the work reflects the deliberate irony of a mask. If in fact this is the case, it requires a fundamental reworking of the whole corpus of criticism of Sabines.

There is in Mexico a long and important tradition of poets obsessed with death, from the poetry of the pre-Conquest Flowering War to its brilliant culmination in the work of José Gorostiza, Xavier Villaurrutia, and Alí Chumacero. No one, however, has made of death the constant theme of his work in quite the same way as Sabines. Villaurrutia, for whom death was totally obsessive, created a personal mythology in which death was personified into a constant daily presence, and his poetry is in large measure an ambivalent erotic song to Death the mistress. Sabines's work is diametrically different, and sees death from a totally distinct vantage point. Death is a presence in the same sense as in Pablo Neruda or Francisco de Quevedo, a constant menace slowly corroding us and ever undoing us. At the same time, in no way does Sabines develop a coherent attitude toward this everpresent death. Much less intellectual—and intellectualizing—than Villaurrutia or Gorostiza, Sabines's

poetry is an emotional outburst, a scream of rage and indigna-
tion in the face of the death of a beloved individual and the
indifference or absence of a caring God.
Frequently, death appears as a metaphor for the generalized
deterioration of life. Human history is the story of this "Lento,
amargo animal":

> Amargo como esa voz amarga
> prenatal, presubstancial, que dijo
> nuestra palabra, que anduvo nuestro camino,
> que murió nuestra muerte,
> y que en todo momento descubrimos.
>
> Amargo desde dentro,
> desde lo que no soy,
> —mi piel como mi lengua—
> desde el primer viviente,
> anuncio y profecía.

Faithful to the ancient Hispanic tradition, Sabines sees life as an
inevitable and always-present process of dying. His use of the
first-person plural throughout the poem catches this collective
suffering in its milenary extent. Death is an integral part of
everyday existence, to the extent that at times we do not even
realize that we are on this path: "Me muero todos los días/sin
darme cuenta" ("Mi corazón me recuerda"). The totality of our
absorption by death, in every aspect of our living, is seen when
the poet says to his beloved, "Tú eres como mi casa,/eres como
mi muerte, amor mío" ("Me tienes en tus manos"). This is no
Baroque conceit; so true is it of us all, that our planet's oxygen
cloak is "el enorme panteón del aire que rodea la tierra" ("Todas
las voces sepultadas").
There are, of course, abundant moments of less intense an-
guish, of resignation or sardonic self-deprecation. Sabines is
such a skeptic that he cannot take seriously even his own
protestations of despair.[15]

> Vamos a morirnos cada quien en su sitio
> calladamente. No hay que darle importancia.
> "Carta a Jorge"

Cuando tengas ganas de morirte
esconde la cabeza bajo la almohada
y cuenta cuatro mil borregos.
Quédate dos días sin comer
y verás qué hermosa es la vida:
carne, frijoles, pan.
Quédate sin mujer: verás.
Cuando tengas ganas de morirte
no alborotes tanto: muérete
y ya.

["Cuando tengas ganas de morirte"]

This process of death is, of course, the process of life. In this
world there are no survivors, "sobrevivientes," only "sobre-
murientes" ("¡Abajo! Viene el viento"). Life is but "esta dulce,
esta llorosa arena/cayendo de las manos," "este bendito corazón
profundo,/manantial de la muerte" ("Lo primero que hay que
decir"). Perhaps the most precise, and certainly the most mov-
ing, recapitulation is these lines from "El cadáver prestado":

¿Qué otra cosa sino este cuerpo soy
alquilado a la muerte para unos cuantos años?
Cuerpo lleno de aire y de palabras,
sólo puente entre el cielo y la tierra.

There is another side to all this, however. Death has another and
less abstract face, one that is sometimes less frightening than
the face of life. In the earlier poetry there is a good deal of
Neoromantic ennui, and at times there is more than an echo of
the poetic past. Sabines dips into tradition in poems like "Sigue
la muerte," where life is a mad dance of death recalling the
medieval satires; and the personification of death in, for exam-
ple, "El poeta y la muerte," is deeply rooted in the Mexican
tradition. But there are moments of deep personal insight into
the poet's own vital and esthetic processes.

Me habló de la mariguana, de la heroína, de los hongos, de la llahuasa.
Por medio de las drogas llegaba a Dios, se hacía perfecto, desparecía.
Pero yo prefiero mis viejos alucinantes: la soledad, el amor, la
    muerte.

["Como pájaros perdidos: XX"]

As the poet approaches middle age, death becomes much more a personal physical possibility, and less a reaction to the tedium of daily life (however much this may have had of affectation or pose) or a metaphysical speculation on the corrosive nature of time. *Maltiempo* (1972) is probably the collection that most succinctly expresses the very real, almost physical, fear of approaching death in prose poems like "Ahora me pongo . . .":

> Ahora me pongo lentes para escribir. Es el 3 enero de 1970. Próximamente cumpliré 44 años.
>
>   Desde hace dos o tres meses digo: ¿Llegaré a fin de semana? No creo que tenga cáncer ni ninguna otra enfermedad incurable, pero siento que de un momento a otro me voy a desplomar. ¡Veo morir a la gente tan fácilmente!

Perhaps in this despairing cry we see most clearly the real nature and extent of Sabines's attitude toward death, in this projection of his own death upon other people in such an immediate fashion.

   This tendency is already visible in *Horal* (1950), in a poem like "Es la sombra del agua," where a nude portrait of a woman becomes fused with the poet's memory of a dead woman and with the "memoria de una ausencia." The impenetrable emotional distance of the woman becomes one with the physical fact of death, so that "nadie podrá saber nunca/—tan muerta estás—cuando mueras" ("Clausurada, sellada"). Sabines's entire poetic production is conscious of this fact of the immediate, concrete, physical fact of death. One of his most deeply-felt themes is the death of close ones, and there are a number of poems written about the lost and loved dead: "Tía Chofi," "Autonecrología," "Algo sobre la muerte del Mayor Sabines," "Doña Luz," and "Tío Chagua." In this last, published in the review *Estaciones* and not included in any book, the point of departure, typically, is the death of a close relative. First we are presented with the speaker's feelings of having been abandoned, followed by the voice of the dead man, first bewildered, then resigned in the face of his own annihilation and the need to come to terms with the abrupt fact of his own death. It is this immediacy of emotion, this total lack of pretentious intellectualizing, that makes "Tío Chagua" or "Tía Chofi" so moving as statements of humankind's impotence in the face of death. One of Sabines's rare political or social poems, "Tlatelolco," captures this same sense; the bitter sarcasm of his attack on the politicians responsible for the murders does not obscure the terrible sense of personal frustration.

Sabines's best known poem is the lament for the death of his father, "Algo sobre la muerte del Mayor Sabines." His capacity for disorienting the critics or exacerbating esthetic differences is visible here in truly devastating fashion, since most regard this as one of his outstanding efforts, while a few others object strenuously. Ana María Hernández speaks of the "lugares comunes, excesos de sentimentalismo y deslices de mal gusto."[16] Others compare the elegy favorably to such monuments of Hispanic literature as Jorge Manrique's "Coplas por la muerte de su padre" and García Lorca's "Llanto por Ignacio Sánchez Mejías. Such comparisons lead nowhere; Sabines's poem is very different from the other two, and is, in any context, an extraordinarily moving poem. Jaime Labastida states, "Aquí aúllan los hospitales y es el hombre la víctima; y Dios mismo, que en Manrique aparecía como esperanza y consuelo, en Sabines se manifiesta como el creador de un dolor en última instancia gratuito y sin sentido: Dios es 'el manco de cien manos', 'el impotente', el 'Omniausente', 'el viejo sordo': estas imprecaciones son inconcebibles en labios de Manrique."[17]

"Algo sobre la muerte del Mayor Sabines" is Sabines's longest and, in a special sense, his most ambitious poem, in that it attempts to capture the impact on the poet's life of the suffering and death, the trauma, of his father. But it is hardly an ambitious poem in the commonest sense of the word; there is no philosophizing, no abstraction onto a metaphysical plane of the significance of our unavoidable individual extinction. Instead, the poem is composed of short fragments, each of which is a glance at the immediacy and the agony of the loss. In VIII, for example, the family is unable to accept as real the dead man's passing because his belongings, which remind them forcibly of him, are still there; or in IX, because "tu nieta más pequeña/te busca en el cuarto,/y todos, sin decirlo,/te estamos esperando."

The second of the two longer sections into which the poem is organized is a meditation on the dead man's passing after he has

been buried, but the agony is not lessened. The senselessness of
the human conditioning is summed up in the lines of II, 4.

> ¿para esto vivir? ¿para sentir prestados
> los brazos y las piernas y la cara,
> arrendados al hoyo, entretenidos
> los jugos en la cáscara?
> ¿para exprimir los ojos noche a noche
> en el temblor obscuro de la cama,
> remolino de quietas transparencias,
> descendimiento de la náusea?
>
> ¿Para esto morir?
> ¿para inventar el alma,
> el vestido de Dios, la eternidad, el agua
> del aguacero de la muerte, la esperanza?
> ¿morir para pescar?
> ¿para atrapar con su red a la araña?

This is no longer neo-Baudelairean ennui, but the absolute and
immediate anguish of a man who has come face to face with the
human situation and finds it absurd, meaningless, indefensible.
   The last section of "Algo sobre la muerte del Mayor Sabines,"
which evokes the vision of the widow, "sola, en su vejez hun-
dida,/sin dolor y sin lástima,/herida de tu muerte y de tu vida,"
is an ironic lead-in to "Doña Luz," although the latter was
actually published a year earlier than the former. "Doña Luz"
begins, "Acabo de desenterrar a mi madre, muerta hace tiempo.
Y lo que desenterré fue una caja de rosas: frescas, fragantes,
como si hubiesen estado en un invernadero." This is remarkably
different from the litany of suffering of "Algo sobre la muerte
del Mayor Sabines," in which the poet in his own pain has
detailed the dying man's suffering, the nature of his agonizing
illness, and the slow process of decomposition in the earth.
"Doña Luz" is an affectionate memoir that treats the poet's
mother as though she had just returned, as though she lived
again at the side of her protective son. Or she will live again in
the spring, reborn "de la amorosa tierra, bajo los árboles lumi-
nosos, en el aire limpio." But even in this traditional response
the poet's sadness is easily visible: "No somos nada, nadie,
madre./Es inútil vivir/pero es más inútil morir." The most

accurate judgment of these two poems is that of José Emilio
Pacheco, when he said, "Gracias a que Sabines no tuvo 'el pudor
del silencio' nuestras videas se enriquecieron con esas dos gran-
des elegías: al mayor Sabines y a Doña Luz. Ambos dejan de ser
personas concretas y se convierten en el padre y la madre de
todos los lectores, en su protesta inútil contra la orfandad, la
enfermedad, la inconsolable humillación de la muerte."[18] The
lack of abstract philosophizing and the capture of the poet's grief
in specific, concrete terms give these poems their quality of
immediacy, which is also, paradoxically, the expression of the
despair of this unavoidable human situation.

At the poem's end, Sabines comes perilously close to perceiv-
ing the sterility inherent in his obsessive theme.

> Todo esto es un cuento, lo sabemos. He querido hacer un poema con
> tu muerte y he aquí que tengo la cabeza rota, las manos vacías. No
> hay poesía en la muerte. En la muerte no hay nada.

Such lines recall others of the first elegy:

> (Me avergüenzo de mí hasta los pelos
> por tratar de escribir estas cosas.
> ¡Maldito el que crea que estos es un poema!)

Sabines is very close here to recognizing the central defect of his
poetry, its dangerous teetering close to self-indulgence and ex-
haustion. In their best moments, these poems are a shriek of
enraged rebellion at cosmic injustice, even though we must
question the final significance of a poet who turns nearly every-
thing he writes, even such fine poems as these, into a protest at
his own imminent death.

An infinity of poets, when faced with their own mortality,
have found solace in love, but Sabines is unable to do so. All too
often the beloved only recalls to him that, like love, the flesh is
perishable. Instead of reacting against death through love,
Sabines declares war on God. Upon occasion, he blasphemes
mightily, and many poems rely heavily on strings of vulgarisms
and oaths. Not so frequently noticed is his heavy reliance on a
vocabulary that is religious and often biblical in its sources. His

conception of life seemingly owes a good deal to the traditional Christian notion of the vale of tears, without, of course, the consolation of an afterlife. In "La caída," an expression of solitude and anguish worthy of César Vallejo in its power, he speaks thus of poetry:

> Esto que vive en mí, esto que muere
> duras muertes conmigo,
> el manantial de gracia, el agua de pecado
> que me deja tranquilo.
> Fuego de la purísima concepción, poesía,
> bochorno de mi amigo,
> sálvame de mi mismo.

The vocabulary and the structure are those of the Christian litany to the Virgin, and although the conception is obviously parodic, it is intriguing to see that the role of the Virgin has been taken over here by poetry. These are far from the only examples; among others, there are "el paño de mi sangre en que reposa/mi corazón esperanzado" ("Con ganas de llorar"); "Sofía virgen, vaso transparente, cáliz" ("Tía Chofi"); the "becerro de oro" ("A un lado de los dioses"); the "Arca de Noé" and the names of Magdalena and Salomé ("He aquí que estamos reunidos") and of José and María ("Tú eres mi marido"); the "jinetes del apocalipsis diario" ("Autonecrología"); and the atrocious bitterness of "Canonicemos a las putas, Santoral del sábado: Bety, Lola, Margot, vírgenes perpetuas, reconstruides, mártires provisorias llenas de gracia, manantiales de generosidad" ("Canonicemos a las putas"). But it is much less this occasional use of terminology than the form of a frequent parodic litany, such as we have seen above, that imprints its stamp on Sabines's poetry. "Con los nervios saliéndome del cuerpo" is virtually a list of the commandments in reverse, and there is the sardonic litany of "Otra carta."

> Bendita entre todas las mujeres
> tú, que no estorbas,
> tú que estás a la mano como el bastón del ciego,
> como el carro del paralítico.

> Virgen aún para el que te posee,
> desconocida siempre para el que te sabe,
> ¿qué puedo darte sino el infierno?

This litany in reverse is a frequent usage, as in "La Tovarich":
"Que todos mueran a tiempo, Señor,/que gocen, que sufran
hoy.//Desampárame, Señor,/que no sepa quien soy." There is a
similar procedure in the violence of "El cadáver prestado."

> Señor del abismo, director de las sombras,
> guía de la víbora, padre de las tarántulas,
> hacedor del sueño, lumbre de la vigilia,
> quemadura del ojo:
> desparece, esfúmate,
> hazte a ti mismo nada,
> gota de agua ahogada,
> burbuja del aire en el pulmón del viento.

This kind of parody is not at all unusual, even to this degree of
verbal violence, as can be seen in one of Sabines's most sarcastic
attacks on the modern world, "Cantemos al dinero," or the
horrifying mock-litanies implicit in the listings of bodily hor-
rors in "La enfermedad viene de lejos" or "Algo sobre la muerte
del Mayor Sabines."

This use of Christian ritualistic language for a reverse pur-
pose is not limited to these parodic litanies. In "Adán y Eva"
Sabines created a characteristically negative version of the
myth of the earthly paradise, which ends—only too typically—
with the death of Eve. Another biblical legend seems especially
important to him, almost obsessive: the story of Lazarus, the dead
man resurrected. It appears in "Campanas de algodón", where the
call for the dead man to rise is unheard; and in "Once y cuarto" the
poet raises the chilling spectre of Lazarus's second death.

> ¿Qué pensaría Lázaro cuando iba a morir por segunda vez? La
> segunda muerte ¿ fue distinta de la primera, como el lunes es
> distinto del martes? ¿A cuántas muertes tenemos derecho cada
> uno? Porque la vida es siempre la misma, pero la muerte . . .

In "Con tu amargura a cuestas," the embittered protagonist
walking the sordid night streets has also been raised from the

dead, and the description of the city is cast in the form of the biblical list of blessings, with, of course, the anticipated reversal: "Para ti son las manos caídas,/para que las estreches con tus muñones." The poem ends in an unusual fashion for Sabines; its recasting of the Lord's Prayer is uncharacteristically open-ended in that it offers the option to choose.

> Para que tú te entregues
> se te están dando todas estas cosas:
> para que dejes tu cuerpo usado
> allí en el polvo donde estabas tendido bocabajo y llorabas;
> para que te levantes a los treinta y tres años
> y juegues con tus hijos y con todas las gentes
> en el nombre del padre y del espíritu santo
> y en el nombre de la gloria del juego del hombre.

There is at last a vision of a possible plenitude beyond the edge of this ailing world, and it is up to us to choose. But this plenitude, if indeed it can exist, is cast in the form of "la gloria del juego del hombre," rather than in any divine dispensation or ordering, and the choice is loaded against us.

Such use of biblical themes is typical of Sabines's poetry and reflects his passionate use of the other side of the tension that so possesses him: the existence, nature, and function of God. It is so much a crucial element that one critic repeatedly calls him deist, pantheist, and even lyrical mystic,[19] and another sees in his work a "peculiar misticismo."[20] Sabines never doubts the existence of God, but for him the supreme being ranges from inept to evil, hardly different from human beings: "Uno es algo que vive,/algo que busca pero encuentra,/algo como hombre o como Dios o yerba." ("Uno es el hombre"). At times Sabines wonders about the relationship between God and other possible prime movers: "Dios mío, ¿qué Dios tienes tú? ¿quién es tu Dios padre, tu / Dios abuelo? ¡Qué desamparado ha de estar el Dios primero, el / último!" ("Doña Luz"). Such speculations are hardly original; they fit neatly into the Neoromantic outlook of the whole body of Sabines's work, along with such well-worn notions as that we are only pieces of a huge machine operated by someone or something else, and that our prized individual freedom "no es sino el aceite con que nos lubrican,/la palmada que

nos de la vida para sentirnos importantes" ("El cadáver pres-
tado"). What is new is the violence of the speaker's personal
relationship with God. This poetry speaks not *about* God but *to*
him directly, hurling insults, epithets, and obscenities. Sabines
is outraged that God should have perpetrated on his creations a
joke of such surpassingly bad taste, and the poetry is an expres-
sion of this resentment. His view of God is slashingly ironic:
"Afuera, Dios roncaba, / Y su vara de justicia, en manos del
miedo ladrón, / dirigía un vals en la orquesta." ("Tarumba").
"Bocota enorme de Dios enorme haciendo payasadas" ("El ca-
dáver prestado"). This is a mediocre God, alien and remote,
whose principal function seems to be to do evil.

> Gloriosos los que mueren en paz. El sapo bajo la pedrada. El piojo
> entre las uñas. El cuello del santo entre las tijeras de Dios.
> (Insisto en la sabiduría de El Que Mata a Tiempo.) Gloriosos los
> que viven bajo las alas de la mariposa torcaz.
>
> ["Va a venir"]

The speaker would be rid of God, and wishes him the same good
luck: "Líbreme Dios de mí/igual que me he librado de Dios"
("Cuba 65"). But implicit in such irony is the other side of the
coin, and this ambiguity toward God is also frequent.

> Te quiero con todo mi odio,
> te perdono con todo el rencor de mi alma.
> Como marido y mujer estamos,
> viéndonos, acechándonos, dispuestos
> a clavarnos las uñas, furiosos de amor y de deseo.
> Ponte faldas, señor-señora,
> vela que te consumes velándome,
> apágate de una vez como un rayo.
> Tu precioso mundo sigue rodando
> en la casa de la locura
> como una canica de barro
> tirada por un niño ciego.
> Y yo te bendigo y te acompaño.
>
> ["El cadáver prestado"]

In the depth of this understanding Sabines overcomes the fear of
death that torments him, and himself realizes what lies behind

his rebellious posture. Beyond the savagery and the mocking, a would-be believer weeps lost in a world without meaning; behind the anger and the mistrust, a mystic yearns for absorption, a yearning that is contaminated by doubt and anger and that finds, as a result, a thoroughly mixed expression. "Tarumba," Sabines's best-known early poem, and one that attracted both considerable attention and a good deal of self-righteous criticism, is an outright talk with God that mixes obscene defiance with the wish to "crecer como una piedra regada todas las mañanas/por el jardinero del sol."

It is quite likely that this search for the totalizing religious or mystic experience or at least relationship explains the characteristic use of the disemic allegory that Andrew Debicki has found throughout so much of Sabines's work.[21] Sabines never loses contact with this world, the scabrous half of his poetry, even while he pursues some meaning that will make all this scabrousness acceptable. This all makes more comprehensible his poetic blasphemies and outrages. He is one of the *poetas malditos,* those who like Rimbaud seek salvation through renunciation. But the renunciation of Sabines's poetry is never as extreme as Rimbaud's; he never cuts off communication with his God. Those familiar only with Sabines's imprecations can be startled by the occasional sudden tenderness. His work never loses the sudden gift of a stunning lyric like "Quiero apoyar mi cabeza."

> Quiero apoyar mi cabeza
> en tus manos, Señor.
> Señor del humo, sombra,
> quiero apoyar mi corazón.
> Quiero llorar con mis ojos,
> irme en llanto, Señor.
>
> Débil, pequeño, frustrado,
> cansado de amar, amor,
> dame un golpe de aire,
> tírame, corazon.
>
> Sobre la brisa, en el alba,
> cuando se despierte el sol,
> derrámame como un llanto,
> llórame como yo.

Lines such as these are startling in the work of the man widely regarded as the great blasphemer of Mexican poetry. And they are not alone; scattered throughout we find such other gentle jewels as "Para tu amor, Señor"—"Para tu amor, Señor, no tengo apenas/otra cosa qué dar que mi tristeza." But for each such, there are dozens of renunciations and denunciations, for this is no easy relationship.

Often in such poets, woman becomes a replacement or substitute for God, and Sabines is no exception in this, but the substitution is never fully effective. Sabines's poetry is a carnal poetry, but the women in it are never completely successful in calming the inner tension between the poet, his God, and death. Sabines's obsession with women often takes the form of a concentration on pregnancy and pregnant women, and, although it is rarely placed in that context, this seems again a variant of the search for the door that will permit him to leave mortality behind. All women become the Woman, in Christian terms the Virgin, ever in the process of bearing the Saviour who will free us from our guilt and mortality, because, at heart, Sabines is a profoundly Christian poet and, as I suggested earlier, his poetic roots lie partially at least in mysticism, which is sometimes expressed in a surprisingly Nerudian fashion through contemplation of the natural world.[22]

For within the anger and rejection which are at the core of Jaime Sabines's poetic vision, there is the seed, barely glimpsed, of a profound joy. At times it finds expression in unexpected fashion, as in "¡Qué alegre el día!", a paean, if not entirely free of irony, to a city whose meanness and sordidness do not completely succeed in obscuring the radiance.[23] A similar attitude lies at the heart of poems such as "Poemas de unas horas místicas," six short lyrics that express the tormented and complicated but very real and absolutely immediate, unabstract relationship between the poet and the God with whom he sometimes succeeds in speaking. Tomás Segovia has said that the "Poemas de unas horas místicas" are "de una autenticidad deslumbrante. Sabines tiene con su Dios verdaderos altercados; se hacen de palabras, se insultan, se adoran."[24] It is not exaggeration to suggest that the search for meaning through woman may be more comprehensible if we realize that the relationship of the poet with his God is much like the relationship with lovers.

Since the publication in 1977 of *Nuevo recuento de poemas,* which added little to what had already appeared five years earlier, Sabines has published little that is new. Critics had always questioned the extremely uneven character of the poetry and the lack of any coherent development. César López recognizes that Sabines's lapses are due to the personal, immediate nature of his poetry, but comments that "Difícilmente se puede encontrar entre nosotros poeta tan desigual. Sus registros están a veces entre los mejores de la lengua. Sus fallos ruborizarían a cualquier poetisa pueblerina."[25] An anonymous reviewer of *Maltiempo* pointed out the volume's achievements and failures: "Poeta expresionista, encontró la 'antipoesía' antes que Nicanor Parra y descubrió, con menos retórica y más fantasía, las violencias y los vértigos del prosaísmo mucho antes que el cardenal Ernesto. Humor como un puñetazo en la cara . . . el sentimentalismo y la cursilería de ciertas líneas y la pose primitivista, 'macha' y antiintelectual de Sabines. Un poeta verdadero y un mal comediante disfrazado de salvaje. Un gran poeta trunco."[26]

Whether Sabines tired of such interpretations of his work or whether there were other operative causes, he appears to have ended this anguished dialogue. There are two crucial texts in *Maltiempo,* the last individually published major volume, which may explain this silence and which, in a poet as autobiographical as Sabines, we may take as literally or at the very least as metaphorically true of his inner world. The first is *Desde la muerte de mi hijo Jaime,"* which begins and ends thus:

Desde la muerte de mi hijo Jaime, de 22 años, no he querido hablar más de la muerte. En esos días escribí un poema de ocho o diez cuartillas, pero lo hice trizas y lo arrojé a la calle. No es posible pasarse la vida hablando de los muertos. Estoy harto. Me da vergüenza. . . . No te ensucies el alma con este mugroso amor terrestre a tu mujer que pelea, a tus padres que regañan, a tus hijos que no agradecen, a tus hermanos que traicionan, a tus amigos que olvidan: dedícate al divino amor de todos, al acuoso amor que perdona las ofensas no recibidas y la gloriosa crucifixión.

The other is the final text of the book, which I include here in its entirety.

He repartido mi vida inútilmente entre el amor y el deseo, la queja de la muerte, el lamento de la soledad. Me aparté de los pensamientos profundos, y he agredido a mi cuerpo con todos los excesos y he ofendido a mi alma con la negación.

Me he sentido culpable de derrochar la vida y no he querido quedar —me en casa a atesorarla. Tuve miedo del fuego y me incinceré. Amaba las páginas de un libro y corría a las calles a aturdirme. Todo ha sido superficial y vacío. No tuve odio sino amargura, nunca rencor sino desencanto. Lo esperé todo de los hombres y todo lo obtuve. Sólo de mí no he sacado nada: en esto me parezco a las tumbas.

¿Pude haber vivido de otro modo? Si pudiera recomenzar, ¿lo haría?

Taken together, these have all the air of a poetic testament, a form which Sabines has used previously, but which here may be definitive or very close to it, for his poetry. Given the probable strong dose of ambiguous irony in the first text and the clear disenchantment in the second, these may be Sabines's farewell to a way of feeling and of writing that was no longer meaningful. Like John Fowles's blind mystic in *The Magus*, Jaime Sabines, after spending many years in dialogue with God, may have realized that the only voice he heard was the echo of his own.

5 RUBÉN BONIFAZ NUÑO
The Shadow of the Goddess

Rubén Bonifaz Nuño, born in Veracruz, Córdoba, in 1923, is unusual if not very nearly unique among contemporary Latin American writers. Like so many others, he studied law and never practiced; for many years he has held positions such as director general of publications of the National Autonomous University of Mexico, and coordinator of humanities of the Faculty of Philosophy and Letters, corresponding to our American faculties of arts and sciences. He is also a member of the Mexican Academy of the Language. But here the similarities with other creative artists, many of whom are also academics, cease resoundingly. A classicist and professor of Latin at the university, Bonifaz Nuño has published a series of important translations: *Antología de la poesía latina*, with Amparo Gaos; the *Cármenes* of Catullus; and the *Georgics* and *Bucolics* of Vergil. Among the more intriguing aspects of this work as translator is Bonifaz Nuño's effort to capture something of the movement of the classical rhythms by employing an accentual syllabic transcription of the original Latin meters.[1] In addition, he has written extensively on Latin literature, with two books, *Tiempo y eternidad en Virgilio: La Eneida, libros I-VI* and *El amor y la cólera: Cayo Valerio Catulo*, in addition to articles on similar subjects in Mexican journals. It is obvious that Bonifaz Nuño's love for classical Latin poetry is both deep and of long standing.

But Bonifaz Nuño is no Latinophile sunk into Mexico's European and classical heritage, with his eyes closed to the other major strand of Mexican culture and ethnography, the Indian legacy. He is, on the contrary, an avid student of this tradition as well, and has studied with Father Angel María Garibay and Miguel León Portilla, the successive deans of Mexican studies of pre-Conquest language, literature, and culture. He has, further-more, written on pre-Hispanic culture, although less than on classical themes, and two of these publications are of basic importance for the understanding of his own original poetry: the essay "La fundación de la ciudad" and his address upon being elected to the Mexican Academy, "Destino del canto."[2] In both, he focuses principally on the similarities and differences, especially the former, between Latin and Aztec poetry. Upon occupying the seat formerly held by José Vasconcelos, polemical politician, educator, novelist, and philosopher, Bonifaz Nuño called Vasconcelos, "aquel en quien se combatían sin tregua enormes fuerzas contrarias que muchas veces fueron inconcilia-bles. Señor de la dualidad, como el dios terrible de los nahuas que se inventaba a sí mismo; poseedor de dos rostros opuestos, como el Jano de Roma, que encendía la guerra frunciendo el ceño colérico y sonreía a la bienaventuranza de la paz."[3] The measure of Bonifaz Nuño's awareness of what he is about in his own creative undertaking is visible in the fact that when he speaks of Vasconcelos, he does so in a fashion that underlines several of the fundamental aspects of that poetry; the struggle of irreconcilable forces, inner duality, and startlingly, the Aztec shadow. In "Fundación de la ciudad," he studies certain charac-teristics of the two cultures' poetry and discovers important resemblances between the *Aeneid* and the *Libro de Chilam Balam de Chumayel*. It is obvious that throughout his work Bonifaz Nuño is fully aware of its double source.

Several factors immediately strike the reader of Bonifaz Nuño's poetry, from the very first pages. One is the precision and exactness of his language, the verbal rigor and control, undoubtedly a heritage of his classical training, which becomes with the passage of time a prevailing sense of structural unity and balance. Each book comes more and more to be organized about a central theme with harmonic variations, and it is possi-ble to see the collected poetry as one long development and refinement of Bonifaz Nuño's obsessive theme. The second constant is the vision of a destructive reality within which we live. The revelation of this reality and its impact on the search for something different and better has been called by Andrew Debicki the "tensión entre una realidad destructora y el anhelo del hombre"[4] Even in the earliest work, the collection *La muerte del ángel* (1945) and the poems included under the heading "Algunos poemas no coleccionados, 1945-1952" in the collected work published under the title *De otro modo lo mismo* (1979), this double thrust is visible, although in attenuated form. These early poems, like so much of Mexican poetry in this century, deal heavily with death, and seem to reflect the influence of Rilke, among others, in the personal lyrics to death and the angelic presences. But even here, and even in poetry so overflowing in images that it is often obscure, the verse forms are tightly handled and often traditional in nature, and the poet is clearly striving for careful control of his rebellious matter. These are youthful verses, but they suffer from many fewer youthful errors than the early works of most poets.

Imágenes, poems written between 1946 and 1951, might be considered the poet's first important book. Like all his succeeding work, it consists of poems organized about a unifying theme; it is literally a book of poetry and not a collection of poems. The theme is solitude, the threat and even at times the very presence of death, and their repercussions on and relations with love. Although the author categorizes *Imágenes* as being part of his period of apprenticeship,[5] the volume alrady demonstrates his technical proficiency and the impeccable use of meter and rhythm. These qualities provoked comment by several critics: Jesús Arellano called the book a search for formal perfection; José Emilio Pacheco used the same phrase; and Ramón Xirau found it perhaps excessively literary,[6] a judgment that seems borne out by time. This formalist insistence is, of course, probably a product of the poet's training in classical verse; it is tempting to regard it as well, following Debicki, as an effort to overcome the vision of the disintegration that surrounded him.[7] This kind of controlling presence is a constant in all the poet's later work, just as some of *Imágenes'* most important technical characteristics also persist. "Ahí también se advierten ciertos caracteres propios de la estructura semántica de su poesía: la preferencia por el uso del verbo, la escasez de adjetivos, que casi siempre denotan texturas, formas, tonos de luz y sombra, sabores y olores."[8]

One of the principal metaphoric constants of Bonifaz Nuño's

poetry is already important here, the use of marine imagery.
Poem number 6 begins, for example, "Hondo en la corriente
pausada fluyen/lentos peces grises." There is a girl seated beside
the stream.

> Pasa, lenta, el agua en sus pies. Espumas
> aglomera turbias, esconde flores,
> y manos y pájaros muertos lleva
> entre lisos lomos y raíces.

This amorphous menace, heightened by the destabilizing, un-
expected syntax that becomes such an important feature of
Bonifaz Nuño's poetry, is a major theme of the book.

> sensaciones líquidas, con ternura
> cercan, insidiosas laten, invaden.
>
> Y seres marinos corren a ciegas
> entre las arenas conmovidas
> por el agua oscura, que suavemente
> mece hinchados cuerpos medio desnudos.
>   [7]
> . . . adioses que se anudan
> de pronto, y sumergen como naufragios:
>
> se diluyen formas, miembros confusos
> bajan y enriquecen la calma oscura
> de eternas corrientes, que trasladan
> barcos hace mucho tiempo perdidos.   [8]

It is important to emphasize that these visions of marine soli-
tude, although they may seem Surrealist visions, are in fact
rooted in a concrete external reality. The skewed nature of the
vision is produced by the poet's point of view. He is not talking
about an *inner* world, but about a highly subjective and even
idiosyncratic way of looking at the *outer* world. This is a para-
doxical land in which "vemos casi alegremente/que se nos
fueron muchas cosas,/y que nada nos queda nuestro" ("Poema
9"), a world in which a creeping viscosity invades all things and
in which we find "El verdadero amor, la torre/de lucientes
muros carcomidos" ("Poema 17").

Included with *Imágenes* in *De otro modo lo mismo* is a group
of poems published separately: "Ofrecimiento romántico,"
"Canciones para velar su sueño," "Canto del afán amoroso."
They are, basically, variations on the lover's attitude, reminis-
cent in some ways of Shakespeare's sonnets, which often take
the same approach; like the sonnets, they are sometimes almost
unbearably lovely.

> Así sea mi amor para tu amor:
> que no sepa de ti, que no te cambie,
> que no transforme las dulzuras íntimas
> de tu fuente cerrada,
> ni de tu viaje el anhelante espacio.
> Que sólo sepa el claro
> instante revivido en el que pases.
> Que no sea mi amor amurallada
> cárcel, ni vaso que recibe,
> sino un cristal transido, un cauce tierno,
> el portal de un camino.
>   [Canto del afán amoroso, 17]

Such verses are a startling contrast with *Imágenes* and with two
poems included in *De otro modo lo mismo* among the section of
uncollected poems from 1954-1955. One is "La rosa," a group of
three sonnets dated 1954 and dedicated to the Virgin in
orthodox Christian symbolism. The other is a vivid contrast:
eight poems under the collective title "Cuaderno de agosto."
The "Cuaderno" is a vision of horror and of evil unprecedented
in Boifaz Nuño and perhaps in all Mexican poetry, and leads
directly to one of the most important facets of *Los demonios y
los días.* We feel the speaker's panic before the unreasonable
menace of something which invades us and transforms us into
"una casa inútil / llena con un huésped que no deseo"
("Cuadernos, 3"). This is a vision that opens, like a door to Hell,
onto an unexpected, unrecognizable and alien world.

> Como si tuviera la boca llena
> de cobre, y los ojos ensangrentados;
> cubierto de pájaros rojos,
> de plumas ardientes, de irremediables

alas que no vuelan y que duelen
["Cuaderno, 5"]

We have left far behind the fruitless love of *Imágenes*; if
"Cuadernos de agosto" has not yet arrived at the extremes of the
infernal vision of certain mature poems, we are well on our way.
With *Los demonios y los días* (1956), Bonifaz Nuño entered
what he himself has called his creative period, in contrast to the
earlier works, which he has called apprenticeship or training.[9] It
is an extraordinarily dense book, with an obviously unified
structural conception behind it, although the exact nature of
this conception is not clear. The volume consists of forty-two
poems or subsections numbered in Arabic numerals, and five
others interspersed given Roman numerals. The structure is not
completely balanced, but the intervals between the sections
with Roman numerals do show a regular pattern: 7, 9, 8, 9, and 7,
with two more after poem V. Poems I through V are tightly
related; they are a vision of a desolate world that recalls the
wastelands of Eliot or Gorostiza. The poet himself has pointed
out influences of the bitter visions of the painters Goya and
Orozco.[10] Poem I begins thus:

Cha cha cha. Bailemos. Hiervan los ruidos.
Siga el vacilón. Bailemos diente con diente.

Y el Desharrapado enrosca la cola
y su cacerola mueve, y atiza
su lumbre. Bailemos.
                    Pobres marranos.

The similarities with Gorostiza's *Muerte sin fin* are imme-
diately obvious. Throughout the five poems, the names of this
malevolent figure change—he is el Desharrapado, el Embustero,
el Enredador, el Bellaco, el Expulsado, el Macaco, el Chapucero,
el Perjuro, el Caudillo—but this is the personification of Evil,
incorporating but transcending the Christian Devil. We are pre-
sented with a nightmare vision of a porcine, grunting, rooting,
swinish existence, a literal Witches' Sabbath in which "Hoy se
casan/un chivo contento y una gallina/negra, totalmente vir-
gen" (III). The bitter vision is punctuated by the irony of calling

the victim of this unholy rite "totalmente virgen," as though
the partial condition were possible, and of saying in a tone
reminiscent of much medieval poetry, "es bueno querer la
mugre,/pues mientras hay mugre hay esperanza" (II).

Counterpoised to this nightmarish song we find others that
are drastically different, at times reminiscent of such classical
figures of Renaissance poetry as Fray Luis de León or Garcilaso
de la Vega in their harmony and clarity, and the lines in Poem III
about what can only be called "el amor malo" strongly recall the
medieval Juan Ruiz, Arcipreste de Hita. The general tone, how-
ever, if not the blasted song of the Roman-numbered poems, is
hardly the graceful Renaissance beauty of Fray Luis or even the
robust sensuality of the Archpriest. Nor do we find the generous
love of some of some of the earlier books of Bonifaz Nuño; here,
love has become "esta pasión inútil, dañina," "esta corrosiva
nostalgia" (3). Many critics have spoken of the social orientation
of *Los demonios y los días,* but this is really hardly the case. It is
much more a volume of solitude than of solidarity. Lines like
"vivimos/viendo que tendemos la mano/y la retiramos siempre
vacía" (4) are far more frequent than any expression of mass
communication, although there is an occasional poem like 23,
which begins,

> Sólo es verdadero lo que hacemos
> par a compartirnos con los otros,
> para construir un sitio habitable
> por hombres.

Much has been made of poems such as 9, which use the gram-
matical forms of the verb to underline the separateness of indi-
viduals, as though the poet were using this as a statement of
solidarity, when the point of the poem is that this separateness
is the true state of things. Poems with any real social content or
commitment are really the exception; much commoner is the
wry ironic vision, so reminiscent of the poetic heritage passed
from Corbiere and Laforgue through Eliot to Novo, Owen, and
others:

> . . . los que fueron invitados
> una vez; aquellos que se pusieron

> el menos gastado de sus dos trajes
> y fueron puntuales; y en una puerta,
> ya mucho después de entrados todos,
> supieron que no se cumpliría
> la cita, y volvieron despreciándose. [24]

Bonifaz Nuño has commented that "En ese tiempo había en México cierta moda de protesta, a la que yo no pude escapar."[11] He escaped more than he believed; on the other hand, he continues by clarifying that he detests protest poetry, and by affirming his belief in poetry as a gratuitous act in which words, not ideas, are the principal element. Clearly, this hardly means that poetry has no semantic charge, but it rejects the concept of poetry subordinated to an intellectual or ideological commitment of any sort. For Bonifaz Nuño, poetry is an act of free will, remote from any effort to forge messages, and the semantic discharge is the result of the complex network of experiences that exists within any poet. In spite of the efforts to see in *Los demonios y los días* a sociopolitical commitment of some sort, it is fundamentally a long poem of human solitude, with its roots in the ironic techniques of an earlier generation, more ironically Neoromantic than Marxist. This does not negate, in any sense, the underlying expression of compassion and the wish for human communion, but the volume is not the simplistic approach some readers have seen (or perhaps wished to see). It is an expression of the poet's identification, but not of identity, with the outsiders, the solitary, those who, like him, feel lost in an enormous plastic city with its "más de tres millones de almas enfermas" (13). One cannot help but wonder what his reaction is to the five or six times as many who live in Mexico City today.

Poem 42 is an effort to break out of this solitude. It is distant from political identity or anything of the sort; rather, it is a typical expression within the line we have already seen in *Los demonios y los días*, the tradition of the modern poets of the ironic vision of the city.

> Estoy escribiendo para que todos
> puedan conocer mi domicilio,
> por si alguno quiere contestarme.
> . . . .

> Escribí al principio: tiendo la mano.
> Espero que alguien los comprenda.

Nothing could be further from a poet of the masses, from the effort to establish the type of immediate contact rooted in a conception of a socially-based oral/aural poetry that we have seen in Efraín Huerta. Bonifaz Nuño's poetry reflects an intense and personal vision of poetry as the expression of the individual's radical solitude, and the only hope for contact is the mutual comprehension of the solipsistic nature of existence.

In 1958 Bonifaz Nuño published *El manto y la corona,* a deceptive volume which misled those few critics who commented on it and which its author called a technical retrogression because it is a book "comido absolutamente por la emoción," "una confesión desvergonzada. Y la poesía no es para hacer confesiones desvergonzadas." José Emilio Pacheco, one of Mexico's finest critics, called it "un canto de amor en varias estancias. Su unidad es la naturaleza contradictoria del sentimiento amoroso que, pese al desplome que trae consigo, es la única manera de trascender la irremediable soledad, el vacío." Mauricio de la Selva saw its double theme as love and the chaotic situation in which humankind of our times moves. For Jesús Arellano, it was a sentimental vision of love as salvation in a mechanized world. De la Selva went into greater detail: "Al amor, en este libro, lo enfoca profundamente desde todas las perspectivas de la contradicción; canta a un amor que todo lo llena pero que también todo lo destruye; del que todo se espera y que a ratos decepciona; tímido a veces y exigente otras; fuerte y débil; pacífico y violento. Lo único que subsiste de esta sucesión de estados de ánimo es la pasion que caracteriza al poeta y su sentimiento."[12]

All of the above is, up to a point, true. On one level, the book is the story of a love, a long unified poem that contemplates one side of the affair from multiple angles and registers the various shadings of the speaker's passion: plenitude and frustration, the demand for total possession of her, and the secret confession.

> Y sólo yo sabré que hubiers a sido
> cabalmente dichoso

> con cualquier cosa que me dieras;
> que era mentira
> que te necesitara toda;
> que cualquier cosa tuya,
> por pequeña que fuera, siendo tuya . . .
> Y que, por no tenerla, estoy muriendo.
>
> [14]

But there is a level here to which the reviewers and the critics have not addressed themselves: the nature and identity of this beloved. Ernesto Mejía Sánchez points out the ambiguous nature of the title, and says of the beloved that she is "la joven amada que ilumina el mundo en torno."[13] But if we examine her carefully, we find that she exists only through the poet, that he speaks of her and to her, but that she has almost no existence of her own that is accessible to the reader. We see only his vision of her, never her own reality. Raúl Leiva alluded to this in speaking of the dialectic "entre el ser y su imagen."[14] He comes closer to the truth when he says, "No se canta aquí a una mujer cualquiera, sino a un ser *que hace cosas,* que no está vanamente en el mundo: ella, corazón siempre encendido, ayuda con su magia a que el poeta viva, a que se descubra en ella, iluminándose. La mujer, aquí, es una verdadera *cómplice,* en el sentido baudelairiano. En ella descubre una belleza necesaria, fatal, diabólica y angélica que *no es de este mundo.*"[15] This is, of course, built into much, if not all, amorous poetry—if indeed not all literature—but here it achieves unexpected dimensions. We never see her mind, only his; we see her only as reflected and filtered by the poet's thoughts and words, as Beatrice exists through Dante. The emotion expressed in these poems is not love, it is adoration, which is quite a different matter. There are several references to the function of language that underline this separation between reader and subject, references that create an odd relationship between the poet and his beloved.

> Ya no pretendo ser yo mismo
> para que tú me veas;
> estoy contento asi, me he contentado
> con ser tu mensajero,
> tu traductor, tu intérprete;

el que toma al dictado lo que dices
para guardarte inalterada.   [9]

This echoes the archaic conception of the poet as disciple and
slave of the beloved-cum-goddess, a concept familiar to the
readers of Robert Graves's *White Goddess*. It is suddenly clear
why their first meeting is described so.

Náufrago, roto, enronquecido,
encendí mis hogueras en la orilla
más alta, sobre el mar, y tú las viste
al pasar, desde lejos, y llegaste
y curaste mi sed, fuiste a mis llagas,
arropaste mi frío,
y me guardaste inerme y consolado
sobre tu corazón.   [7]

However much these lines may refer to a more-or-less specific
woman and a more-or-less concrete external reality, they are
framed in familiar words. The allusions are ancient, and to an
episode that is more closely associated with a goddess than with
a woman of flesh and blood. When she leaves, she does so
because he has not sung her sufficiently. Like the ancient bards,
his function is to praise her in song; any negligence or derelic-
tion produces the awful possibility that she will abandon him.
And when she is there, his attitude is again one of adoration.

Desde antes de nacer estabas hecha
para ser contemplada.
Horas enteras, días, años,
desnuda, contemplada, comprendida.
[20]

We should not be surprised that the book is called *El manto y la
corona*, because its protagonist is a goddess. She exists to be
contemplated, she is free, and he exists to defend and to praise
her, to interpret her through his poetry.

Amiga a la que amo: no envejezcas.
Que se detenga el tiempo sin tocarte;
que no te quite el manto

de la perfecta juventud. Inmóvil
junto a tu cuerpo de muchacha dulce
quede, al hallarte, el tiempo.   [16]

he llegado a cegarme en el orgullo
de contemplar la púrpura y el oro
de tu fastuoso amor.   [28]

She may be sheer invention, she may be a vision that lies behind
and beyond a more concrete woman of ordinary flesh who has
inspired the poet to this creation, but in any case, this beloved
partakes of the goddess, of the terrible adored figure who comes
to dominate so much of the later work. It is proper that Bonifaz
Nuño should have made clear their respective roles in one of his
most stunning poems.

Y cuando me haga viejo,
y engorde y quede calvo, no te apiades
de mis ojos hinchados, de mis dientes
postizos, de las canas que me salgan
por la nariz. Aléjame,
no te apiades, destiérrame, te pido;
hermosa entonces, joven como ahora,
no me ames; recuérdame
tal como fui al cantarte, cuando era
yo tu voz y tu escudo,
y estabas sola, y te sirvió mi mano.
                                    [16]

In an unpublished dissertation, John Bennett has come to some-
what similar conclusions. He suggests that the tension basic to
Bonifaz Nuño's work is the struggle between the concepts of
union and the battle between opposing elements, and that the
figure of the woman, whom he calls a "kind of generalized
female force", is intimately linked to this theme.[16] Certainly
this woman who becomes slowly but inevitably more impor-
tant with the passage of years, is a combination of elements. If
she represents the beloved—concrete, ideal, or fleeting—, she
recalls more and more the two figures of the goddess/mother of
Mexico's and Bonifaz Nuño's double cultural inheritance:
Coatlicue and the Virgin Mary.[17] She does not yet achieve the

syncretic fusion that appears in later books, but the affiliation is undeniable.

Fuego de pobres (1961) is remarkably, and surprisingly, different from *El manto y la corona,* and its commentators are unanimous in recognizing its nearly impenetrable hermeticism. Inexplicably, a few have seen it as social poetry, a reading which seems indefensible, and which Bonifaz Nuño regards as frankly aberrant. A considerable part of the difficulty is that the book seems to operate on two levels: there is a thread of despair, expressed thematically by what appears to be the revery of a man lying in bed listening to night sounds. In one of the earliest attempts at exegesis of the book, Fausto Vega declared that the primary plane is that of "un hombre, que en la noche, mientras llueve, ya acostado, recuerda y espera que amanezca."[18] Contrapuntally, there is a series of what seem to be visions of horror, many of them rooted in the Nahua pictorial and sculptural tradition, a source noted by the poet.[19] But there is another double thread to this volume, a thread that follows the poet's interest in the binary heritage of all Mexicans: the Hispanic and the indigenous. It bears a double epigraph, from the *Iliad* and the Codex Florentine, which Henrique González Casanova renders as follows:

> Los dolores, sin embargo, dejemos aún yacer en el ánimo, estando afligidos: pues ninguna ganancia se saca del triste llanto.
> *Iliad,* XXIV, v. 522-24.

> Y si tal vez así fuera; si tal vez saliera verdadero; si así estan las cosas sobre la tierra. ¿Acaso por eso estaremos amedrentados? ¿Acaso por eso viviremos con miedo? ¿Acaso por esto llorando viviremos?
> *Códice Florentino,* Lib. VI, cap. XVIII, fol. 75r.

The two sources share the stoicism that is so often alleged to be characteristically Mexican, as though the poet were saying that the two strands of the double inheritance reinforce each other to create a characteristic national spiritual patrimony. It is doubtful, however, whether the poems of *Fuego de pobres* in their entirety or even in any major portion can really be called stoic. Rather, there is a strong echo of the European tradition of soli-

tude and despair—existentialism was still a powerful force in
literature and thought when these poems were written—and
against it the hallucinated thematic counterpoint of what can
only be described as visions, like something from a half-buried
past. We must not underestimate the intertextual complexity of
this fabric; there are memories of the Latin poets, of López
Velarde and of Villaurrutia, with echoes of folksong and the
typical daily language of the Mexican. And, most important of
all, the innumerable allusions to pre-Hispanic poetry, from the
repetitive imagery based on flowers and precious stones to the
constant presence of the serpent. Some of the poems vividly
recall the pre-Hispanic sculptures that abound in Mexico:
"Collar del movimiento, sangre/nacida, sierpe de plumajes, ór-
bitas,/calavera de azúcar del ombligo" (25).

There appears to be a further contrapuntal organization of
the two traditions. The first is the vision of modern man lost in a
rainy world of solitude and boredom, a world in which images of
death fill the city streets:

> . . . es el tiempo de ponerse,
> encenizado de colillas fúnebres,
> a velar con cerillos
> algún recuerdo ya cadáver . . .
> [1]

Interwoven with this perspective is another more temporal and
more horrifying vision, as though our modern despair were only
a barely perceived sense of something more terrible and more
eternal, something expressed here through symbols from the
ancient Aztec rite.

> Deshabitado el traje suspendido,
> suena con un temblor de piel que busca
> su bestia desollada, su materia
> de bestia próxima pudriéndose.
> Oh, muerta, muerta, muerta.   [6]

The figure alluded to here—or invoked—is the Aztec god Xipe
Totec, the Flayed One. There are other and equally appalling
visions, which at times are so close to the archaic spirit that the

poet speaks in lines that might have come directly from Aztec
poetry, as in "Sólo mientras vivimos merecemos,/sólo mientras
estamos, mientras somos,/al menos, alguien que ha nacido"
(12). These lines echo much of pre-Hispanic lyric poetry, with its
concentration on the brevity of this existence, often in deliber-
ately obscure language that hid a religious or metaphysical di-
mension accessible only to the priests. Bonifaz Nuño has,
however, given them a contemporary thrust by shifting the
focus of the image so that instead of pointing out the brevity of
life and the inevitability of whatever may come next, here we
find a lament precisely because of that brevity. What the poet
has done here is to use themes, images, and vocabulary from the
metaphysical Aztec poetry of ritual human sacrifice and despair
in the face of inevitable death to communicate a personal sense
of loss in the face of our impending death here and now. Simul-
taneously, there is the deeper sense of almost-seen horror, of an
apocalyptic perception that speaks to us of flayed bodies, of eyes
and mouths sewn shut, and of unspeakable reptilian horrors.
Behind the fear we each know lies something far greater, more
terrible. Perhaps this is what still gives a chill to these echoes of
the Aztec ancients' lines: "Hay noches en que tiemblan/—agua
ciega, inestable—las paredes/de las casas" (20). Strangely, and
only very rarely, there are hints of another and much different
tradition in the references to crosses and olives, to Holy Thurs-
day and Palm Sunday. The most intriguing aspect of such refer-
ences is that they tend to appear in lines that seem to be written
in some sort of arcane private symbolism, in which allusions are
recognizable, but the sense is obscure:

> Viéramos, amarilla, construirse
> la corona sulfúrica de humo
> en la huella del chivo, y floreciera
> la doliente señora del incienso
> con el siete de espadas.
>   Viernes santo.
>   [11]

The goddess of *Fuego de pobres* is revealed to us in her
manifestation as Coatlicue, the goddess of death and finality
with her skirt of skulls; the other half of the Aztec divinity, the

goddess of love and creativity, is almost entirely absent. Agustín Yáñez noted this when he said, "Por el camino y sobre la traza engrandecida de *Los demonios y los días*, el ardor de Coatlicue—creadora, destructura—indujo a su poseído a construir *Fuego de pobres*, y allí alojó a los viejos dioses del pueblo." Bennett has pointed out how the roots of the metaphoric system of the text are found in Nahua mythology: Quetzalcóatl's serpent, Tezcatlipoca's mirror, the jaguars and eagles of the military orders of nobility.[21] This does not mean that these metaphors have a single semantic charge; on the contrary, part of the richness and at the same time difficulty of Bonifaz Nuño's poetry is the constant polysemia. The serpent is an Aztec symbol of cosmic movement related to the creation myth, but it also never ceases to be a phallic symbol as well, and the two signifieds are balanced in this complex poetry. In the same way, fire, and above all in its manifestation as the burning water, represents the "guerra florida," the Aztec war of conquest to obtain sacrificial victims. This becomes in Bonifaz Nuño a metaphor for his own inner war between the two poles of life and death, salvation and damnation, love and horror. But it also carries the Christian symbolism of purification through sacrifice, a meaning that it had as well in pre-Hispanic mythology, thus closing the circle. In this way, Bonifaz Nuño's poetry becomes more and more intricate in its search for expression of this complicated atemporal network of realities, until it becomes an intertextual web of extreme complexity. In "La fundación de la ciudad," the poet speaks of the temporal and atemporal levels, the plane of time and the plane of eternity, which are found in the *Aeneid* and the *Chilam Balam*. We might say the same of his poetry, which strives, by means of this elaborate framework, to transmute the anguish of a Mexican of today into the expression of the terror of all humankind of every epoch.

Much of this can only be read in terms of each reader's corpus of responses, his own *personal* poetic competence, since the book is formulated in a sort of symbolic code.[22] In an interview with John Bennett in 1968, the poet commented in detail on poem 17 of *Fuego de pobres*, pointing out that it is composed of a series of complicated allusions to astrological signs and the Bible, particularly the Apocalypse.[23] One has the impression that Bonifaz Nuño deliberately attempted to create the book in this fashion, utilizing his materials consciously, an impression fostered by Acuña when he speaks of the poet's "precisión de relojero suizo."[24] At this point in time it is exceedingly doubtful that anyone still really takes very seriously the idea that a poet works like a watchmaker, however much a disciple of Eliot or Mallarmé he may be. No poet is fully conscious of more than a fragment of what he is about, and Bonifaz Nuño's use of a semiprivate code, along with his effort at meticulously conscious creation, are really ways of enriching, rather than intellectualizing, the basically supraintellectual nature of poetic communication. *Fuego de pobres* is a fascinating and exasperating book; even more than with most poetry, however hermetic, the reader feels that he is only dimly grasping the interrelations of the poetic symbols.

Included in *De otro modo, lo mismo*, is a group of uncollected poems written between 1962 and 1965, between publication of *Fuego de pobres* and that of *Siete de espadas* (1966). Although they do not seem to involve a central generating principle, they embody the same series of themes that was becoming so dominant. Increasingly they utilize demonic imagery; the marine images that were so important earlier have all but vanished. The poet seems overcome by fire imagery with its obvious corollary of purification. There are frequent references to *escamas*, as snake figures become increasingly central, at the same time that several of the poems show once more clear resemblances to pre-Conquest poetry. At times this resemblance becomes simply overwhelming, as in "El envío":

> Y un sol en cruz para salvarme,
> y un collar degollado y una sarta
> de calaveras, y tendría
> la mazorca de dientes amarillos
> y las hambrientas órbitas.

There is a curious overlap between a poem like "El principio," with its "la extranjera, la muy blanca," which seems to express both a love relationship and the imminence of death, a theme not far removed from European Postromanticism, and "Idilio," whose title immediately recalls the superb poem by Manuel José Othón. Despite the profound differences between the two idylls, there are striking similarities, and Bonifaz Nuño seems to be suggesting that behind the erotic terrorism of the Indian woman of Othon's poem lay something very like the goddess who inhabits his own work. The same is true of "La consumación," which again evokes Othón's desperate vision of the mistress who enslaves the persona of his poem. The persona of Bonifaz Nuño has also been enslaved, although his goddess is somewhat more metaphysical and less tangible for the reader.

Siete de espadas adopts the same hermetic stance as *Fuego de pobres;* it is an extraordinary and extremely difficult book that makes one think of a frenzied and profoundly erotic *Waste Land.* Like Eliot, Bonifaz Nuño is attempting to leave behind superficial notions of time in order to arrive at a totalizing contemplation of existence. The difficulty is that the vision is so piercing and the creative imagination so dazzling that the poems are difficult to penetrate. The 143 seven-line stanzas appear to be a fabric of memory, perhaps the recollection of a dream, within which the speaker searches for the permanent in the flux of the eternal versus the momentary. Bennett has said that instead of describing the experience, the book recreates it from within.[25] Behind this there is a Dionysiac note mingled and simultaneously contrasting with the despair of recognizing the ephemeral nature of existence. The presiding figure is once again the mysterious great mother goddess.

> La elegida desciende, y en mis hombros
> —pata de cabra, escoba del conjuro—
> pliega sus alas de hoja seca.
> Y en las fauces lentas de las flores
> de presa, entre las sábanas hendidas
> —encrucijada, crisma, fiebre—
> me consagra en vilo y me deshuesa.
> [1]

If *Siete de espadas* reads almost like a battle between the heritage of Dante and that of the Aztec sacrificial rituals, it is because the volume creates an extraordinary inner reality. Be-

hind each aspect of the poem we perceive the imprecise shadow
of an alien but fascinating alternative world.

> Caballo blanco, venado del cielo,
> hierro en cruz virulenta. Y ya perdida
> mi tumba solar, muerte en batalla;
> tú, mi deleite, mi florido
> collar de macho. De la ceiba pende
> —ajorcas de ceniza, lengua—
> por los pies mi corazón ahorcado.
>   [11]

> Tendida en el maizal, prolífica
> en su dicha terrible, aúlla
> la joven reina de los hombres
> siempre desposada; mi señora
> madre de toda muerte. Y en la sangre
> nupcial vertida y en el parto, acopla
> las voces y agavilla el coro.   [143]

Such an atrocious vision defies translation into Occidental
cultural terms, and this is precisely the point of its appearance
here. The poet is seeking a more complex and more authentic
reality, beyond everyday surfaces and the simplistic one-dimen-
sional figures of the Manichean Occidental tradition, which is
prone to divide existence into clearly separated poles of good
and evil. There is despair in *Siete de espadas* in its recognition of
the inevitability of death, in a world in which "Los matan de
fiesta, como a ciegos" (16). As a response to this despair, the poet
alludes repeatedly to the pre-Conquest tradition of the poetry of
stoicism: "sólo sueños/aquí, amigos, sembramos" (124).

El ala del tigre (1969) follows the same line established in
Fuego de pobres and *Siete de espadas:* tightly constructed and
unitary in conception, it consists of eighty five poems, each of
them of three sestets, although there does not appear to be a
single dominant central theme. Whatever the creative pro-
cedure employed in these later books by Bonifaz Nuño, for the
reader there is no recognizable logical referent, and the poems
give the impression of transcribing an internal battle, organized

and made at least partially comprehensible by the poet's pro-
digious capacity for producing images. The book contains many
of the themes we have already seen, and the volume seems to
recall a voyage through memory. Death waits at every turn of the
road: "la muerte/mira, agazapada, en el instante/donde apaga su
lengua roja/ algún dolor que fuimos" (7). Literally or figuratively,
the enigmatic woman object of his poetry and his desire has
died, but she is also present to assure herself that the poet's
death too is a certainty.

The whole presentation of death here is thoroughly ambigu-
ous, and there is even one poem, 37, which seems to sing the
glories of the ritual death prized by the Aztecs. There is again an
abundance of pre-Hispanic imagery, particularly the precious
stones and the jaguar-eagle figures so important in the Nahuatl
lyric. Some poems, like 31, could well come from Garibay's or
León Portilla's translations of the Aztec originals. This is not at
all literary archaeology, but the profound and solidly based
immersion in a poetic tradition in order to communicate related
problems. The Aztec world may seem to us remote and in many
senses incomprehensible, but its prevailing consciousness of
doom, of time running out and cyclically renewed only because
the gods are as indifferent to our survival as to our extinction, is
not alien to our own modern sense that time slips away from us
as well. In the frenzy of the images that Bonifaz Nuño adapts
from the ancient tradition, one feels the desperation, the loss, of
a man gravely wounded by existence: "Herido estoy de ser" (15).
At times this perception of loss erupts in apocalyptic verses,
such as poem 40, which capture the full horror of man, Aztec or
modern, trapped in a cosmic riddle whose only solution is his
own dissolution.

> Solapados soles y planetas
> devoradores de basura;
> sistemas lunares, indigentes
> siglos de manos traicionadas
> comen de mí, me desconsuelan,
> en torno me arrastran, me acarrean.
>
> Pero ¿Quién soy yo? ¿Quién ha pensado,
> al despertar, que era de día?

> ¿El que prometió? ¿Quien se ha dolido
> de cumplir, a penas, la promesa?
> ¿A quién arrastran, despojado?
> ¿Quién de aquel 'quien' se condolece?
>
> Comida de cósmicas larvas
> que giran en tronos desolados,
> noche de amor de moscas, presa
> de planetarias tripas, savia
> soy del tronco mendigo y ávido
> que con flacas lunas me devora.

This is a vision of the annihilation of self, of identity, of reason to be and of possibility of being. With reason the poet speaks of "la calavera/roja que me sigue y me precede" (41).

If the poet is driven to constant allusion to a violent archaic form of life, it may be because the life that surrounds him today is equally violent; this is the vision we see constantly. Certainly, in its terrifying panorama of senseless death, poem 55 recalls the slaughter of Tlatelolco,[26] with its echoes of ancient cultures and ancient barbarism mixed with modern savagery. In several of the poems we see the poet's vision of his valley today and the difficulty of making bearable a life in which "me esfuerzo, me pagan/por podrirme, cada quince días" (71). Once more there is an abundance of reptilian imagery, of coils and rings. In the two traditions underlying these poems, the European and the Nahua, these patterns are in conflict. The European tends to consider such images as representative of the sensual, in the Freudian or Christian senses, while the pre-Hispanic cultures seem to have conceived of them as symbolic of the simultaneity and identity of life and death and to have manipulated them in this fashion in their poetry and art. Thus, from the same imagery we derive a paradoxical content that refers simultaneously to both life and death. Coatlicue appears in her two manifestations, as befits the great mother and murderess. These are awesome poems, and the perception they offer, alluding once more to the tradition of Mexican poetry from Gorostiza through Sor Juana Inés de la Cruz back to the Aztecs, is penetrating: "Y clavado a mi pared, me quedo:/soy el ojo que mira; el ojo/mirado soy, y lo que él mira" (64). What the poet sees and describes, that is what the poet is—and so are we.

The latest collection included in the collected work is *La flama en el espejo,* originally published in 1971. Like all Bonifaz Nuño's mature poetry, it is carefully structured: ten poems numbered 1 through 10, interspersed with a series of others lettered *a* through *z*. Each of these internal divisions has three poems except number 5, which is accompanied by four poems lettered *l* through *n*, which are the book's formal structural center. The volume's epigraph is from the *Purgatorio,* "Gli occhi suoi già veder parmi," "Already I seem to behold her eyes," Virgil's words of Beatrice. (It is tempting to see in the tripartite organization of the lettered sections an homage to Dante's *terza rima*.) Despite this continued severe formal structure and the persistence of the pre-Hispanic symbolism to which we have become accustomed, *La flama en el espejo* constitutes a radical change from the several preceding collections. The orientation is much more Christian and much more preoccupied with salvation through love. Its tutelary deities are no longer Coatlicue and Xipe Totec but the pantheon of Christian poets who strove, as does the Mexican, to encounter meaning and salvation in a chaotic and dangerous world: Eliot, Dante, St. John of the Cross. This does not suppose that the poet has undergone some sort of late conversion, but the lady who presides over this anguished search is far from the devouring goddess who struck fear into the other books. In her place we find a poetized beloved who "encarna el anhelo del hombre y del poeta de elevarse a una visión trascendente."[27] She is hardly a traditional religious figure; however, the poems are much too erotic for that. She may well be the lady/goddess whose presence has been the controlling factor in so much of Bonifaz Nuño's poetry, but transformed here into a symbol, or perhaps the cause, of salvation and love.

> Verdadera, desnuda, erguida,
> nada teme ni oculta nada.
> Sin pesar ni miedo ni desdicha,
> vencedora sin tregua, ejerce
> alta y humilde los secretos
> de la resurrección; la clave
> de la vida inmortal preserva.

> Y es vano, mi alma, tu deseo
> de gracia, si la gracia en ella
> no quieres hallar, si no la encuentras
> en su regazo donde alberga
> la luz y el amor que la limitan.   [y]

All this mention of resurrection, the life immortal, the soul, and grace is startling for the reader accustomed to the poetic language of the earlier books, coming as it does directly from orthodox Christianity, but the luminous figure of the woman/goddess is too reminiscent of the bronze divinity of Othón, honored at length some ten years earlier in "Idilio," to fit comfortably into accepted theology. In some of the poems, notably b, there is again a synthesis of Aztec and Christian symbolism in the treatment of redemption through sacrifice.

The center and source of this entire volume is the woman, who seems to incarnate both Christian and non-Christian characteristics as the guide to salvation of some kind. Christian allusions abound; lines like "Y con la humildad, a cuanto mira/—glorioso el que la vio primero—/en el agua del fuego alumbra/y por el bautismo resucita" (e) are much closer to Christian orthodoxy than the poet's earlier work, and one is reminded of St. John of the Cross in "De noche la busco; se levanta/mi corazón de noche; exalta/flores de aromas entre brasas" (f) or of Eliot in "Eje inamovible de la rosa/giratoria" (t). Certainly, Christian conceptions of salvation appear to be the source of the first lines of poem 9, with their annunciation and the allusions to the resuscitation of Christ.

> El que estuvo muerto, vive. Lumbre
> de la anunciación requema el vientre
> pleno del sepulcro; entra en las órbitas
> recorridas de ojos planetarios.

But there are other poems as non-Christian as these appear to be Christian. All of poem 5, for example, reverts to the systematic use of demoniac imagery—there is again a strong suggestion of the zodiacal system which the poet has used earlier—and there are basic contrasts. Almost at the formal center of the book we

find a poem like *n*, which is a traditional Marian presentation of
the Virgin as giver of life and salvation. Immediately following
it, poem 6 portrays what appears to be the same figure in serpent
imagery, and indeed imagery of particular power.

> De tersa potestad enrosca,
> bella de escamas como plumas,
> la espalda; los pechos claros alza
> a la luz; los fríos cascabeles
> agitados resuena; abierta
> contra el cielo, la solemne boca
> vibra al aire la trisulca lengua.

It is extraordinary to see this juxtaposition of seemingly
contradictory visions of the great goddess. *La flama en el espejo*
is, once again, a difficult book, but it seems to incorporate
several of Bonifaz Nuño's favorite themes: the stubborn search
for salvation and the perception of the role of the great goddess/
woman through whom alone such salvation can be achieved.
The book is so organized that the numbered poems almost
appear to be the record of a process or perhaps an experience of
illumination of a kind that the mystics would understand, al-
though of a nature somewhat different from what they would
experience. The lettered sections appear to be a kind of com-
mentary on the principal process, although this is only a hypo-
thetical interpretation. But there is nothing hypothetical about
our belief that *La flama en el espejo* is a decisive stage in the
process that characterizes Rubén Bonifaz Nuño's poetry, and
that it offers an integration of Christian and Aztec elements
such as no other Mexican writer has proposed. At the con-
clusion of this passionate pilgrimage, the speaker comes to this
perception of the meaning of the search: "Y eras parte del orden
suyo,/de la majestad benigna donde,/mi alma, por fin te reconoces"
(z). With this perception comes also self-recognition because this
drama of the mind is of the same nature as the *Divine Comedy* or
the tragedies of Sophocles: our voyage toward the understanding
which must inevitably also be the acceptance of our mortality.

> Se vuelve aérea, vibra diáfana
> la losa del sepulcro; leve,

despega con las alas mansas
de la respiración; los párpados,
incendiados por alegres lumbres,
la ceguera aprietan, sepultada;
la rompen. El resucitado
remonta la memoria; mira
en la tercera luz del alba.   [10]

This specifically Christian formulation applies, on dramat-
ically different levels, to both Christ and Lazarus, but also to the
speaker, the poet/persona, who, after his prodigious voyage
through memory, appears to have found the understanding he
sought.

In 1978, one year before the publication of *De otro modo, lo
mismo*, a collection of the author's complete poems, including a
good deal of unpublished material, there appeared a slender
volume titled *Tres poemas de antes*.[28] It is impossible to deter-
mine exactly what significance to attribute to the name,
whether they are three unpublished poems written somewhat
earlier or three new poems that refer to an earlier period or
episode, and there is no indication why they do not appear in the
collected work. The book contains some allusions and meta-
phors that lead us to suspect that the poems were written
relatively shortly before publication: "has crecido/como una
flor en llamas" ("Cuando caigan los años,2"). The three poems
or sections into which the book is divided are "Acaso una
palabra," "Llagas, flores caducas", and "Cuando caigan los
años," and they consist of seven, seven, and eight subsections,
respectively. The first and last present love failed, of a par-
ticularly striking bitterness if we recall the process we have seen
in the prior work. "Llagas, flores caducas: 1" contains some-
thing that is very close to a confession of what poetry is for its
author: "Llagas, flores caducas, poesía,/lámpara de terror con
que me alumbro." "Llagas . . . , 2" is more in line with what we
might anticipate in this description of the beloved:

Nadie llamó. Silencio. Abrí la puerta
y estabas tú. Recuerdo: te cercaba,
ya desde entonces, una luz que daba
al alma el centro de una dicha incierta.

When this love too ends and she leaves, she also leaves a curious and familiar memory.

> Estás lejos, relumbras en tu risa
> pensando en no sé qué; lejos, ausente,
> y gozo y paz y voz y luz repartes.
>
> Pero tu imagen brilla en la sumisa
> sombra de la memoria; está presente
> conmigo, sola y siempre. En todas partes.

This is a love once again desolate, a "doliente pozo/del sueño angosto." ("Llagas . . . , 3"), but it also leaves in the reader an impression of the splendor that recalls to us exactly who is hidden behind each of these evanescent beloveds.

Ten years passed after the publication of *La flama en el espejo* before another major new work appeared: *As de oros*.[29] Once again it is a book with an almost mathematical structural principle: it opens with five poems, after which there is a series of eleven bearing the names of classical or biblical figures, separated each from another by two poems. The volume ends with four poems bearing no titles. The obvious and immediate temptation is to seek the organizing theme in the named poems, and in fact they have in common that they are all memoirs dealing with a consuming love, a love that is in the majority of cases adulterous, incestuous, or associated with some sort of treachery. The myths of Hippolytus and Oedipus are universally known, with their wake of incestuous adulteries; of the others, Judah had two children with his daughter-in-law Tamar, Ciniras was the father of Adonis by his own daughter, and Ammon raped his half-sister Tamar (not the same Tamar of Judah). Thyestes is at the center of a whole network of incestuous intrigues, father of Aegisthus by his daughter Pelopia, and seducer of Aeropé, wife of his brother Atreus. Somewhat less drastic is the case of Theseus, who kidnapped the queen of the Amazons and on her fathered Hippolytus, in addition to betraying her with her sister. Ulysses is best known as the usually faithful husband of Penelope, but he appears here as a man who desperately wishes that he had not closed his sailors' ears to the sirens' song. Isaac seems to represent an extraordinarily durable love; at age forty he married Rebecca, who presented him with twins twenty years later—unless we are to suspect a somewhat more cynical intention on the part of the poet. Capaneo was one of the seven againt Thebes; when he was killed by Zeus for the blasphemy to which his pride led him, his wife Evadné committed suicide. The last is Aeneas, mythical prince of Troy who betrayed Dido, queen of Carthage. All these figures have in common a capacity for passion and perhaps even for great love, in addition to their clearly mythical or legendary character. Although by no means entirely certain, the whole volume appears to share the recollection of love that in the named poems led to terrible and portentous events. And present always is the consciousness of time; the past appears, with its painful memories understood and distilled, as a renewing element that purifies the poet and grants him the strength and courage to continue forward.

The women of *As de oros* are all quite mysterious, as we might expect, rather memories of love than present and passionate mistresses. There is no real objective reality to them, even if we include the widely-known settings they are given in the named poems. It seems likely that love here, and the presence of the goddess who is forever quietly behind this poetry, have been given an altered situation, perhaps even a new identity. "Escalas sin término la música," for example, seems a deliberate allusion to Fray Luis de León's "Oda a Salinas" and the Neoplatonic concept of the music of the spheres, through which one might contemplate perfection. But in the work of the Mexican, the music and its perfection bring, rather than a mystical experience, the recollection of a woman.

> Y en este momento vuelve todo:
> aquel vestido suyo, aquella
> sortija abierta oscuramente;
> la sal de aquel júbilo obstinado
> transparentándose en sus párpados.

But it would be an error to draw a rigid line between the mystical and the nonmystical. Mystics like St. John of the Cross, among others, systematically used erotic imagery in their effort to express the ineffable union with the divine. It would appear that

for Bonifaz Nuño, at least in this context, the erotic and the
ineffable are one.

> Y ella en los vértices de todo,
> y en medio y en torno, es y refleja
> y junta la cima y las escalas,
> la alianza y el astro de la alianza.
> Y el alma preñada para siempre.
>
> ["Escalas sin término"]

We can perceive here a kind of plentitude which we all too often
simplistically assign to divine love exclusively, but which can
also be found in love of a more profane kind. *As de oros* follows
the same line which has become increasingly important in this
poetry, of salvation and illumination through the mysterious
woman/goddess. Here, it seems to be illumination through
memory of a great love, rather than through her actual presence.
The flame that is a constant motif looks ever more like the
mystic rose of Christian symbolism. Thus, if the despair of the
city is "la polvorienta rosa amarga" ("Abren sin cesar"), the
soul's wakening—to love? to danger?—is the "mar aéreo de una
rosa/de fuegos girantes," and the rivers of memory, "olas de
piedra" ("Ambiciosa túnica de alas"), are "fijos como el re-
molino/incesante de la rosa oscura,/cansada de ser tan sólo
rosa." "En los umbrales de la piedra," which possesses fascinat-
ing resonances of initiation, ritual, and sacrifice, shows how
"fija sus duros pétalos el alma." In the same poem, this rose is
clearly identical with the flame; in addition to the obvious
Christian references, the whole poem bears remarkable echoes
of the Aztec rite of human sacrifice, in which the heart torn
from the body of the ritual victim was known as the "flor
amarilla." Illumination, or whatever it may be that is transpir-
ing here, is closely related to the purifying flame.

In another and significantly titled poem, "¿De dónde este
terror?", the nightmare vision of the city is soothed at the end.

> La oscuridad pone al desnudo
> el manar sonoro de la fuente,
> y en la noche recién poblada
> su flor levanta el invisible

> surtidor, el ramo redivivo;
> la flama azul, sobreviviente
> última de alguna especie extinta.

This rose may be many things, but whatever it signifies to the poet, it is somehow related to a more transcendental significance for the world about us. At the same time, it is connected to the unnamed woman.

> . . . escucho el nombre
> pleno con la gracia del silencio
> de la flama azul con que me exploran:
> el ardiente nombre que la llama.
> ["Con la oreja en las cintilaciones"]

Whoever she may be, she possesses a supernatural or semidivine quality that connects her with the road to understanding.

All this does not imply that *As de oros* presents a vision of a rose-colored reality. On the contrary, in the envenomed city, the apocalyptic vision still menaces. We are a good deal less than we might wish to have been; our lives are assemblages of the disappeared who wander through the mirrors' "galerías/ciegas del azogue carcomido" ("Año por año, cada día"). Our efforts at communication are foiled: "Y sólo son claras las palabras/que nada designan; que no dicen/nada" ("Otro día ha sido sepultado"). Perhaps the most appalling aspect of all this is its lack of even redemptive pain; the speaker sees the changes wrought in him.

> Y he cambiado. Sordo, encanecido,
> una oficina soy, un sueldo;
> veinte mil pesos en escombros
> y un volkswagen, y la nostalgia
> de lo que no tuve, y el insomnio,
> y cáscaras de años devaluados.
> ["Yo amé"]

Time plays a double role here; if our mirrors recall all those we have known and loved, they also tell us what we have become: hair that has lost even its artificial tint, wrinkles which imprison us, "alguien que no soy yo" ("Del azogue ansioso"). We are trapped between the necessity to continue the struggle and the danger of the struggle itself, between time the assassin and time that may just possibly bear us to the plenitude which is the object of the struggle. And, so that we may remember that this goddess of such complex origins exists not only on a metaphysical plane, at times it is her body that brings "la gracia inalterable" ("En pie, la ley de la miseria").

At the core of *As de oros* is this experience, expressed sometimes as plenitude, sometimes as grace, sometimes as self-recognition and perception. Whatever we may call it, it is the experience that confers a meaning beyond all meaning, that makes the experience of daily living both bearable and worthwhile, because it is an experience that ennobles us and makes us better than we were. Although this experience is sometimes expressed in terms that openly recall Christian symbolism and the whole mystical tradition, it would be a mistake to attempt to relate it too closely to these sources. It is far closer to the recognition that lies at the root of the tragic experience.

> Y aquí, entre el aire inseminado
> de flamas, entre inmensas urnas
> de blandos labios, se levantan
> mis párpados, los ojos miran,
> y tras ellos voy, y ocupo un rostro
> herrado de lumbres; y es el mío.
> ["¿Qué vino de alas, qué semilla"]

As "Jocasta" makes clear, she, rose, and flame are one, a single element that absorbs and confers meaning, even at the cost of suffering.

"Hacia el placer las noches giran," one of the last poems of the volume, is almost a recapitulation of all the above. Before the goddess, the poet offers himself to her as the milenary sacrifice, delivering himself and at the same time receiving from her hands his true face. The similarities with the pre-Hispanic ritual could not be clearer, but instead of a sacrifice with the ultimate purpose of giving sustenance to the gods, this sacrifice sustains and revives the poet. Thanks to the mistress/ woman / goddess, he recovers from the poisoned city, from the mirrors that betray us by showing us what we have become.

From everything evil that life may possess, he is rescued. Rubén Bonifaz Nuño has created an extraordinary poetic symbiosis between elements of the Christian and the Nahua mythopoeses, to express the torment and the glory of modern humankind, just as he communicates the worry, the terror, the internal dissension, through the battle and the voyage and the conflict. This is the poet's extraordinary achievement: the creation of an idiom and a poetics of a dazzling and unique originality.

6 ROSARIO CASTELLANOS
The Search for a Voice

The single most important choice for any writer, more important even than questions of content or ideology, is the selection of a voice, that peculiar personal and idiosyncratic expression of the author's individuality in the face of the leveling effect of the mass *langue*. This option, which is hardly an entirely conscious one, conditioned as we all are by the complex social and personal factors that go into our makeup, is complicated further by the need to adopt an authorial stance, that is, a relationship *toward* the created work. The possibilities for such stances are considerable, if not unlimited, but the ultimate selection is not usually stumbled upon by chance. In the case of Rosario Castellanos, the history of her poetry is in many ways the history of her search for such a stance and the changes effected in it by circumstances foreign to the poetry itself. Her solitariness, her breakthrough into awareness of her role as woman in an oppressively male-dominated society, and her championing of the oppressed and deprived Indians of her native state of Chiapas are all well-known.[1] Such was her commitment that she gave her inherited lands to the Indians who worked them, and she spent some years living in Chiapas writing didactic puppet plays and, among other things, "un resumen de la Constitución para que los indios conocieran sus derechos y un libro de lectura para los niños recién alfabetizados."[2] Her master's thesis in philosophy at the University of Mexico, examining the question of whether a female culture exists apart from the dominant traditional male-oriented culture, has been called "uno de los primeros—si no el primer—intento en lengua castellana de enfocar un problema feminista bajo una perspectiva filosófica."[3]

All this is widely known, but not all readers are aware of the extent to which her poetry was influenced throughout her life by autobiographical factors, even though Castellanos denied it, alleging that "el pudor me impide referirme a esos temas."[4] As we shall see, despite her statement, quite the reverse seems to be true, and this "pudor" lies at the heart of her search for her own voice. Curiously, in view of the statement just quoted, she was not inhibited from discussing details of her private life quite openly in interviews. An acquaintance with these details helps us to comprehend the process of her search, as in this revealing quotation from *El uso de la palabra:*

Abandonada durante mi adolescencia a los recursos de mi imaginación, la orfandad repentina y total me pareció lógica. Permanecí soltera hasta los treinta y tres años durante los cuales alcancé grados de extremo aislamiento, confinada en un hospital para tuberculosos, sirviendo en un instituto para indios.

Luego contraje un matrimonio que era estrictamente monoándrico por mi parte y totalmente poligámico por la parte contraria. Tuve tres hijos, de los cuales murieron los dos primeros. Recibí el acta de mi divorcio (cuyos trámites se habían iniciado ya con la debida anticipación) ya en mi casa de Tel Aviv.[5]

These autobiographical facts are also recurrent elements in her poetry. Indeed, Castellanos was a remarkably self-conscious artist, and aware both of exactly who she was and of the implications of the process of searching for her own voice. This process was complicated by these factors of her personal life and by the verbal facility with which she struggled and which she felt was an obstacle to her writing. ". . . descubrí a muy temprana edad que corazón y pasión, amor y dolor eran terminos inseparables, puesto que rimaban bien, y esto me condujo no sólo a una temática y a un estilo infectos, sino también a una concepción de la vida y del mundo de la cual aún padezco las consecuencias . . .[6]" Much of Rosario Castellanos's work as a poet—she was also an important novelist and an acute critic and essayist—lies in the effort to create a poetic persona, a mask that would serve a double purpose. First, it would give some degree of objectivity or distance to her work, because of the wish to hide or at least disguise the extent to which the work reflected autobiographi-

cal features. At the same time, through this distancing it would
help her to control her language. Nothing could be further from
the confessional poet than this earlier period of her work. As
Jaime Labastida has said, "En múltiples ocasiones su voz ad-
quiere el rasgo del oráculo; como para volver más distante lo que
está demasiado cerca de su carne."[7] That she later almost aban-
doned this kind of poetic disguise and adopted another voice is,
at least in part, a recognition that she had created so well that
unless she developed another kind of persona, she would be-
come frozen behind a mask that had served its purpose. Mean-
while, she achieved, in the words of José Emilio Pacheco,

su verdadera voz, esa característica no formal sino esencial e intrínseca
que permite a un poema ser lo que es y hace a todas las cosas poética-
mente reconciliables al dar a la experiencia un significado que sin el
poema pasaría inadvertido. Con ella se afianzó en la poesía mexicana
una corriente que podríamos llamar 'realista,' directa, coloquial (pero no
prosaica), en cierto sentido antimetafórica, y se cumplió la gran ruptura
de la generación de 1950 con el simbolismo.
    Apareció también el recurso de la distancia: el afán de objetivar
confesiones y observaciones en un monólogo que se atribuye a un
personaje reconocible o inventado. Y todo lo hizo con tal inteligencia
que nunca incurrió en el despeñadero que acecha a este género: parecer
traducción de un idioma que se desconoce a otro que tampoco se
domina.[8]

This is not a process that appears as though by magic or
proceeds out of sheer inspiration; the sources from which
Rosario Castellanos learned are many and often unexpected. In
a text dated 1965, she spoke of her debt to several of Latin
America's most renowned women poets, several of whom are
quite remote from her stylistically. In some cases, it would
appear that the influence consisted of learning what *not* to do.
"Pero debo a Juana de Ibarbourou mi incurable desconfianza
hacia los temas sensuales; a Delmira Agustini mis precauciones
contra la grandilocuencia, y a Alfonsina Storni el hallazgo de la
ironía como perspective interesante y el afán de experimenta-
ción, de ruptura de los moldes establecidos y de aceptación de lo
desagradable como posibilidades válidas.[9]" Of Gabriela Mistral,
Castellanos said that she admired "el patetismo, la humildad de

los objetos elegidos para expresar sus estados de ánimo."[10]
Many other sources have been cited by critics; Sor Juana lnés de
la Cruz is a favorite, based on certain coincidences of attitude
and some verbal echoes, although they are in truth hardly sim-
ilar. Labastida has summed it up very well. "Su poesía, recon-
centrada y grave, se ha nutrido en el cultivo de los versos
dilatados que evidencia, de inmediato, la identidad con formas
todavía anteriores a la poesía castellana: los clásicos griegos y
latinos, la Biblia, el libro del Consejo (Popol-Vuh)."[11]

Castellanos's poetry does not divide easily into periods, al-
though she said that she passed from closed subjectivity to the
discovery of the other and from that to social reality.[12] Nor does
her work usually reflect drastic long-lasting shifts from one
book to the next. Although there are frequently rather consid-
erable changes, she tends to return to earlier modes, at least
partially, in succeeding volumes. What is clear is that over the
total course of her production there is a visible evolution, al-
though not quite the one pointed out by the author herself. Her
first published works, *Apuntes para una declaración de fe* and
Trayectoria del polvo both appeared in 1948. There is little in
them to distinguish one from the other, as Castellanos herself
recognized when she commented that although they appear in
this order in the collected poetry, *Poesía no eres tú, Trayectoria* is
the earlier and that no one had noticed the error because of their
similarity.[13] *Apuntes* is a relatively long attempt at a syncretic
poetic vision of the history of humanity and of the world, a
vision of the possibility of hope for the hemisphere in spite of
apparent present decadence. Later, the author spoke mockingly
of the poem's presumptuous conception and pretentious word-
iness,[14] but even so there is a tone that would characterize the
very last poems, as María del Carmen Millán noted: "Desde
Apuntes para una declaración de fe, se anuncia el tono que le será
más grato. El color gris, en sus matices metálicos, presidirá el
'paisaje de escombros' que trazó la soledad original del mun-
do."[15]

One of the most surprising notes of this early volume is the
importance of ironic humor, which would then nearly disappear
and not again play an important role until almost the very last
poems. There is much in *Apuntes* that recalls the Salvador Novo

of "Elegía," a poet for whom Castellanos repeatedly expressed her admiration; images like the biblical serpent who "debía tener manos/para frotarlas, una contra otra,/como un burgués rechoncho y satisfecho" could be typically Novo. *Trayectoria del polvo* lacks the irony that is the principal poetic virtue of *Apuntes*, and often the author resorts to an incantatory, almost biblical, tone of limited success. This may represent the influence of *Muerte sin fin* of José Gorostiza, of which she said, "Bajo su estímulo inmediato, aunque como influencia no se note, escribí en una semana *Trayectoria del polvo*."[16] Yet the poem achieves far greater success than *Apuntes*, particularly in the earlier sections, because the focus is more personal and the expression denser. There is nothing in *Apuntes* to match verses like "Nací en la hora misma en que nació el pecado/y como él, fui llamado soledad." The expression is more concentrated, less diffused by the conscious effort to write philosophically or grandly, and in a brilliant image the author fuses humanity's search for self with the personal voyage in search of definition that would be the theme of so much of her own work: "Yo, sedienta de mí, me detenía en estatuas duplicando el instante fugitivo en cristales y luego reiniciaba mi marcha de Narciso."[17] The ironic vision of humanity facing life and its inevitable corollary recalls key sections of *Muerte sin fin* and the tone of Novo, but it also indicates a vision that would surface again years later, and seems to hint at Castellanos's own ambivalence toward the experience of life.

> La fiesta cosquillea en los talones.
> Vamos todos a ella cantando y sonriendo.
> Vamos todos a ella cogidos de la mano
> como quien sale al campo a cosechar claveles.

De la vigilia estéril (1950) represents a considerable step forward, avoiding in large measure the youthful rhetoric of the two books published only two years before. It establishes the themes for the more mature work: solitude, sadness, death. There is also a marked religious tone that soon disappears, as well as a significant love element and a few poems in which motherhood, actual or anticipated, plays an important role. This last is from

sources recognized by Castellanos, who had deliberately read
Mistral and the Bible in order to overcome the abstractness of
her earlier books. Unfortunately, these influences also became
stylized to the point of becoming another rhetoric. The best
poems are those that deal with immediate matters in concrete
specific imagery: "La casa vacía" or "Destino." Castellanos said
that she had wanted to create poems whose images referred to
concrete objects, but she was less than pleased with the result,
as she expressed with her characteristic sense of humor: "*De la
vigilia* exuda retórica, según se llegó a decir. Y es que, por esos
años, poseía una facilidad siniestra para alargar los poemas, y me
dejaba llevar por ella."[18] That she was at least partially suc-
cessful is evidenced by poems such as "Distancia del amigo" in
which she abandons the mannerisms of much of the book in
favor of a rhythmic colloquial tone that presents a religious
content in deceptively simple terms.

Much of *De la vigilia estéril* seems to bear an autobiographi-
cal stamp. Despite Castellanos's remarks about "pudor," her
attempt to create a mask that would let her express her inner
vision without revealing it to the reader had not yet been fully
developed. For example, in "Tinieblas y consolación," although
the situation is referred directly to God, it recalls what we know
of Castellanos's childhood, when she was relatively forgotten in
her parents' absorption with her younger brother. There is some-
thing abruptly pathetic in lines like "¿Olvidaría el padre/a su
hija más pequeña?" or "Adolescencia gris con vocación de
sombra,/ con destino de muerte:/las escaleras duermen, se der-
rumba/la casa que no supo detenerte" ("La casa vacía"). There
are a few moments when this hinted identification of the poem
with the poet and her sad childhood become overt, as when she
speaks of "esta celda hermética que se llama Rosario" ("Dos
poemas"). Not surprisingly, there are anticipations of such ma-
jor poems as "Lamentación de Dido," especially in the three
"Elegías del amado fantasma," but in the "Dos poemas" there is
an important new note: the poet's realization that there exists a
world outside her, composed of other suffering human beings:
"Vine a saberlo aquí: el amor no es la hoguera/ para arrojar en
ella nuestros días/a que ardan como leños resecos u hojarasca."
And even the reference to herself as a "celda hermética" in the

second of the two poems bespeaks a new attitude; the cell must open, since "Yo no tendré vergüenza de estas manos vacías/ni de esta celda hermética que se llama Rosario." She has become aware of the existence of her fellows, a fact that was to be of crucial importance in her novels, but that would also impact in a major fashion on the poetry.

This discovery led to *El rescate del mundo,* a short volume of fourteen poems published in 1952. They are concerned exclusively with indigenous and popular themes: people and occupations—"A la mujer que vende frutas en la plaza," "Lavanderas del Grijalva," "Escogedoras del café en el Soconusco," "Tejedoras de Zinacanta," "La oración del indio"—or with the simple things that are a fundamental part of rural life—"El árbol que hay en medio de dos pueblos," "A fiesta," "Cofre de cedro," "El río." The rhythms are simpler and are popular in origin: "Ay, del que junto al río/no quiere llamarse sed" ("Estrofas en la playa"). Or this evocation of "El tejoncito maya," which recalls some of Carlos Pellicer's most famous lines:

> Cubriéndote la risa
> con la mano pequeña,
> saltando entre los siglos
> vienes, en gracia y piedra.

Or the brilliance of "Silencio acerca de una piedra antigua," with its sudden realization of the millenary heritage.

> Y los signos se cierran bajo mis ojos como
> la flor bajo los dedos torpísimos de un ciego.
> Pero yo sé: detrás
> de mi cuerpo otro cuerpo se agazapa,
> y alrededor de mí muchas respiraciones
> cruzan furtivamente
> como los animales nocturnos en la selva.

El rescate del mundo is a slender volume, but it indicates the course of a drastic change that would take place in Rosario Castellanos's development as poet. This change was not yet complete; *Poemas* (1957) is one of her most important collections and represents in some ways the culmination of earlier tendencies. There are several poems written in short meters and with a vaguely popular tone, especially several of the sections of the "Misterios gozosos," which are composed primarily of poems with no fixed referent in the objective world, but the most important characteristic of the volume is the shattering sense of nostalgia that imposes itself on the reader. In addition to the emotion of loss, the poems of the collection reflect a movement that takes on mythic migratory dimensions, as in "Exodo," "Destierro," or "Relación del peregrino." Common to virtually all is the sense of timelessness, of being unrelated to daily reality. Frequently they may be read from a Christian point of view ("El ungido," "El hermano mayor") but this is not true of all. They seem rather the expression of the vision of all of humanity as temporal voyager, alone with the purified emotionalism of the voyage and a few others who share the need to pursue the journey. More than anything else, these poems are reminiscent of St. John Perse for the sense of timelessness of these mythic migrations, and of Jaime Torres Bodet for the direct presentation of the emotional implications of such a situation. One of the most interesting of the poems here is a lovely "Elegía" that recalls the opening of *Rescate*.

> La cordillera, el aire de la altura
> que bate poderoso como el ala de un águila,
> la atmósfera difícil de una estrella caída,
> de una piedra celeste ya enfriada.
>
> Esta, ésta es mi patria.
>
> Rota, yace a mis pies la estera que tejieron
> entrelazando hilos de paciencia y de magia.
> O voy pisando templos destruidos
> o estelas en el polvo sepultadas.
>
> He aquí el terraplén para la danza.
>
> ¿Quién dirá los silencios de mis muertos?
> ¿Quién llorará la ruina de mi casa?
> Entre la soledad una flauta de hueso
> derramando una música triste y aguda y áspera.
>
> No hay otra palabra.

Unlike the poems of *Rescate,* this is not an affirmation of the consciousness of a living way of life, but a lament for something gone; it is the silence of her dead, broken only by the desolate music of the bone flute. The poem is anchored in the broken remnants of the small concrete details of life of nontechnological civilizations: sleeping mats, bone flutes. . . . It begins at the cosmological level: a fallen star, cold now. Firmly rooted in the immediate level, the poem can contrast it with the larger cultural manifestations: temples, now destroyed; trodden earth for the communal dance, abandoned now; paths, buried beneath the dust. "Elegía" is saved from archeologism or abstraction by its base in the homely detail that gives it immediacy. This specific subject matter does not again appear in *Poemas,* but the nostalgic tone pervades the volume. More to the point, unlike the remainder of the volume, "Elegía" gives the situation a specific Mexican referent. The sadness is no longer a remote and placeless generalized sense of longing, but rooted in the Mexican *meseta.* Anyone who has traveled the central highlands of Mexico will recognize the description. As we have seen, Castellanos was preoccupied with the need to deal with concrete images and specific objects. Here she applies this technique to a poetic theme that normally uses such techniques to prevent the sense of timelessness from deteriorating into sheer vagueness, but in "Elegía" rather than simply use objective correlations more or less at random, she has anchored them in a specific contextual reality. She has said of these poems that they represent a return to religiosity, but not to an orthodox Catholicism. "Volví a una especie de religiosidad ya no católica, a una vivencia religiosa del mundo, a sentirme ligada a las cosas desde un punto de vista emotivo y a considerarlas como objetos de contemplación estética. Me producía raptos de verdadero júbilo transformar en poemas lo que estaba junto a mi . . . . Los objetos, sumamente puros, pugnaban por revelar sus secretos. Es algo que no se puede concretar en ideas sino en imágenes. Imágenes traspasadas por una emoción gozosa y que los críticos juzgaron como dolorosa."[19]

The high point of the volume is two of her best poems, and quite possibly two of the best produced by her entire generation in Mexico: "Resplandor del ser" and the splendid "Lamentación de Dido." They present a remarkable contrast; "Resplandor del ser" is as close as Castellanos ever comes to achieving the moment of total immersion in the felicity of the universe. The motive, if there is a specific one, is not made clear. It appears to be the sheer joy of the word and of the creative act, but this creativity is also hinted at in more personal or physiological terms, and it may very well be the double fecundity of the word and of biological birth about which she speaks. In any event, the poem captures a moment that is rare in Castellanos's poetry. It avoids the abstraction that is a major peril for this kind of statement by beginning with very concrete images of the natural world that reflect the emotional state of the speaker: " . . . estoy labrando, como con cien abejas,/un pequeño panal con mis palabras." The joy opens out from this initial image, but the poem returns periodically to such natural imagery as a sort of underpinning to its more metaphysical developments. At the poem's end, we have come full circle and are once again before the renewed joy, expressed here in the image of the returning life of the cyclical natural world.

> La hoja que el otoño desprende de la rama
> conoce los caminos del regreso.
>
> La juventud recuerda su querencia.
> La golondrina vuelve del destierro.
>
> No te despidas nunca, porque el mundo
> es redondo y perfecto.

"Lamentación de Dido" is another matter entirely, a poem all fire and passion. It presents Castellanos's view of the failed love of Dido and Aeneas as presented by Vergil in Book IV of the *Aeneid*. The "Lamentación" is much briefer than its Latin model, only slightly more than five pages, and highly condensed, which is one of the principal reasons for its power. It was written about 1955, at a time when the author spent a year ill with tuberculosis; it may be that this enforced free time gave her sufficient opportunity to work this complicated poem out in detail. The theme is an obsessive one in her work: the betrayal by an absent lover, for whatever reasons, seems to have haunted her. As she herself said, "He escrito mis poemas de amor con cenizas. El concepto del amor tal como se expresa en algunos de mis poemas . . . es un concepto trágico: algo que pone en crisis lo que nos parece seguro, lo que rompe el egoísmo que nos proteje de las heridas. De esas heridas es de lo que hablo. La única misión del amor es precisamente esa: exponernos a la herida y luego desaparecer."[20] It is obvious that this is no theoretical account; in the same interview Castellanos openly admitted that the poem reflected an autobiographical episode, another example of her willingness to discuss openly what she seemingly made every effort to veil in her poetry. It seems quite clear that this discretion in her poetry is really more an effort to avoid the excesses of emotionalism, especially if we recall what she had earlier called her "sinister facility." "En este poema quise rescatar una experiencia, pero no me atreví a a hacerlo sino al través de una imagen dada en lo eterno, en la tradición: la imagen de Dido. La desgracia amorosa, el abandono, la soledad después del amor, me parecieron tan válidos y absolutos en Dido que los aproveché para expresar, referidos a mí, esos mismos sentimientos. Al través de ellos pude contar mi propia historia, que era, desde luego, bastante más pobre."[21] The myth of Dido, as Vergil had presented it, provided Castellanos with the kind of objective correlative to her own feelings that would allow her to control them, to objectify them in a poetic mask. Jaime Labastida has pointed out how Castellanos changes the focus of the poem so that Dido is the center, not Aeneas.[22] It is, in the best of senses, a poem distilled from autobiographical experience and controlled by the use of poetic tradition.

"Lamentación de Dido" also uses a distinctive verse form, an irregular line that looks more like rhythmic prose than verse. It consists of an irregular series of units predominantly of seven and eleven syllables, organized in long lines, at times as though a whole verse had been run on in prose fashion. María del Carmen Millán emphasizes the effectiveness of this line to express "la vida fatigosa de una mujer que debe ganar su sitio paso a paso, atenta a los problemas domésticos, a las celebraciones rituales y a las responsabilidades civiles."[23] Manuel Durán has come to the same conclusion, when he speaks of her "Poesía grave y seria, que sin embargo nos reserva a veces sorpresas verbales, cambios de dirección, remolinos del pensa-

miento y de la emoción."[24] Castellanos was consciously at-
tempting to achieve what these two critics have cited, a solemn
but musical line she called a "versículo" that would serve to
hide her personal and emotional investment behind the mask of
a traditional theme and a classical-seeming meter, and would
permit her to avoid the excesses of confessional poetry. "El tema
es el que condiciona la forma. El empleo del versículo permite
una respiración más ancha que en el verso tradicional, posibilita
un mayor número de imágenes y, también, una libertad más
amplia para colocarlas—casi como en la prosa. Por los acentos y
el número total de sílabas conserva una musicalidad que tiene
mucho de solemne."[25]

Castellanos seems to have been looking for an equivalent to
the line used by two of her favorite poets, Claudel and Perse, a
line that would express her belief, stated three years after the
writing of "Lamentación de Dido," that "hace tiempo que el
universo ha dejado de ser un todo ordenado susceptible de caber
en una forma estricta. Al través de la variedad infinita de los
fenómenos hay una armonía, más vasta, más poderosa, más
difícil de captar. Exige la respiración ancha del versículo, las
combinaciones métricas yuxtapuestas, el contrapunto."[26]

This consciousness of the formal aspect of poetic creativity
is the other side of her own vision of her mission as a writer.
Rosario Castellanos quite clearly wished to be a "major" poet,
as is visible in the overreaching of *Apuntes* and *Trayectoria*, both
works conceived as encompassing visions of life and human
existence, far too great a task for such a young poet. Even so
early she had been reaching for a kind of stately but flexible
language, something like a combination of Perse and the Bible.
When she achieved it, she was so fearful that it might become a
recipe for concocting poems that she reacted against it strongly
in later books, although echoes remain until the end. But her
work through the best-known poems reveals this search, and it
is illuminating to examine her translations of three of her favor-
ite poets, Claudel, Perse, and Emily Dickinson. The two French
authors often used a long, stately line which Castellanos re-
produced rather closely, but her translations of Dickinson are
quite another matter. She has a problem with the short, sharply
rhythmic character of Dickinson's verse, and the Spanish ver-

sions use a more measured, less staccato line. Where the orig-
inals are frequently made up of four iambs, the translations tend
toward a steady seven-syllable line, but she alters and expands
Dickinson's crabbed and intricate syntax, with the result that
the translations lose a good deal of movement and agility. Where
Castellanos is closest to Dickinson is in those of her own later
poems where she abandoned the search for stateliness and re-
turned to a more popular traditional verse.

Obviously, the success of "Lamentación de Dido" has little
to do with these specifics of the possible sources of the line; this
is important only in that it provided her with a measured con-
trol against which she plays the uncontrolled passion of the
anguished Dido. After the slow regal measures of her lament,
Dido's confession comes as a chilling cry.

Esto que el mar rechaza, dije, es mio.
Y ante él me adorné de la misericordia como del brazalete de más
    precio.
Yo te conjuro, si oyes, a que respondas: ¿quién esquivó la adversidad
    alguna vez? Y quién tuvo a desdoro llamarle huésped suya y preparar
    la sala del convite?
Quien lo hizo no es mi igual. Mi lenguaje se entronca con el de los
    inmoladores de sí mismos.

El cuchillo bajo el que se quebró mi cerviz era un hombre llamado
Eneas.

The nearly normal spoken rhythms permit Castellanos to han-
dle this passion with effective moderation and occasional tell-
ing understatement, while at the same time she controls the
outbursts of the agonized queen. The overwrought emotions
with which the poem deals contrast with the almost colloquial
speech, a contrast that is implicit in that of the legendary tragic
queen with her modern counterpart. A vocabulary rich in
terms like booty, daggers, "el de la corva garra de gavilán," "nave
de airosas velas," rapidly establishes the barbaric atmosphere of
a remote semimythical kingdom, only to be contrasted again
with the restraint of Dido's statements. The result is a poem in
which the betrayed queen speaks in remarkably modern
rhythms and words, and we realize doubly that Dido is much

more than a convenient figure about whom to compose a paean to the past.

There is another dimension to this technique. Certain obsessive themes recur in Castellanos's work, among them the situation of Dido, the abandoned lover. It is not unlikely that the repeated effort to create the nearly classical line she uses here, the progressive abandonment of a specific external referent in so much of her poetry, and the adaptation of the figure of Dido are a masking of the real circumstances, whatever they may have been, that led to this obsessive usage. Castellanos's Dido, unlike Vergil's, shuns suicide—"Ah, sería preferible morir. Pero yo sé que para mí no hay muerte./Porque el dolor—¿y qué otra cosa soy más que dolor?—me ha hecho eterna"—but this will not always be the case.

This tendency toward impersonal poetry as a masking device is carried to an extreme in *Al pie de la letra* (1959). Few of the volume's eighteen poems have any visible individual reference or are placed in the mouth of a speaker who could by any stretch of the imagination be a double for Rosario Castellanos. This is particularly surprising when we learn the volume's origin: "Más que textos liricos, los poemas pueden considerarse como retratos . . . Los poemas están basados en personas concretas, pero intentan ir más allá, quieren llegar a los rasgos de carácter que predominan en esas personas."[27] She has again attempted to mask the specific circumstances that gave rise to the poems in order to attain a less individual expression, one that would also obscure her own participation as a *character* within the poems, as well as their author. The majority of the poems deal with subjects that are impersonal, broadly human, or apparently external to the author, and in several she deals once more with themes reminiscent of Perse's fables of migration. One of the most interesting is "Crónica final," the history of an unidentified group of people—writers, nation, or generation?—who systematically avoided their responsibilities and must now face the fact that "Nuestra historia la escribe/reptando entre cenizas la serpiente." A curious characteristic of the poem is that the avoidance of objective referent leads to a condemnation of inauthenticity and of betrayal of the ideal in the most general of terms, even though the poem itself is conceived and expressed in very concrete imagery. The "años de la cobardía,/cuando toda la tierra hedió de las entrañas/podridas del augur y enormes animales/mugieron en los páramos nocturnos," the lie that became "madrastra nuestra y fue/dispensadora del pan amargo, escanciadora del agrio vino,/dueña, en fin, de la celda y de la triste lámpara," are firmly anchored in reality, although a reality of a kind alien to the majority—I would suspect all—of her readers, so that the poem gives the odd feeling of being somehow remote and barbaric.

"Monólogo de la extranjera" uses the same kind of structure, but it has an obvious personal reference, albeit one that is never identified in the poem itself. The poem is presented in terms of a woman who returns to her land converted into an outsider; from the first line, we are given her situation. "Vine de lejos. Olvidé mi patria. / Ya no entiendo el idioma / que allá usan de moneda o de herramienta." The poem is developed without autobiographical references; if we were not aware of Castellanos's return to her home state of Chiapas and the impact this trip had on her, this poem too would seem as starkly impersonal as the others. But the reader can glimpse behind the mask and see the suffering that is otherwise carefully concealed, even though it is only by inference from other sources that we are able to perceive the real source of this agony.

> Basta. He callado más de lo que he dicho.
> Tostó mi mano el sol de las alturas
> y en el dedo que dicen aquí 'del corazón'
> tengo un anillo de oro con un sello grabado.
>
> El anillo que sirve
> para identificar los cadáveres.

One of Castellanos's most typically Persean poems is also one of her most effective, "Relato del augur." It uses all the characteristic images: the peoples in migration, leaders designated by titles or abstract terms, the use of concrete details to give a sense of immediacy and to avoid overabstraction. But the uncharacteristic element here is that the people are easily identifiable as the Mexica, the ancestors of today's Mexicans. Here are the mythic march and the final arrival: "He aquí la heredad:

el valle, el valle. / Cerros donde los dioses se quebraron las manos, / lava de las catástrofes antiguas." This is obviously the Valley of Mexico, Anahuac, land of the smoking mountains. Without ever identifying a place or a person, the poem recapitulates the trauma of the Conquest which would put an end to the Mexicas' power and authority.

> Se multiplican voces:
> del mar vendrá la tempestad. Del mar.
>
> Ay, todo lo que vemos
> tiene un temblor funesto de presagio.
>
> ¡Del mar vendrá la tempestad! ¡Del mar!
>
> No es mentira. No invento lo que digo.
>
> Sólo estoy recordando.

And so Rosario Castellanos recapitulates the history of the founders of the Empire of Tenochtitlan in a parable that shows how fleeting are all the empires of humankind. It is perhaps indicative of the future works that two of the best poems are precisely those that begin to move away from distancing of the poet from her subject and that most clearly offer an external referent.

Nearly all the books mentioned thus far are characterized by a tension between short personal poems and the longer attempts at a poetic persona, but *Lívida luz* (1960), winner of the Villaurrutia Prize, marks a substantial break. The volume consists primarily of brief and highly personal lyrics that are simultaneously a statement of the author's social commitment, as though this emerging commitment had provided her with a means to react poetically against her own efforts at masking her emotions. It is not chance that the volume bears an epigraph from the work of Simone Weil, with whose mystical activism Castellanos was much in sympathy. She says of the change that the new poems signified for her:

En ellos reflexiono sobre el mundo, ya no como objeto de contemplación estética sino como lugar de lucha en el que uno está comprometido. Allí se reflejan las experiencias que obtuve en Chiapas en mi trabajo para el Instituto Indigenista. En esos lugares la lucha ha llegado a extremos desgarradores de brutalidad. En esos poemas también figuran mis experiencias en ciertos ambientes de la ciudad de México. Asimismo, lecturas sobre los temas sociales y políticos que, por entonces, comenzaron a interesarme de manera muy particular. Todo ello está implícito en los poemas, aunque no se descubra a primera vista.[28]

But this newly apparent commitment does not produce euphoria; the light of the title, as Raúl Leiva pointed out, "no es clara, [que] no es radiante, sino más bien pálida, amoratada, azulosa, como preludio de tragedia, como anuncio de muerte. No es la luz de la primavera y el amor sino el mortecino resplandor de la duda, de la vacilación, de la desesperanza."[29] Much less is it the communal march to the radiant future that some would have preferred; the poems are more anxiously individual than before. Castellanos may have varied the masks she used to protect herself from the exposure her poetry would otherwise have meant, but she could not use the mass mask of the proletarian poet hymning doctrinaire slogans. She was too thoughtful and self-aware, too conscious of her individuality and her role as writer to be able to mesh into a collective communal voice. In two fundamental texts, she clarified her conception of the conflictive nature of poetry and the artist's commitment.

La inteligencia está perdida, dice Simone Weil, desde el momento en que se expresa con la palabra *nosotros*. Su ejercicio es una responsabilidad estrictamente privada.[30]

Estoy del lado del arte comprometido. Ahora, ¿comprometido con qué? Esencialmente con lo que uno considera que es la realidad. El compromiso es transcribir, con los medios estéticos más adecuados, más ricos, más llenos de matices, esa realidad que nosotros alcanzamos a contemplar, a descubrir, y que queremos transmitir a los demás; entonces, el compromiso esencial del artista no debe ser hacia una consigna dictada desde fuera por nadie, ni por ningún partido político, ni por una doctrina religiosa, ni por una escuela estética, sino por sus propias experiencias.[31]

In *Lívida luz*, then, there are no prefabricated formulae leading to the "only" road to the future. We find, on the contrary,

pessimism and frustration in the face of ingratitude and vio-
lence, a world in which "El ciervo va a beber y en el agua
aparece/el reflejo de un tigre" ("Destino"). It is as though the
masks were all beginning to crack and leave the poet naked
before the accumulated suffering of all time. At moments the
frustration is expressed in almost everyday language, as in "El
excluido."

> A menudo, si un hombre recibe bien de otro
> se le despierta un ímpetu homicida
> —rostro secreto de la gratitud—
> y el insulto que calla lo envenena.
>
> El favor lo ha marcado
> y no cabe en el mundo en que es ley de las cosas
> la lucha, el exterminio.
>
> A menudo . . . A menudo . . .

This frustration is apparent everywhere, as in the second of
the "Tres poemas," which presents a pure vision of an enormous
fish whose eyes never close, fixed always on someone, some-
thing, incapable of doing any more than observing, a comment
on humankind's incapacity that leads us inevitably to the apoc-
alyptic vision of "Los distraídos."

> Nadie escuchaba. Nada podía detenerse.
>
> Era el tiempo de las emigraciones.
>
> Todo ardía: ciudades, bosques enteros, nubes.

This is a poetry that becomes more and more pessimistic, more
and more the expression of a perception of the tragic nature of
existence. In an article published six years after the publication
of *Lívida luz*, Castellanos spoke of this perception and of
poetry's duty to record it. "¿Qué aprehende la poesía sino el
instante que aspira a convertirse en eternidad? ¿Qué muestra
sino la conciencia torturada por el transcurrir inexorable del
tiempo que nos deteriora, que nos cambia de lo que éramos en lo
que somos, en lo que vamos a ser? Nostalgia sin consuelo ante la
certidumbre de lo irreversible. Nunca, lo dijo Heráclito, nos

bañaremos dos veces en el mismo río."³² The growing nega-
tivism of her poetry is due only in part to a socially-based
pessimism; whatever other personal factors were influencing
the process, the inexorability of advancing time and the loss of
any hope of the instant of plenitude were also at work.

But there is an important new element in *Lívida luz.* Several
poems include direct comments, in first person singular, as if
the author were suddenly to be transformed into a confessional
poet in the manner of Robert Lowell, for example. Another
important theme is solitude, which at times is metamorphosed
into an obsession with the sterility of not producing life.
"Monólogo en la celda," for example, starts with a solitary
expression not very different from the beginning of a number of
earlier poems.

> Se olvidaron de mí, me dejaron aparte.
> Y yo no sé quien soy
> porque ninguno ha dicho mi nombre; porque nadie
> me ha dado ser, mirándome.

But there is an unexpected twist.

> Dentro de mí se pudre un acto, el único
> que no conozco y no puedo cumplir
> porque no basta a ello un par de manos.

This is connected thematically with the most impressive poem
in the volume, "Jornada de la soltera," the clearest, most inti-
mate poetic expression to date of Castellanos's often-expressed
personal feelings. Indeed, the poem is so intensely personal, and
Castellanos spoke so often and so freely of her private life, that
one is tempted to suspect the creation of another and different
persona. One of the Mexican poets most admired by Castellanos
was Salvador Novo, who perfected the art of appearing to be a
confessional poet revealing his most personal feelings while in
fact adopting an ironic self-mocking mask. There is a thread
that recurs in a number of these poems: a speaker who is more
observer than participant, remote from those about her (or him),
whose suffering is somehow disconnected: "Yo soy de los que
mueren solos, de los que mueren/de algo peor que vergüenza./ /

Yo muero de mirarte y no entender" ("Agonía fuera del mun-
do"); "Y los vi desde lejos/ocultar lo que roban y reír" ("El
despojo"). This new persona is a solitary or "Encerrado" or
condemned to a "Monólogo en la celda." Even in as intensely
personal a work as "Jornada de la soltera," the poem is written in
third person, paradoxically distancing it from the author herself.
In the swing from the mask of Dido, Castellanos has here
created the mask of a third person, never really identified as
Rosario Castellanos, never quite willing (or able) to take the
definitive step into autobiographical or confessional poetry, yet
drawn obsessively to certain themes that clearly concerned her
deeply. One of these was the looming shadow of death, of possi-
ble suicide, which was to become a constant, almost obsessive,
presence. In "Canción de cuna" it appears strangely linked with
the theme of maternity and the figure of the Tempter:

> ¿Es grande el mundo?—Es grande. Del tamaño del miedo.
> ¿Es largo el tiempo?—Es largo. Largo como el olvido.
> ¿Es profunda la mar?—Pregúntaselo al náufrago.
>
> (El Tentador sonríe. Me acaricia el cabello
> y me dice que duerma.)

This same Tempter is behind the last lines of the brief "Noctur-
no." "No es posible sino soñar, morir, / soñar que no mor-
imos / y, a veces, un instante, despertar." Little by little this
poetry is becoming absorbed by these questions, as in the an-
guished "¿Qué se hace a la hora de morir?" of "Amanecer." Of
the overtly socially-oriented human solidarity that had been so
important only a few years earlier, there remain barely traces.

Perhaps as a reaction against the extreme personalism of
Lívida luz, Materia memorable (1969) is in a much calmer and
apparently more objective mode, as though the poet were engag-
ing in a sort of dialectic to-and-fro in her struggle to discover the
most effective and at the same time the least revealing poetic
idiom and stance. The title comes from the final stanza of
"Toma de conciencia," a poem that expresses much of the
familiar recognition of the solitude and frustrations of a woman
who regularly faces the "mínimas tragedias cotidianas," but
there is also, as the poem's title indicates, a new perception. She

is no longer entirely alone; she forms part of all creation, known
and unknown to her. She participates in all living kind, in a
new—or recalled?—solidarity which defies the ever-present
Tempter. This returning sense of participation makes it possible
for her to write a poem that would earlier have been inconceiva-
ble, "Las dádivas":

> La mano que se abrió sobre mis días
> es una mano grande como el cielo.
> Me dió raíz, memoria, y para respirar
> una herida que llaman la rosa de los vientos.

There are some ambiguities that will not permit the poem to be
taken as a simple expression of happiness, but the basic idea is
new, as is the startling "Sobremesa," which converts a perfectly
ordinary and even anodyne moment, such as the women's
gathering after dinner for the usual chores, into the astonishing
vision of "Para su plenitud este instante no quiere/más que ser y
pasar." This quotidian immanence appears again in "Quinta de
recreo": "Esta es la morada en que el día se despoja/de su
armadura y sólo resplandece." Small epiphanies, perhaps, but
that is what most of us must settle for.

Emerging in *Materia memorable* is a new kind of poem which
fuses the longer line and use of a poetic persona of the earlier
works with a calmer, more colloquial idiom approximating the
rhythms of normal speech. The rhetoric of the earlier years is
definitely gone, and the tensions of subjectivism and wordiness
are effectively harmonized. "Nocturno," for example, consists
of irregular combinations of seven and four syllables, with the
majority of lines ranging around eleven; it echoes quite clearly
the form of "Lamentación de Dido," but the subject matter is
much more openly modern and personal. It is one of Cas-
tellanos's most controlled performances, with short phrases
balanced against longer combinations. The poem is a straight-
forward portrait of two people who have quietly betrayed their
pact, until now there is no further opportunity. In a perfectly
calm tone, the speaker asks for a truce. But the chief charac-
teristic of the poem is its vocabulary, which, like the form, still

echoes the migration-epic based earlier works. Their life to-
gether is phrased in ritual terms: "desde que los mayores nos
pusieron la sal/sobre la lengua/y nos soplaron al oído un
nombre"; "atados mano contra mano."

> Nos partimos el mundo. Para ti
> ese fragmento oscuro del espejo
> en que sólo se ve la cara de la muerte;
> los hierros, las espinas del sacrificio, el vaso
> ritual y el cascabel violento de la danza.

"Nocturno" is again a potentially highly personal and revealing
poem; Castellanos has chosen to express the strictly *personal*
aspect—"acaso/para nosotros dos ya no hay mañana"—against a
background that both highlights the major theme and at the
same time removes it from confessionalism. The poet is still
struggling with the dual temptation to confess openly her per-
sonal life and to screen it against a distancing background.

The extent to which *Materia memorable* is anchored in the
ongoing struggle is visible in the persistence of the creation of
masks. "Testamento de Hécuba" uses as a framework the leg-
end of the Trojan queen, mother of Paris, enslaved by Ulysses
after the fall of Troy. Castellanos's version follows closely the
classical outline and does not seem to have been adapted di-
rectly to her personal circumstance, although clearly the fallen
queen's hinted equivalence between her slavery and her pre-
vious life struck an echo in Castellanos. Considerably different
is "Metamorfosis de la hechicera" in that it has no fixed refer-
rent and does not rely on a historical setting. It is impossible to
identify any source for the unnamed "hechicera" who, for what-
ever reasons, "se marchó por esa calle/—que tan bien conocía—
de los adioses," but we discover a series of the obsessive figures
we have seen earlier: the need to achieve name, that is, to attain
an identity, and the fish as symbol and symptom of a chaotic
world.[33] There is reason to wonder whether Rosario Castellanos
did not create in this mysterious figure of the *hechicera* some-
thing of herself when she speaks of "Mujer, tuvo sus máscaras y
jugaba a engañarse/y a engañar a los otros."

The Indian heritage reappears in "El talismán" and "Ultima

crónica." The latter is phrased in a thoroughly mythic fasion and communicates attendance at—and participation in?—a millenary rite of initiation into

> . . . ese culto secreto en el que se renueva
> la sangre ya caduca,
> en que se vivifican las deidades,
> en que el árbol se cubre de retoños.

There are allusions to the flowering war and other hints of an Aztec background, but the disturbing aspect of the poem is the total lack of any significance or meaning to this barbarous rite. It is obviously the central ritual that gives meaning and form to the nameless civilization, and it remains incomprehensible. The poem is thrown into a jarring context by the last verse:

> Y continúo aquí, abyecta, la tarea
> de repetir *grandeza, libertad, justicia, paz,*
> *amor, sabiduría*
> y . . . y . . . no entiendo ya
> este demente y torpe balbuceo.

Here the poet uses the mythic framework to pave the way for the stunning ironic twist of the last lines, when the uncomprehending babbling of the political catchwords of our time makes the time and place of these savage rites only too clear.

"El talismán" uses the same idiom and the same mythic conception, with its protagonist in search of her own face in a land of stones and cataclysms. But although the poem is couched in mythic, ahistorical terms, it is also easily legible as Castellanos's return to and awakening into the indigenous culture of Chiapas. It is a fine example of the kind of controlling form she sought in the use of these poetic structures. This tendency is carried to its logical outcome in "Acción de gracias," in which the poet begins by saying,

> Antes de irme—igual en cortesía
> al huésped que se marcha
> quisiera agradecer a quien se debe
> tantas hermosas cosas que he tenido.

The tone established, although more ironic than we might have expected, is once more that of the pilgrim who has been here only temporarily. Again we see the distancing mythic structure, with mention of Nausicaa, Raquel, Penélope. The idiom and vocabulary are equally typical; her presence has been received by "la voluntad de la tribu, de darle/calor al peregrino." Daily life is structured in terms of this same saving formal conception, in a brilliantly ironic distancing of the everyday meal.

> Los pucheros borbollan
> sustanciosos de res sacrificada,
> de hortaliza escogida, de corral abundante.
> Y pasan a la mesa, interrumpiendo
> la charla baladí o la palabra áspera.
> Bajo su especie humilde comulgamos
> y el señor distribuye las raciones
> con equidad y juicio.

The description is worthy of a rural epic in its atmosphere and general tone, and the impression of an archaic patriarchy is reinforced by the description of the presiding husband as "el señor." But the word's ambiguous allusion to God is also strengthened through the verb "comulgamos," so that the poem is both an ironic view of what is essentially a humdrum domestic rite and a bitter vision of the role of the married woman in a male-dominated society in relation to the omnipotence of the husband. There is no doubt that Castellanos was using the mythic framework to heighten the autobiographical element; directly between the verses that establish the framework by naming Nausicaa, et al. and the strophe that describes the meal in terms of a ritualized tribal ceremonial, occur these revealing and touching lines: "Ay, aire bautizado por los nombres más próximos: / hijo Pablo, Gabriel hijo, Ricardos / —el padre, el primogénito—" These are all easily identifiable as the poet's husband, son, and two stepsons. The effect is doubly impressive, given the contrast between the two framing stanzas and the personal outburst of the framed lines which foregrounds in brilliant fashion the poem's ironic message.

It is important to stress the presence of death in this volume, even in the relatively peaceful poems. Castellanos's insistence on finding her own name is prefigured ironically and, given the

circumstances of her premature death, tragically, in a poem like
"Tránsito," when she says, "No, no moría. No supe/cómo borrar
el nombre de Rosario." Suicide is never really absent from her
poems, after the earliest ones, and *Materia memorable* includes
the overt "Privilegio del suicida," in which the sufferer is the
survivor, condemned to life.

Materia memorable was the last separate volume of poetry
published during the life of Rosario Castellanos; the collected
poems, *Poesía no eres tú*, appeared in 1972, two years before her
death. It includes four sections of previously unpublished
poems: *En la tierra de en medio, Diálogos con los hombres más
honrados, Otros poemas*, and *Viaje redondo*. It would seem that
the multiple obligations of which she wrote so often—wife,
mother, columnist, teacher, and finally diplomat—had inter-
fered with her creative work.[34] There is nothing here of the
sustained power of the mature longer poems, which does not
mean at all that there are not poems here which do her honor.
Perhaps the most striking aspect is the almost complete disap-
pearance of the masks we have noted so often. *En la tierra de en
medio*, a title that reflects her increasing vision of this world as a
no-man's-land, bears as epigraph Eliot's "Human kind/cannot
bear very much reality." For the first time, Castellanos is writ-
ing overtly autobiographical poetry or, at the very least, poetry
whose speaker bears a life that conforms to the outward details
of Castellanos's own life. The tone is of resigned, ironic sadness,
acceptance of the fact that her existence has become hopelessly
mediocre and her poetry what María del Carmen Millán had
called a "despiadado inventario de la mediocridad que vivimos,
de los mitos que alimentamos, de la demagogia que padecemos,
de la inexistencia que propiciamos," all seen tragically through
the poet's experience, which was always an "experiencia de
lucidez, de inteligencia y desafío."[35] Life has become a game of
chess between those who "éramos amigos y, a ratos, nos
amábamos" ("Ajedrez") but who now meditate on the final
move that will definitely annihilate the other. There is the
stunned recognition of "Desamor."

> Me vio como se mira al través de un cristal
> o del aire
> o de nada.

> Y entonces supe: yo no estaba allí
> ni en ninguna otra parte
> ni había estado nunca ni estaría.
>
> Y fui como el que muere en la epidemia,
> sin identificar, y es arrojado
> a la fosa común.

There could hardly be a more devastating perception, especially for one so concerned with the search for her own identity and individuality. And there are the painful confession, without mask or disguise, of "Pequeña crónica" and the reliance on "Valium 10." Rarely does the poet use her old trick of the poetic mask of mythic structures; it is visible only in the unseen absence of "Bella dama sin piedad," or the familiar story of the Aztec princess in "Malinche." There is no longer any need for such forms; Castellanos has learned to control her rhetorical exuberance, and the result is an "Autorretrato" where the tutelary voice is no longer Claudel or Perse but the master ironist, Salvador Novo. No longer does Castellanos take refuge behind lengthy rhetorical verses dealing with remote people and remoter places. In "Autorretrato" she can use clearly autobiographical materials—"Soy madre de Gabriel"—as she creates her ironic self-portrait as a housewife advancing in years whose stable life is in danger of collapse.

> En cambio me enseñaron a llorar. Pero el llanto
> es en mi un mecanismo descompuesto
> y no lloro en la cámara mortuoria
> ni en la ocasión sublime ni frente a la catástrofe.
>
> Lloro cuando se quema el arroz o cuando pierdo
> el último recibo del impuesto predial.

And always the theme that was becoming more and more obsessive.

> Si sonríe, sonríe desde lejos,
> desde lo que será su memoria y saluda
> desde su antepasado pálido por la muerte.
>   ["Bella dama sin piedad"]
>
> Y la vena
> —mía o de otra ¿qué más da?—en que el tajo

suicida se hundió un poco o lo bastante
como para volverse una esquela mortuoria.
[*"Pequeña crónica"*]

Pero cuando no estaba . . . Bueno, en fin,
hay que ensayar la muerte puesto que se es mortal.
[*"Narciso 70"*]

Two poems deserve further comment in that they return to a deeply humane commitment. "Poesía no eres tú" is an extension of what we have already seen in *En la tierra de en medio*, but there is also the formulation of a commitment and of the belief that poetry can no longer be the expression of the intimate lyric, even though during this stage of her career Castellanos herself was writing predominantly intimate lyrics. It is impossible to say how much the attitude was influenced by the trauma of 1968, but one of the strongest poems of the volume is the denunciation of the massacre, "Memorial de Tlatelolco." She avoids high-pitched political rhetoric; instead, she portrays in a controlled voice the complete absence of any record of the crime, of any official or public recognition that it had ever transpired. Nor does she cast exclusive blame on the government that perpetrated and then covered up the slaughter; like Octavio Paz, she finds something ancestral in it all. "No busques lo que no hay: huellas, cadáveres, / que todo se le ha dado como ofrenda a una diosa: / a la Devoradora de Excrementos."

Castellanos's remaining works do not give the impression of being finished collections. *Diálogos con los hombres más honrados* is a group of semiaphorisms, responses to lines by other writers, ironic comments rather than poems. Others are longer but they share the same wry pessimism. They are all pretexts for commenting on the life and character of the Mexican, but even here death is ever present. It would be difficult to find a more explicit statement of the poet's steady progress toward acceptance of death, as though she knew or anticipated what was shortly to happen.

"Me quiero despedir de tanta pena"
igual que tú, Miguel, pero soy mexicana
y en mi país tenemos ritos, costumbres, modos.

Si la pena me dice que se va, me desvivo
por ser hospitalaria.
¿Se le ofrece un café? ¿Una copita?
Que se quede otro rato.
Aún no es tarde y afuera hace mal tiempo
y hay tanto de qué hablar todavía. Hablaremos.

Alguna vez se va a poner de pie,
a pesar de mis súplicas,
y llegaremos juntas a la puerta
y la abriremos y, a los cuatro vientos,
como aquí suele hacerse, seguiremos charlando.

Y temo que mi adiós—si es que hay adiós—
se confunda con una bienvenida:
la que preparo ya para la muerte.

Otros poemas is a group of eleven poems, several of which
share a tendency to comment on the modern scene, at times in a
meter and vocabulary that recall the mythic poems, as in
"Telenovela," which pillories the "Gran Caja Idiota" that now
occupies the place left vacant by Homer and Scheherazade. The
collection is much more serious and introspective than is *Di-
álogos,* and a principal theme is self-inflicted death: "el gramo
de cianuro/que escondía entre sus joyas" ("Evocación de la Tía
Elena"); "No me toques el brazo izquierdo. Duele/de tanta
cicatriz" ("Advertencia al que llega"). The final group is *Viaje
redondo,* nine poems written during or at least inspired by her
trip to Israel, where she was to take up her duties as ambassador.
They are in some cases amusing, in some perceptive, often self-
deprecating. The final poem in the volume, and in this sense her
testament, is "El retorno," a clear-eyed contemplation of life's
hypocrisy and fanaticism, of the uselessness of stock responses
to the existential situation: religion, work, art, political action,
love. . . . She comes to a conclusion that is more chilling than
anything else in her work.

Acepta nada más los hechos: has venido
y es igual que te hubieras quedado o que si nunca
te hubieras ido. Igual. Para ti. Para todos.

Superflua aquí. Superflua allá. Superflua

exactamente igual a cada uno
de los que ves y de los que no ves.

Ninguno es necesario
ni aun para ti, que por definición
eres menesterosa.

This is Rosario Castellanos's bitter epitaph. We have seen
how the struggle to control her own verbal facility lead a charac-
teristic style, how this style gradually evolved into a much more
personal vision of the individual, and how this vision, with its
view of human solidarity and responsibility, slowly gave ground
before an increasingly despairing vision. More and more her
poetry is the expression of the search for a real self as a reaction
against the slogans and recipes with which we are surrounded,
with no exit except the universal one. In the words of José
Emilio Pacheco, "Una y otra vez nos recordó que la existencia no
es eterna y el sufrimiento no es una molestia accidental sino la
condición misma de la vida."[36] Until finally she was silent.
Perhaps the best elegy is these words of Pacheco.

Para quienes tuvimos el privilegio de tratar a Rosario Castellanos hubo
inevitablemente dos personas distintas: una escribía los poemas más
trágicos y dolorosos de la literatura mexicana; otra se presentaba al
mundo bajo un aspecto de tal manera gentil y risueño que sólo es
posible recordarla con palabras que se dijeron de otro poeta: "Su presen-
cia era mágica y traía la felicidad."[37]

The most tragic irony of all is that Rosario Castellanos should
have left as her final word this vision of her own superfluity,
when those who were her friends and those who know only her
poetry can give testimony that never was there one less super-
fluous.

7 Conclusions: The Double Strand

The five poets examined in this volume may well seem very different one from another, and there are indeed considerable differences between them. It would be difficult to imagine writers seemingly more remote from one another than Chumacero and Bonifaz Nuño on the one hand, and Huerta and Sabines on the other, with Rosario Castellanos occupying some sort of middle ground. Even more, it would be exaggerated to see the hermeticism of the first two as though it were the same thing. They are, in fact, very distinct in the reasons for their intensely closed poetry. Essentially, both deal with the poet's own inner processes. Chumacero is concerned almost exclusively with a growing recognition of the manner in which the human mind is locked within itself and cannot communicate with anyone outside, while Bonifaz Nuño's poetry is an intricately contrived hymn of praise to the great woman-goddess. In the same way, Sabines and Huerta have much in common, but where the former is primarily a religious poet, in a broad sense, for whom the role of woman is really tangential, the older poet is deeply concerned with the role of woman in the erotic relationship and the connections between this relationship and the wider question of freedom. Against this background, Castellanos deals primarily with her own sense of inadequacy and the technical problem of expressing these emotions without lapsing into overtly sentimental confessional poetry.

But in spite of these differences, there are also considerable and sometimes unsuspected resemblances. Within each of the poets there is an operative principle of contradiction, which makes of their poetry the expression of the tensions generated by these oppositions. For one thing, they are all, in one way or another, engaged in a struggle with the word, a battle which is also a voyage of discovery. Chumacero's poetry, in a very important sense, is the stubborn but losing struggle to find an accommodation with his own sense of sterility, and the final discovery that the poet's mind is closed off from any kind of meaningful communication. Bonifaz Nuño laboriously constructs complicated verbal structures in the effort to break through to the goddess. His discovery is not really very different from that of Chumacero; he is led slowly to the recognition that life is a process of slow loss. The distinction is that in Bonifaz Nuño's poetry we come to realize that beneath the dull and vulgar daily surfaces there is another and truly horrifying reality. Sabines makes a related discovery: that life is only a slow process of approaching death, and that death is not some abstract sense but an immediate and awful fact that snatches away those closest to us. Castellanos's voyage is in many ways the most touching of all, in her struggle to develop an original and effective means to express accurately and coolly her emotional dilemma. Huerta is, in one fashion, unlike the others; whatever else his poetry may be, it is constant and inflexible in its conviction. At the same time, it is a serious exploration of the not always obvious and certainly not always lovely relations between political and sexual freedom and violence.

There is, of course, another and very clear resemblance. These are all poets of love; each of them is seeking some kind of plenitude through one aspect or another of love. In each of the five, even Huerta, love is in some way an absence, ranging from the metaphysical remoteness of Chumacero to the real betrayal chronicled by Castellanos. This is in all five cases a passionate love that follows its path to the end, even when that end may be very different from what was originally intended. In Bonifaz Nuño and Chumacero, the vision is internalized; we see the beloved only through the poet's eyes, and love is a road to a tragic self-perception. In Chumacero's poetry love struggles with sterility, as does the word, and the effort leads finally to the realization that there can be no love and no communication. Eroticism is the only escape, but the body leads only to death. Woman can be only an abstraction, an absence, and even the routine escape through a fleeting relation is of no service. For Chumacero, the recognition of love is that there can be none. Bonifaz Nuño is the closest of the five to a traditional love poet, in the sense that the overwhelming majority of his poetry is directed to the beloved. But this is no traditional mistress; she is the great goddess through whom we are led to the final revelation. If she is Beatrice, she is also Coatlicue, and the revelation is both of her splendor and of our own insignificance. Rather than love, this poetry sings the poet's adoration of the goddess.

The other three conform somewhat more to our notions of the poetry of love, but only apparently, for they too are highly individualistic. Rosario Castellanos deals repeatedly with the frustration of love betrayed, and if her subject matter is often taken from classical myth, beneath the distant goddesses it is sometimes possible to perceive the present woman. Finally, she abandons these masks and develops a coolly ironical manner that does not hide the piercing edge of loss. Huerta is a love poet in a very special sense: for him, woman, his beloved Mexico City, and political freedom are inextricably blended, so much so that at times it is not at all clear of which he is writing, or whether he makes any poetic distinction between them. Whereas love is sometimes abstract for Chumacero, Bonifaz Nuño, or even Castellanos, for Huerta it is immediate and direct. Jaime Sabines too deals with an immediate love in direct fashion, but woman plays a minor role, as a possible temporary escape. She is, at best, a memory of an absence. Sabines's poetry deals with the basic struggle of love versus death; it is an expression of his dismay and anger at the immediacy of our dissolution. He cannot accept that those he loves and ultimately himself can be annihilated by a God who is at best unfeeling. In its core, even when it is being written as parody, his is a poetry of religious love outraged.

But there is another way in which these five Mexican poets are very much alike, the double strand of my title. They are all heirs to the Occidental literary tradition. They write in Spanish and their meters are, basically, those learned in the European models. Their work bears echoes of the European masters, and Eliot is a presence in several of them. In Bonifaz Nuño there is more than simply a memory of Dante; his work is charged with progressively greater allusions to the entire conception of

Dante's love poetry and Beatrice's role. Chumacero owes a debt to modern French poetry, and Castellanos modelled a good deal of her work on Claudel and Perse, as well as using mythological figures as a key element in her effort to create a persona. Sabines and Huerta seem closer to other Latin Americans such as Neruda and Vallejo, but Huerta, at least, gives whole lists of his favorite poets from the European tradition, and they both awaken echoes of Villon and the medieval dance of death.

At the same time, these poets are very much Mexican, participants in the complex culture that has roots both in the European Christian tradition and in the Aztec world of kings, priests, warriors, and sacrificial ritual. Repeatedly their work echoes that of other Mexican poets: Gorostiza, Villaurrutia, Novo, López Velarde, Othón. The peculiarly mocking familiarity with death is one of the most visible aspects of Mexican literature and society. If on the one level we have the songs of the Revolution—"Si me han de matar mañana, que me maten de una vez"—on another we have the metaphysical intricacies of Gorostiza's *Muerte sin fin* and the anguish of Villaurrutia's *Invitación a la muerte* and *Nostalgia de la muerte*. It is intriguing to note that the 1946 edition of the latter was published by Editorial Mictlán, which was the name of the Aztec land of the dead. Given the routinely repeated allegations that Villaurrutia was guilty of excessive francophilia, it is tempting to see that this "poeta de la muerte," as he is also routinely called, was pointing out in typical elliptical fashion his awareness of his own sources.

Our five poets are also, each in his/her own way, poets of death as befits the recipients of this inheritance. Chumacero's poetry deals constantly with the desolated awareness that love is in fact the other face of death and that its reality is the absence that leads to death. Behind Bonifaz Nuño's intricate formal structures there is a vision of a monstrous alternative world; the great goddess to whom he sings is also the mother of death. His sources are the Christian poetry of Dante, obsessed by love and the other world, and the Aztec lyric, a poetry of ritual sacrifice. Sabines is the most obvious of the five; he is overwhelmed by the physical fact of death and his fear of it. For Huerta, death is another aspect of his obsessive theme; it is the lack of freedom.

Rosario Castellanos may well be the most extreme example, given the circumstances of her tragic end (she was electrocuted while changing a light bulb) and the extent to which, during her last years, death, particularly death by suicide, came almost to monopolize her writing.

It is not only that these five poets lie within the Mexican tradition of the poetry of death. Their work contains easily identifiable allusions to pre-Hispanic poetry and culture. It is clearest in Bonifaz Nuño, who uses Nahua sources directly and consciously. He refers repeatedly to Coatlicue, the double goddess of love and death. His work is saturated with allusions to Aztec poetry and sculpture, and he repeatedly uses imagery based on these allusions: flint, flowers, hearts, knives, serpents. But Bonifaz Nuño is not alone; Huerta has written *El Tajín*, where the images from Nahua poetry express modern ruin and desolation. In other poems he too uses Coatlicue and the Aztec sacrificial imagery: obsidian knives, hearts, flowers. Rosario Castellanos also uses his imagery of the flowering war, and she refers as well to Coatlicue in a poem that directly connects the modern violence at Tlatelolco with the ancient tradition; several of her migration-based mythic poems are clearly related to the Mexica. The references are fewer in Chumacero and Sabines, but there too they exist. The poetry of Mexico, like its people and its society, reflects the fusion of two worlds, and these complex poets of the double strand operate freely and imaginatively within it.

Notes

CHAPTER 1. THE BACKGROUND

1. José Emilio Pacheco, "Introducción," *Antología del modernismo, 1884-1921* (Mexico: Universidad Nacional Autónoma, Biblioteca del Estudiante Universitario-90, 1970), 1:xi.

2. José Joaquín Blanco, *Crónica de la poesía mexicana*, 3d. ed. Mexico: Katún, 1981, 54.

3. See ibid., esp. 139-44, for an interesting exposition of this idea, although here, as well as in his treatment of the Modernists, Blanco's pronounced hostility toward any writer he suspects of supporting conservative governments leads him into rather dubious declarations.

4. Ramón Xirau, *Tres poetas de la soledad* (Mexico: Antigua Librería Robredo, 1955), 44-45.

5. Andrew Debicki, ed., *Antología de la poesía mexicana moderna* (London: Tamesis, 1977), 27 ff.

CHAPTER 2. ALÍ CHUMACERO

1. Not included in the *Poesía completa* is "Paloma de tristeza," published in the literary review *Fuensanta*, 2a. época, 1 (July-Aug. 1952): 4. The dates of composition or of any possible prior publication are not given, but the poem is formally and thematically much simpler and more traditional than most of Chumacero's work and is probably quite early.

2. Andrés Henestrosa, "Contestación al discurso de Alí Chumacero," in *Acerca del poeta y su mundo* (Mexico: Academia Mexicana, 1965), 30.

3. Interview by Tamara Kamenszain, "Alí Chumacero: La palabra postergada," *La Letra y la imagen*, supl. to *El Universal* 55 (Oct. 12, 1980): 2.

4. Alí Chumacero, "Antonio Machado, poeta de España," *Tierra Nueva* 2, no. 7 and 8 (Jan.-April 1941): 74.

5. Ibid.

6. Alfredo A. Roggiano, "Ser y verdad en los sueños e imágenes de Alí Chumacero," in his *En este aire de América* (Mexico: Edit. Cultura, Biblioteca del Nuevo Mundo-5, 1966), 177-87.

7. Chumacero, "Antonio Machado," 75.

8. Chumacero, "La poesía de Luis G. Urbina," *Letras de México* 5, no. 127 (Sept. 15, 1946): 321.

9. Interview by Elvira García, "Escribo muy poco y procuro no hacerlo," *La Semana de Bellas Artes* 175 (April 8, 1981): 7.

10. Chumacero, "Jorge Cuesta o la traición de la inteligencia," *Estaciones* 3, no. 10 (Summer 1958): 142.

11. See Chumacero, "Antonio Machado," esp. 76-77, for his intriguing comments on subjectivized and objectivized poetry and their role in Mexican letters.

12. José Emilio Pacheco, review of *Páramo de sueños, seguido de Imágenes desterradas, Rev. Universidad de México* 15, no. 1 (Sept. 1960): 30.

13. Debicki, *Antología*, 213.

14. Chumacero, review of Carlos Pellicer's *Recinto, Tierra Nueva* 9-10 (May-Aug. 1941): 176.

15. García, "Escribo muy poco," 7.

16. All textual references and quotations from the poems are from *Poesía completa*, 3rd. ed., prologue by Marco Antonio Campos (Mexico: Premiá Editora, Los libros del bicho-10, 1982).

17. Ramón Xirau, *Poetas de México y España* (Madrid: Porrúa Turanzas, 1962), 161.

18. Debicki, *Antología*, 213.

19. A. A. Roggiano has pointed out the coincidence of symbols, vocabulary, and even of resolution between "Olas" and Valéry's "Cimetière marin"; see his *En este aire de América*, 184-85. It is worth noting that Chumacero translated Bremond and Buffon and that "Amor entre ruinas," one of his most important poems, is preceded by a quote from Mallarmé, a poet of legendary difficulty and one whose technique of composition appears to have been somewhat similar to Chumacero's. The whole question of Chumacero's relations with French letters is in need of further study.

20. *La Gaceta*, nueva época, 8, no. 86 (Feb. 1978): 7; also in the *Poesía Completa*.

21. Raúl Leiva, *Imagen de la poesía mexicana contemporánea* (Mexico: Universidad Nacional Autónoma, Centro de Estudios Literarios, 1959), 264.

22. Kamenszain, "Alí Chumacero: La palabra postergada," 2.

23. Leiva, *Imagen*, 261.

24. Jesús Arellano, "Poesía mexicana en 1956," *Metáfora* 14 (May-June 1957): 11. It is interesting to note Chumacero's comment that Jorge Cuesta was so committed to the intellectual approach that it damaged his poetry, exactly the charge made by Arellano about Chumacero at almost the identical time.

25. Debicki, *Antología*, 213.

CHAPTER 3. EFRAÍN HUERTA

1. Mauricio de la Selva, *Algunos poetas mexicanos* (Mexico: Finisterre, 1971), 48.

2. Naomi Lindstrom, review of *Circuito interior, Chasqui* 7, no. 1 (Nov. 1977): 74.

3. Julio Ortega, "La poesía de Efraín Huerta," *Rev. Universidad de México* 23, no. 11 (July 1969), Hojas de crítica, 2. See Andrew Debicki's *Poetas hispanoamericanos contemporáneos* (Madrid: Gredos, Biblioteca Románica Hispánica, 1976), 246-49, for a study of Huerta's use of irony and point of view in order to avoid the sentimentality intrinsic to such a conception.

4. Lindstrom, review of *Circuito interior, Chasqui,* 75.

5. Rafael Solana, "Efraín Huerta," *Letras de México* 5, no. 110 (April 1945): 50.

6. Ibid., 49.

7. José Emilio Pacheco, "Efraín Huerta," *Rev. Universidad de México* 22, no. 11 (July 1968): 6.

8. Octavio Paz, "Prólogo," *Poesía en movimiento* (Mexico: Joaquín Mortiz, 1966), 20.

9. Efraín Huerta, "Breve explicación," *Poesía, 1935-1968* (Mexico: Joaquín Mortiz, 1968), 7.

10. (Mexico: Instituto Nacional de Bellas Artes, 1955), 98-99.

11. Jesús Arellano, "El poeta proscrito: Efraín Huerta," *Nivel* 43 (July 1966): 5.

12. Andrés González Pagés, "Efraín Huerta: Perfil del poeta vivo," *Plural* 7, no. 67 (April 1977): 57.

13. José Emilio Pacheco, "Efraín Huerta," *Nivel* 72 (Dec. 1968): 7.

14. Efraín Huerta, *Poemas prohibidos y de amor* (Mexico: Siglo XXI, Col. Mínima 62, 1978), 79.

15. Paz, *Poesía en movimiento,* 20.

16. Rafael del Río, *Poesía mexicana contemporánea y otros escritos* (Torreon: Revista Cauce, 1955), 28.

17. Ricardo Aguilar, "Efraín Huerta y los poemínimos," *La Semana de Bellas Artes* 73 (April 25, 1979): 2.

18. Ibid.

19. Víctor M. Navarro, "Huerta, de profanaciones y otros gestos," *La Semana de Bellas Artes* 72 (April 18, 1979): 15.

20. Leiva, *Imagen,* 230.

21. Efraín Huerta, "Elegía de Noviembre," *Plural* 9, no. 105 (June 1980): 4-5.

22. Jaime Labastida, "La poesía mexicana (1965-1976)," *Rev. Universidad de México* 30, no. 12 (Aug. 1976): 8-9.

23. Ricardo Aguilar, "La dualidad en la obra de Efraín Huerta," *La Palabra y el Hombre,* nueva época, 27 (July-Sept. 1978): 32-42.

Chapter 4. Jaime Sabines

1. Ammen Alwar, "Jaime Sabines in Translation," *Review* 20 (Spring 1977): 61.

2. With this manuscript in completed form, I learned of the existence of Sabines's *Poemas Sueltos,* a volume of twenty poems and twenty-nine pages published in Mexico in 1981 by Papeles Privados in a limited edition. Although I have been unable to consult the collection, a review by Oscar Wong, published in *Plural* 130 (July 1982): 79-80, makes clear that if there has been any evolution since the publication of his last major work, it has been in the direction of a return to simplicity of expression.

3. Armando Armengol, "La iniciación poética de Jaime Sabines," *La Semana de Bellas Artes* 71 (April 11, 1979): 2-7

4. Jomi García Ascot, "Sobre Jaime Sabines," *Rev. Universidad de México* 20, no. 6 (Feb. 1966): 9.

5. Andrew Debicki, "La sugerencia, el punto de vista y la alegoría: La poesía concreta y universal de Jaime Sabines," in *Poetas hispanoamericanos contemporáneos,* 191-211.

6. Alí Chumacero, "La poesía," *La Cultura en México* 46 (Jan. 2, 1963): V.

7. José Emilio Pacheco, "Aproximación a la poesía mexicana del siglo XX," *Hispania* 48, no. 2 (May 1965): 215.

8. Mauricio de la Selva, *Algunos poetas mexicanos* (Mexico: Finisterre, 1971), 148.

9. Jaime Sabines, "Sobre la poesía," *Pájaro Cáscabel* 2 (Nov. 1962): 1.

10. Ibid.

11. Sabines, *Poesía de la sinceridad* (Tlaxcala: Alcance al número 31 de *Huytlale,* vol. 5, 1959). I am indebted to Dr. Kenneth Brett for his kindness in providing me with this information and for a copy of this almost unknown work.

12. Ibid., 7.

13. Ibid., 8.

14. Ibid.

15. Sabines's use of colloquial language and the angry mockery that suffuses his poetry are reminiscent of Huerta and the Chilean poet Nicanor Parra, whose "antipoetry" has a good deal in common with both Huerta and Sabines, as well as with other younger Mexicans influenced by the two latter. Although it is not my purpose here to examine in detail such possible relationships, it seems quite clear that neither of the Mexicans knew of Parra's work until relatively late and that theirs is an independent development owing more to the general situation, both social and poetic, than to any external influences.

16. Ana María Hernández, review of *Nuevo recuento de poemas, Hispamérica* 7, no. 20 (Aug. 1978): 119.

17. Jaime Labastida, *El amor, el sueño y la muerte en la poesía mexicana* (Zacatenco: Instituto Politécnico Nacional, 1969), 101-2.

18. Pacheco, review of *Nuevo recuento de poemas. Vuelta* 9, no. 1 (Aug. 1977): 36.

19. Jesús Arellano, "Raíces poéticas de Jaime Sabines," *Nivel* 33 (Sept. 1961): 2, 6.

20. César López, "El mundo poético de Jaime Sabines," *Casa de las Américas* 5, no. 30 (1965): 89.

21. See Debicki, "La sugerencia."

22. Music plays an important role in several of Sabines's poems. "La música de Bach mueve cortinas" recalls Fray Luis de León's "Oda a Salinas" in the suggestion of mystical union through music.

23. It would be worthwhile, although beyond the limits of this study, to examine this important aspect of Sabines's work in the light of the disemic allegory discovered by Debicki.

24. Tomás Segovia, "Recuento de Sabines," *Rev. Mexicana de Literatura* 9-10 (Sept.-Oct. 1962): 53.

25. López, "El mundo," 89.

26. Anonymous, "Corazón de león y saladino," *Plural* 3 (Oct. 1972): 41.

CHAPTER 5: RUBÉN BONIFAZ NUÑO

1. For much better informed commentary on this intriguing subject, see Rafael Moreno's "Nuevo virgilio mexicano," *La Cultura en México* 81 (Sept. 4, 1963): V-VIII, and a review by R. M. M. of the *Antología* published in *Rev. Universidad de México* 12, no. 7 (March 1958): 29.

2. Rubén Bonifaz Nuño, "La fundación de la ciuded," *Diálogos* 9, no. 2 (50) (March-April 1973): 10-16; *Destino del canto*, with a response by Agustín Yáñez (Mexico: Universidad Nacional Autónoma, 1963).

3. Bonifaz Nuño, *Destino del canto*, 8.

4. Debicki, *Antología*, 222.

5. See Mario Puga, "El escritor y su tiempo: Rubén Bonifaz Nuño," *Rev. Universidad de México* 10, no. 10 (June 1956): 19.

6. Jesús Arellano, "Drama poético en la obra de Rubén Bonifaz Nuño," *Nivel*, 2a. época, 4 (May 1963): 5; José Emilio Pacheco, "Aproximación," 214; Ramón Xirau, "Nuevos poetas de México," in his *Poetas de México y España*, 171.

7. Debicki, *Antología*, 222.

8. Henrique González Casanova, "Rubén Bonifaz Nuño," *La Cultura en México* 7 (Aug. 7, 1963), VI.

9. Puga, "El escritor y su tiempo," 19.

10. René Acuña, "Rubén Bonifaz Nuño: Una aproximación a *Fuego de pobres*," *Mester* 4, no. 1 (Nov. 1973): 44.

11. Ibid., 41.

12. Ibid., 42; Pacheco, "Aproximación," 214; de la Selva, *Algunos poetas mexicanos*, 13; Arellano, "Drama poético," 5; de la Selva, 13-14.

13. Ernesto Mejía Sánchez, review in *Rev. Universidad de México* 13, no. 5 (Jan. 1959): 29.

14. Raúl Leiva, "La poesía de Rubén Bonifaz Nuño: Desde *Imágenes hasta El manto y la corona*," *Cuadernos Americanos* 30, no. 1 (Jan.-Feb. 1971): 181.

15. Leiva, review in *La Palabra y el Hombre* 3, no. 10 (April-June 1959): 320.

16. John Michael Bennett, "Coatlicue: The poetry of Rubén Bonifaz Nuño," Ph.D. dissertation, University of California at Los Angeles, 1970, 134.

17. Although they lie beyond the intent of the present study, there are considerable and highly visible possibilities in a Jungian study of this provocative poetic figure.

18. Fausto Vega, "Aproximaciones," *Nivel* 34 (Oct. 1961): 2.

19. Acuña, "Rubén Bonifaz Nuño," 44.

20. González Casanova, "Rubén Bonifaz Nuño," VI.

21. Yáñez, *Destino del canto*, 47; Bennett, *Coatlicue*, 164-68.

22. The word "competence" is used here basically in the sense employed by Jonathan Culler in his *Structuralist Poetics* (Ithaca: Cornell Univ. Press, 1975).

23. Cited by Acuña, "Rubén Bonifaz Nuño," 45.

24. Ibid., 49.

25. Bennett, *Coatlicue*, 138.

26. As indicated in my preface, in 1968 a combination of right-wing terrorists, police and soldiers attacked a student demonstration at the Plaza of the Three Cultures in the district of Mexico City known as Tlatelolco. Although to this day the government seems to have made no effort to fix the blame or even to recognize that the episode took place, it is alleged that hundreds of students were killed. The slaughter awakened massive outrage in literary and intellectual circles and has come to be used as a reference point in literary developments.

27. Debicki, *Antología*, 223.

28. (Mexico: Universidad Nacional Autónoma, 1981).

29. (Mexico: Universidad Nacional Autónoma, 1981).

CHAPTER 6. ROSARIO CASTELLANOS

1. Victor Baptiste's excellent *La obra poética de Rosario Castellanos* (Santiago, Chile: Ediciones Exégesis, 1972) includes a very informative chapter on the themes of Castellanos's poetry.

2. José Emilio Pacheco, preliminary note to Castellanos's *El uso de la palabra* (Mexico: Ediciones de Excélsior, 1974), 11.

3. Graciela Hierro, "La filosofía de Rosario Castellanos," *Plural* 10-13, no. 120 (Sept. 1981): 30.

4. Interview by Emmanuel Carballo, "La historia de sus libros contada por ella misma," *Siempre* 44 (Dec. 19, 1962): 3.

5. Castellanos, *El uso de la palabra*, 257.

6. Ibid., 16.

7. Labastida, *El amor, el sueño y la muerte*, 60.
8. Pacheco, *El uso de la palabra*, 12-13.
9. *Los narradores ante el público* (Mexico: Joaquín Mortiz, 1966), 93.
10. Ibid., 94.
11. Labastida, *El amor, el sueño y la muerte*, 60.
12. Castellanos, *Mujer que sabe latín* (Mexico: Secretaría de Educación Pública, Sep-Setentas, 1973), 203.
13. Ibid., 205.
14. Carballo, "La historia de sus libros," 2, and Castellanos, "Una tentativa de autocrítica," in her *Juicios sumarios* (Xalapa: Universidad Veracruzana, 1966), 430-34, esp. 430.
15. María del Carmen Millán, "Tres escritoras mexicanas del siglo XX: Rosario Castellanos," *Cuadernos Americanos* 34, no. 5 (Sept.-Oct. 1975): 177.
16. Carballo, "La historia de sus libros," 2.
17. Castellanos, *Mujer que sabe latín*, 206.
18. Carballo, "La historia de sus libros," 3.
19. Ibid.
20. Ibid., 4.
21. Ibid.
22. Labastida, *El amor, el sueño y la muerte*, 61-63.
23. Millán, "Tres escritoras," 178.
24. Manuel Durán, "In Memoriam: Jaime Torres Bodet, Salvador Novo, Rosario Castellanos," *Rev. Iberoamericana* 41, no. 90 (Jan.-March 1975): 83.
25. Carballo, "La historia de sus libros," 4.
26. "Mujeres de México: Rosario Castellanos," *Nivel* 21 (Sept. 1960): 2.
27. Carballo, "La historia de sus libros," 3.
28. Ibid.
29. Leiva, review of *Lívida luz* in *La Palabra y el Hombre* 5 (1966), no. 7: 183.
30. Castellanos, *Juicios sumarios*, 405.
31. María Luisa Cresta de Leguizamón, "Entrevista a Rosario Castellanos," *La Palabra y el Hombre*, nueva época, 19 (July-Sept. 1976): 4.
32. Castellanos, "José Emilio Pacheco," *Rev. Universidad de México* 20, no. 11 (July 1966): 31.
33. Despite the occasional religious orientation visible in some of Castellanos's poetry, she does not use this traditional Christian symbol in anything resembling a Christian fashion. It is, rather, a double-edged play on the symbol since in Castellanos the fish represents rather the amorphous nature of reality.
34. Castellanos was a convinced feminist and held strong views about the future of a just society. See, for example, her commentary, "A esto, pues, conduce un feminismo bien entendido: a hacer de las mujeres colaboradoras eficaces de los hombres en la construcción de un

mundo nuevo, luminoso, habitable para aquellos en quienes lo mejor de la humanidad se manifiesta: la inteligencia, el amor, la justicia, la laboriosidad" (*Juicios sumarios*, 346). See also, among others, Martha Paley de Francescato's "Women in Latin America: Their Role as Writers and Their Image in Fiction," in *Women in Latin America: A Symposium* (Amherst: University of Massachusetts International Studies Program, Program in Latin American Studies, Occasional Papers, no. 1, 1979), 1-14, esp. 6-7; and Gabrielle de Beer, "Feminismo en la obra poética de Rosario Castellanos," *Revista de Crítica Literaria Hispanoamericana* 7, no. 13 (First semester 1981): 105-12.

35. Millán, "Tres escritoras," 179.

36. Pacheco, *El uso de la palabra*, 13.

37. Ibid., 8.

Selected Bibliography

Section I of this bibliography consists of selected general studies and anthologies, many of which include critical materials, and background material for Chapter 1. Section II includes the books of poetry by the authors studied and important critical studies of their work, including a few reviews of particular significance. Volumes of poetry which are included in collected works or similar publications do not appear separately.

SELECTED ANTHOLOGIES AND GENERAL STUDIES

Aguilar Melantzón, Ricardo. "Efraín Huerta and the New School of Mexican Poets." *Latin American Literary Review* 11, No. 22 (Spring-Summer 1983): 41-55.

Almoina, José. *Díaz Mirón. Su poética.* Mexico: Jus, 1958.

Arrom, José Juan. *Esquema generacional de las letras hispanoamericanas.* 2d. ed. Bogotá: Instituto Caro y Cuervo, 1977.

Aub, Max, ed. *Poesía mexicana, 1950-1960.* Mexico: Aguilar, 1960.

Blanco, José Joaquín. *Crónica de la poesía mexicana.* 3d. ed. Mexico: Katún, 1981.

Brushwood, John S. *Enrique González Martínez.* New York: Twayne, 1969.

Campbell, Federico. *Conversaciones con escritores.* Mexico: Secretaría de Educación Pública, Sep-Setentas 28, 1972.

Carballo, Emmanuel. *Jaime Torres Bodet.* Mexico: Empresas Editoriales, 1968.

Cohen, Sandro, comp., prol. y notes. *Palabra nueva.* Mexico, Premiá, Libros del Bicho-20, 1981.

Cuesta, Jorge, ed. *Antología de la poesía mexicana moderna.* 2d. ed. Mexico: Contemporáneos, 1952.

Dauster, Frank. *Breve historia de la poesía mexicana.* Mexico: Edics. de Andrea, Manuales Studium, 1956.

———. *Ensayos sabre poesía mexicana.* Mexico: Edics. de Andrea, 1963.

———. *Xavier Villaurrutia.* New York: Twayne, 1971.

———, ed. *Antología de la poesía mexicana.* Zaragoza: Clásicos Ebro, 1970.

Debicki, Andrew. *La poesía de José Gorostiza*. Mexico: Edics. de Andrea, 1962.

———. *Poetas hispanoamericanos contemporáneos*. Madrid: Gredos, Biblioteca Románica Hispánica, 1976.

———, sel., intro., comentarios y notas. *Antología de la poesía mexicana moderna*. London: Tamesis, 1977.

Durán, Manuel. *Genio y figura de Amado Nervo*. Buenos Aires: Edit. Universitaria, 1968.

———, ed. *Antología de la revista "Contemporáneos."* Mexico: Fondo de Cultura Económica, 1973.

Fein, John M. *Toward Octavio Paz: A Reading of His Major Poems, 1957-1976*. Lexington: Univ. Press of Kentucky, 1986.

Fernández, Sergio. *Homenajes*. Mexico: Secretaría de Educación Pública, Sep-Setentas 36, 1972.

Forster, Merlin H. *Los Contemporáneos (1920-1932)*. Mexico: Edics. de Andrea, 1964.

———. *Fire and Ice: The Poetry of Xavier Villaurrutia*. Chapel Hill: North Carolina Studies in the Romance Languages and Literatures, 11, 1976.

———. "Four Contemporary Mexican Poets." In M. Forster, ed., *Tradition and Renewal*. Urbana: Univ. of Illinois Press, 1975.

———. *Historia de la poesía hispanoamericana*. Clear Creek, Ind.: The American Hispanist, 1981.

García Terrés, Jaime. *Poesía y alquimia: Los tres mundos de Gilberto Owen*. Mexico: Edics. Era, 1980.

Gómez del Prado, Carlos. *Manuel Gutiérrez Nájera: Vida y obra*. México: Edics. de Andrea, 1964.

Karsen, Sonja. *Jaime Torres Bodet*. New York: Twayne, 1971.

Labastida, Jaime. "La poesía mexicana (1965-1976)." *Rev. Universidad de México* 30, no. 12 (Aug. 1976): 2-9.

———, pról. and selección. *El amor, el sueño y la muerte en la poesía mexicana*. Zacatenco: Instituto Politécnico Nacional, 1969.

Leiva, Raúl. "La generación última y la poesía mexicana del siglo XX." *Cuadernos de Bellas Artes* 4, no. 9 (Sept. 1963): 11-20.

———. *Imagen de la poesía mexicana contemporánea*. Mexico: Universidad Nacional Autónoma, Centro de Estudios Literarios, 1959.

Magaña Esquivel, Antonio. *Salvador Novo*. Mexico: Empresas Editoriales, 1971.

Martínez, José Luis, ed. *La obra de Enrique González Martínez*. Mexico: El Colegio Nacional, 1951.

Martinez Peñaloza, Porfirio. *Algunos epígonos del modernismo y otras notas*. Mexico: Camelina, 1966.

Méndez Plancarte, Alfonso. *Díaz Mirón: Poeta y artífice.* Mexico: Antigua Librería Robredo, 1954.

Miller, Beth Kurti. *La poesía constructiva de Jaime Torres Bodet.* Mexico: Porrúa, 1974.

———, ed. *Ensayos contemporáneos sobre Jaime Torres Bodet.* Mexico: Universidad Nacional Autónoma, 1976.

Monsivais, Carlos, notas, sel. y resumen cronológico. *La poesía mexicana del siglo XX.* Mexico: Empresas Editoriales, 1966.

Moretta, Eugene. *Gilberto Owen en la poesía mexicana.* Mexico: Fondo de Cultura Económica, 1985.

———. *La poesía de Xavier Villaurrutia.* Mexico: Fondo de Cultura Económica, 1976.

Mullen, Edward J. *Carlos Pellicer.* New York: Twayne, 1977.

———, ed. *La poesía de Carlos Pellicer: Interpretaciones críticas.* Mexico: Universidad Nacional Autónoma, 1977.

———, sel., notas y prólogo. *Contemporáneos: Revista mexicana de cultura.* Salamanca: Anaya, 1972.

Pacheco, José Emilio. "Aproximación a la poesía mexicana del siglo XX." *Hispania* 48, no. 2 (May 1965): 209-19.

———, sel., intro. y notes. *Antología del modernismo, 1884-1921.* 2 vols. Mexico: Universidad Nacional Autónoma, Biblioteca del Estudiante Universitario, 90, 1970.

———, notas, sel., y resumen cronológico. *La poesía mexicana del siglo XIX.* Mexico: Empresas Editoriales, 1965.

Paz, Octavio. "Antevíspera: Taller (1938-1941)." *Vuelta* 7, no. 76 (March 1983): 6-12.

———. *La búsqueda del comienzo.* Intr. de Diego Martínez Turrón. Madrid: Fundamentos, 1974.

———. *Cuadrivio.* Mexico: Joaquín Mortiz, 1965.

———. *Sombras de obras.* Barcelona: Seix Barral, 1983.

———. *Xavier Villaurrutia en persona y en obra.* Mexico: Fondo de Cultura Económica, 1978.

———, ed. *An Anthology of Mexican Poetry.* Transl. by Samuel Beckett. Bloomington: Indiana University Press, 1958.

———; Alí Chumacero; José Emilio Pacheco; and Homero Aridjis, sel. y notas. *Poesía en movimiento: México, 1915-1966.* Mexico: Siglo XXI, 1966.

Phillips, Allen W. *Ramón López Velarde: El poeta y el prosista.* Mexico: Instituto Nacional de Bellas Artes, 1962.

Phillips, Rachel. *The Poetic Modes of Octavio Paz.* New York: Oxford University Press, 1972.

Río, Rafael del. *Poesía mexicana contemporánea y otros escritos.* Torreon: Rev. Cauce, 1955.

Rodríguez Padrón, Jorge. *Octavio Paz*. Madrid: Jucar, 1976.

Roster, Peter J. *La ironía como método de análisis literario: La poesía de Salvador Novo*. Madrid: Gredos, 1978.

Rubin, Mordecai. *Una poética moderna: "Muerte sin fin" de José Gorostiza*. Mexico: Universidad Nacional Autónoma, 1966.

Selva, Mauricio de la. *Algunos poetas mexicanos*. Mexico: Finisterre, 1971.

Sheridan, Guillermo. "México, los 'Contemporáneos' y el nacional-ismo." *Vuelta* 8, no. 87 (Feb. 1984): 29-37.

Strand, Mark, ed. Selected with notes by Octavio Paz, Alí Chumacero, José Emilio Pacheco and Homero Aridjis. *New Poetry of Mexico*. New York: Dutton, 1970.

Valdés, Héctor, antología, intro. y notas. *Poetisas mexicanas: siglo XX*. Mexico: Universidad Nacional Autónoma, Dir. Gral. de Publicaciones, 1976.

Wilson, Jason. *Octavio Paz: A Study of His Poetics*. Cambridge: Cambridge University Press, 1979.

Xirau, Ramón. *Mito y poesía*. Mexico: Universidad Nacional Autónoma, 1973.

———. *Octavio Paz: El sentido de la palabra*. Mexico: Joaquín Mortiz, 1970.

———. *Tres poetas de la soledad*. Mexico: Antigua Librería Robredo, 1955.

Zaid, Gabriel, ed. *Asamblea de poetas jóvenes de México*. Mexico: Siglo XXI, 1980.

———, presentación, compilación y notas. *Omnibus de poesía mexicana*. 2d. ed. Mexico: Siglo XXI, 1972.

Zavala, Jesús. *Manuel José Othón: El hombre y el poeta*. Mexico: Imprenta Universitaria, 1952.

WORKS BY AND ABOUT THE POETS

ALÍ CHUMACERO

POETRY

Poesía completa. 3d. ed. Pról. de Marco Antonio Campos. Mexico: Premiá Editora, Los Libros del Bicho-10, 1982.

SELECTED CRITICAL STUDIES.

Campos, Marco Antonio. "La poesía de Alí Chumacero." *Diálogos* 6, no. 90 (Nov.-Dec. 1979): 40-42.

García, Elvira, entrevista de. "Escribo muy poco y procuro no hacerlo." *La Semana de Bellas Artes* 175 (April 8, 1981): 7.

Garfield, Evelyn Picon. "La poesía de Alí Chumacero: Cuarenta años después de *Tierra Nueva.*" *Rev. Universidad de México* 38, no. 20 (Dec. 1982): 15-19.

Henestrosa, Andrés. "Contestación." In Chumacero, *Acerca del poeta y su mundo*, Mexico: Academia Mexicana, 1965.

Kamenszain, Tamara, entrevista de. "Alí Chumacero: La palabra postergada." *La Letra y la imagen*, supl. of *El Universal* 55 (Oct. 12, 1980): 2-6.

Pacheco, José Emilio. Review of *Páramo de sueños. Rev. Universidad de México* 15, no. 1 (Sept. 1960): 30.

Roggiano, A. A. Review of *Páramo de sueños. Rev. Iberoamericana* 28, no. 54 (July-Dec. 1962): 413-20. In his *En este aire de América.* Mexico: Edit. Cultura, Biblioteca del Nuevo Mundo-5, 1966, 177-87.

Xirau, Ramón. "Alí Chumacero." In his *Poesía iberoamericana contemporánea.* Mexico: Secretaría de Educación, Sep-Setentas, 1972, 149-54. In his *Poetas de España y México.* Madrid: Porrúa Turanzas, 1962, 157-62.

EFRAÍN HUERTA

POETRY

Circuito interior. Mexico: Joaquín Mortiz, 1977.

Los eróticos y otros poemas. Mexico: Joaquín Mortiz, 1974.

Poemas prohibidos y de amor. 3d. ed. Mexico: Siglo XXI, Col. Mínima-62, 1978.

Poesía, 1935-1968. Mexico: Joaquín Mortiz, 1968.

Transa Poética. Mexico: Edics. Era, 1980.

SELECTED CRITICAL STUDIES

Aguilar, Ricardo. " 'Avenida Juárez,' Un poema comprometido." *Plural* 10-11, no. 119 (Aug. 1981): 33-40.

———. "La dualidad en la obra de Efraín Huerta." *La Palabra y el Hombre*, nueva época, 27 (July-Sept. 1978): 32-42.

———. "Efraín Huerta y los poemínimos." *La Semana de Bellas Artes* 73 (April 25, 1979): 2-5.

———. "La estructura en la poesía de Efraín Huerta." *Plural* 8, no. 96 (Sept. 1979): 12-19.

Arellano, Jesús. "El poeta proscrito: Efraín Huerta." *Nivel* 43 (July 1962): 5.

De la Selva, Mauricio. *Algunos poetas mexicanos.* Mexico: Finisterre, 1971.

Fernández, Angel José. "Circuito interior, nuevo jubileo y presagio." *La Palabra y el Hombre* 23 (July-Sept. 1977): 71-72.

Flores Olague, Jesús. "Circuito interior." *Comunidad* 12, no. 60 (May-July 1977): 314-15.

González Pagés, Andrés. "Efraín Huerta: Perfil del poeta vivo." *Plural* 67 (April 1977): 56-67.

Hernández, Francisco, and Pedro Orgambide. "Efraín Huerta, el poeta en el ojo del ciclón." *Casa de las Américas* 24, no. 139 (July-Aug. 1983): 21-26.

Leiva, Raúl. "El poeta Efraín Huerta." *Nivel* 72 (Dec. 1968): 1-2, 10.

Lindstrom, Naomi. Review of *Circuito interior. Chasqui* 7, no. 1 (Nov. 1977): 74-76.

Mora, Carlos; Eliseo Diego; Nancy Morejón; Lisandro Otero; Julio Valle Castillo. "Notes en torno a Efraín Huerta." *Casa de las Américas* 22, no. 132 (May-June 1982): 139-55.

Navarro, Victor M. "Huerta, de profanaciones y otros gustos." *La Semana de Bellas Artes* 72 (April 18, 1979): 15.

Ortega, Julio. "La poesía de Efraín Huerta." *Rev. Universidad de México* 23, no. 11 (July 1969): Hojas de critica, 2.

Pacheco, José Emilio. "Efraín Huerta." *Nivel* 72 (Dec. 1968): 7.

———. "Efraín Huerta." *Rev. Universidad de México* 22, no. 11 (July 1968): 6-7.

Solana, Rafael. "Efraín Huerta." *Letras de México* 5, no. 110 (April 1945): 49-50; *Nivel* 26 (Feb. 1961): 1, 4.

———. "Prólogo." In Huerta, *Homenaje: Antología poética*, Guanajuato: Edics. del Gobierno del Estado, 1977.

Trejo Villafuerte, Arturo. "Efraín Huerta: obscenamente amoroso y feliz." *Rev. Universidad de México* 31, no. 10 (June 1977): 42.

Wong, Oscar. "Obra vial de poesía." *Plural* 73 (Oct. 1977): 81-83.

JAIME SABINES

POETRY

Nuevo recuento de poemas. Mexico: Joaquín Mortiz, 1977.

SELECTED CRITICAL STUDIES

Alwar, Ammen. "Jaime Sabines in translation." *Review* 20 (Spring 1977): 61.

Anon. "Corazón de león y saladino." *Plural* 13 (Oct. 1972): 41.

———. "Entrevista con Jaime Sabines." *Espejo* 8 (1969): 87-88.

Arellano, Jesús. "Raíces poéticas de Jaime Sabines." *Nivel* 33 (Sept. 1961): 2, 6.

Armengol, Armando. "La iniciación poética de Jaime Sabines." *La Semana de Bellas Artes* 71 (April 11, 1979): 2-7.

Casahonda Castillo, José. "Introducción" in Sabines, *Poesía de la sinceridad*. Tlaxcala: Alcance al núm. 31 de Huytlale, vol. 5, 1959.

Chumacero, Alí. "La poesía." *La Cultura en México* 46 (Jan. 2, 1963): V.

Dietrick, Charles P. "Breaking Myth, Making Myth: 'Así es' by Jaime Sabines." *Chasqui* 4, no. 1 (Nov. 1974): 34-39.

——. Review of *Maltiempo*. *Chasqui* 3, no. 1 (Nov. 1973): 54-57.

Durán, Manuel. "Dos grandes poetas mexicanos de hoy: Sabines y Montes de Oca." *La Cultura en México* 483 (May 12, 1971): VII-X.

——. "Jaime Sabines and Marco Antonio Montes de Oca: A Study in Contrasts." *Mundus Artium* 3, no. 2 (1970): 44-55.

García Ascot, Jomi. "Sobre Jaime Sabines." *Rev. Universidad de México* 20, no. 6 (Feb. 1966): 9-11.

García Ponce, Juan. "Sabines y nuestro mundo." *Rev. Mexicana de Literatura* 9-12 (Sept.-Dec. 1961): 43-45.

Hernández, Ana María. Review of *Nuevo recuento de poemas*. *Hispamérica* 7, no. 20 (Aug. 1978): 119-20.

Klahn, Norma. Review of *Tarumba*. *Review* 29 (May-Aug. 1981): 86-87.

López, César. "El mundo poético de Jaime Sabines." *Casa de las Américas* 5, no. 30 (1965): 88-89.

Mansour, Mónica. "Jaime Sabines, malestares y desconciertos." *Plural* 136 (Jan. 1983): 38-45.

Monterde, Francisco. Review of *Recuento de poemas*. *Anuario de Letras* 3 (1963): 347-49.

Pacheco, José Emilio. Review of *Nuevo recuento de poemas*. *Vuelta* 9, no. 1 (Aug. 1977): 34-36.

Rivero, Eliana. Review of *Nuevo recuento de poemas*. *World Literature Today* 52, no. 3 (Summer 1978): 440-41.

Segovia, Tomás. "Recuentos de Sabines." *Rev. Mexicana de Literatura* 9-10 (Sept.-Oct. 1962): 50-54.

Sendoya, Luis Enrique. "Análisis de un poema de Jaime Sabines." *Nivel* 119 (Nov. 1972): 1-2.

Wong, Oscar. Review of *Poemas sueltos*. *Plural* 130 (July 1982): 79-80.

Xirau, Ramón. *Poesía iberoamericana contemporánea*. Mexico: Secretaría de Educación Pública, Sep-Setentas 15, 1972.

RUBÉN BONIFAZ NUÑO

POETRY

As de oros. Mexico: Universidad Nacional Autónoma, 1981.

De otro modo lo mismo. Mexico: Fondo de Cultura Económica, 1979.

Tres poemas de antes. Mexico: Universidad Nacional Autónoma, 1978.

SELECTED CRITICAL STUDIES

Acuña, René. "Rubén Bonifaz Nuño: Una aproximación a Fuego de pobres." *Mester* 4, no. 1 (Nov. 1973): 41-53.

Andueza, María. Review of *Tres poemas de antes*. *Rev. Universidad de México* 33, no. 6 (Feb. 1979): 39-41.

Anon. "Bonifaz Nuño, Premio Nacional de Letras." *Rev. Universidad de México* 29, no. 5 (Jan. 1975): 25.

———. "Letras mexicanas: Rubén Bonifaz Nuño." *Letras de ayer y de hoy* 2, no. 14 (Oct. 1966): 10.

Arellano, Jesús. "Drama poético en la obra de Rubén Bonifaz Nuño." *Nivel*, 2a. época, 4 (April 1963): 5.

Bennett, John Michael. "Coatlicue: The Poetry of Rubén Bonifaz Nuño." Ph.D. dissertation, University of California at Los Angeles, 1970.

Cohen, Sandro. "Benifaz Nuño: La intima guerra fría." *Rev. Universidad de México* 34, no. 9 (May 1980): 44-45.

González Casanova, Henrique. "Rubén Bonifaz Nuño." *La Cultura en México* 7 (Aug. 7, 1963): V-VII.

Leiva, Raúl. "La poesía de Rubén Bonifaz Nuño: Desde *Fuego de pobres* hasta *El ala del tigre*." *Cuadernos Americanos* 30, no. 2 (March-April 1971): 167-83.

———. "La poesía de Rubén Bonifaz Nuño: Desde *Imágenes* hasta *El manto y la corona*." *Cuadernos Americanos* 30, no. 1 (Jan.-Feb. 1971): 165-86.

———. Review of *El manto y la corona*. *La Palabra y el Hombre* 3, no. 10 (April-June 1959): 326-31.

Mejía Sánchez, Ernesto. Review of *El manto y la corona*. *Rev. Universidad de México* 13, no. 5 (Jan. 1959): 29-30.

Mendiola, Víctor Manuel. "Bonifaz Nuño: Tres poemas de antes." *La Semana de Bellas Artes* 180 (May 13, 1981): 14.

Michel, Manuel. Review of *Los demonios y los dias*. *Rev. Universidad de México* 10, no. 11 (July 1956): 30-31.

Puga, Mario. "El escritor y su tiempo: Rubén Bonifaz Nuño." *Rev. Universidad de México* 10, no. 10 (June 1956): 19-20.

Rius, Luis. "Rubén Bonifaz Nuño." *Rev. Universidad de México* 20, no. 11 (July 1966): 31.

Selva, Mauricio de la. Review of *El manto y la corona*. *Cuadernos Americanos* 18, no. 1 (Jan.-Feb. 1959): 282-84.

———. Review of *Siete de espades*. *Cuadernos Americanos* 25, no. 4 (July-Aug. 1966): 267-68.

Vega, Fausto. "Aproximaciones." *Nivel* 34 (Oct. 1961): 10.

Villela, Victor. "Destino del canto." *La Cultura en México* 96 (Dec. 18, 1963): XVIII-XIX.

———. Review of *El ala del tigre*. *Revista de Bellas Artes* 321 (Jan.-Feb. 1970): 62-63.

Yáñez, Agustín. "Contestación." In *Destino del canto*. Mexico: Universidad Nacional Autónoma, 1963.

Zarate, A. Review of *Siete de espadas*. *Revista de Bellas Artes* 2, no. 9 (May-June 1966): 102.

ROSARIO CASTELLANOS

POETRY

Poesía no eres tú. Mexico: Fondo de Cultura Económica, 1972.

SELECTED CRITICAL STUDIES

Agosín, Marjorie. "Rosario Castellanos ante el espejo." *Cuadernos Americanos* 43, no. 2 (March-April 1984): 219-26.

Ahern, Maureen, and Mary Seale Vásquez, eds. *Homenaje a Rosario Castellanos*. Valencia: Albatros-Hispanófila, 1980.

Baptiste, Victor N. *La obra poética de Rosario Castellanos*. Santiago, Chile: Edics. Exégesis, 1972.

Benedetti, Mario. "Rosario Castellanos y la incomunicación racial." In his *Letras del continente mestizo*. 2d. ed. Montevideo: Arca, 1969, 165-70.

Calderón, Germaine. *El universo poético de Rosario Castellanos*. Mexico: Universidad Nacional Autónoma, Cuadernos del Centro de Estudios Literarios, 1979.

Carballo, Emmanuel, entrevista de. "La historia de sus libros contada por ella misma." *Siempre, La Cultura en México* 44 (Dec. 19, 1962): II-V.

Cresta de Leguizamón, María Luisa. "Entrevista a Rosario Castellanos." *La Palabra y el Hombra*, nueva época, 19 (July-Sept. 1976): 4-8.

de Beer, Gabrielle. "Feminismo en la obra poética de Rosario Castellanos." *Rev. de Crítica Literaria Latinoamericana* 7, no. 13 (First semester 1981): 105-12.

Domínguez, Luis Adolfo. "Entrevista con Rosario Castellanos." *Rev. de Bellas Artes* 25 (Jan.-Feb. 1969): 16-23.

———. "La mujer en la obra de Rosario Castellanos." *Rev. Universidad de México* 25, no. 6 (Feb. 1971): 36-38.

Durán, Manuel. "In memoriam: Jaime Torres Bodet, Salvador Novo,

Rosario Castellanos." *Revista Iberoamericana* 41, no. 90 (Jan.-March 1975): 79-83.

Dybvig, Rhoda. *Rosario Castellanos: Biografía y novelística.* Mexico: n. p., 1965.

Fraire, Isabel. Review of *Lívida luz. Rev. Mexicana de Literatura,* nueva época, 16-18 (Oct.-Dec. 1960): 75-76.

Godoy, Emma. "Rosario Castellanos." *Abside* 39 (1975): 350-54.

González Guerrero, Francisco. *En torno a la literatura mexicana.* Mexico: Secretaría de Educación Pública, Sep-Setentas 286, 1976. Pról. y recop. de Pedro F. de Andrea. Incl. "Rosario Castellanos, De la vigilia estéril," 179-84.

Hierro, Graciela. "La filosofía de Rosario Castellanos." *Plural* 10-13, no. 120 (Sept. 1981): 30.

Labastida, Jaime. "El amor en algunos poetas mexicanos." *Rev. de Bellas Artes* 25 (Jan.-Feb. 1969): 53-64.

Leiva, Raúl. Review of *Lívida luz. La Palabra y el Hombre* 5, no. 17 (Jan.-March 1961): 180-83.

Millán, Mara del Carmen. "Tres escritoras mexicanas del siglo XX." *Cuadernos Americanos* 34, no. 5 (Sep.-Oct. 1975): 163-81.

Miller, Beth. "La poesía de Rosario Castellanos: Tono y tenor." *Diálogos* 13, no. 2 (March-April 1977): 28-31.

———. "Voz e imagen en la obra de Rosario Castellanos." *Rev. Universidad de México* 30, no. 4 (Dec. 1975-Jan. 1976): 33-38.

Miller, Martha LaFollette. "A Semiotic Analysis of Three Poems by Rosario Castellanos." *Revista/Review Interamericana* 12, no. 1 (Spring 1982): 77-86.

Miller, Yvette. "El temario poético de Rosario Castellanos." *Hispamérica* 29 (Aug. 1981): 107-15.

Los narradores ante el público. Mexico: Joaquín Mortiz, 1966.

Nelson, Esther W. "Point of View in Selected Poems by Rosario Castellanos." *Revista/Review Interamericana* 12, no. 1 (Spring 1982): 56-64.

O'Hara, Edgar. "¿Acaso tú, Rosario Castellanos?" *Plural* 139 (April 1983): 45-47.

Pacheco, José Emilio. Nota preliminar. In Castellanos, *El uso de la palabra.* Mexico: Edics. de Excélsior, 1974.

———. "Rosario Castellanos o la rotunda austeridad de la poesía." *Vida literaria* 30 (1972): 8-11.

Paley de Francescato, Martha. "Women in Latin America: Their Role as Writers and Their Image in Fiction." In *Women in Latin America: A Symposium.* Amherst: University of Massachusetts International

Studies Program, Program in Latin American Studies, Occasional Papers, No. 1, 1979, 1-14.

Plaza, Dolores. "El culto a los otros en la obra de Rosario Castellanos." *La Palabra y el Hombre* 11 (July-Sep. 1974): 13-15.

Reyes Nevares, Beatriz. *Rosario Castellanos*. Mexico: Secretaría de la Presidencia, Departamento Editorial, 1976.

Rodríguez Peralta, Phyllis. "Images of Women in Rosario Castellanos' Prose." *Latin American Literary Review* 6, no. 11 (Fall-Winter 1977): 68-80.

Rojas, Lourdes. "La indagación desmitificadora en la poesía de Rosario Castellanos." *Revista/Review Interamericana* 12, no. 1 (Spring 1982): 65-76.

Selva, Mauricio de la. "Cuatro libros de poesía." *Cuadernos Americanos* 31, no. 6 (Nov.-Dec. 1972): 255-62.

———. Review of *Materia memorable*. *Cuadernos Americanos* 29, no. 1 (Jan.-Feb. 1970): 219-21.

Xirau, Ramón. *Mito y poesía*. Mexico: Universidad Nacional Autónoma, 1973.

———. "Nuevos poetas mexicanos." In his *Poetas de México y de España*. Madrid: José Porrúa Turanzas, 1962, 167-93.

Zaid, Gabriel. "Poetas ejemplares." *Plural* 36 (Sept. 1974): 91.

Index